American Poetry since 1945

New Casebooks

Collections of all new critical essays

NOVELS AND PROSE

DAVID ALMOND
Edited by Rosemary Ross Johnston

MELVIN BURGESS
Edited by Alison Waller

ROBERT CORMIER
Edited by Adrienne E. Gavin

ROALD DAHL
Edited by Ann Alston & Catherine Butler

JOHN FOWLES
Edited by James Acheson

C. S. LEWIS: *THE CHRONICLES OF NARNIA*
Edited by Michelle Ann Abate & Lance Weldy

PHILIP PULLMAN: *HIS DARK MATERIALS*
Edited by Catherine Butler & Tommy Halsdorf

J. K. ROWLING: *HARRY POTTER*
Edited by Cynthia J. Hallett & Peggy J. Huey

J. R. R. TOLKIEN: *THE HOBBIT & THE LORD OF THE RINGS*
Edited by Peter Hunt

VIRGINIA WOOLF
Edited by James Acheson

POETRY

TED HUGHES
Edited by Terry Gifford

GENRE

AMERICAN POETRY SINCE 1945
Edited by Eleanor Spencer

MEDIEVAL ENGLISH LITERATURE
Edited by Beatrice Fannon

Further titles are in preparation

For a full list of published titles in the past format of the New Casebooks series, visit the series page at www.palgravehighered.com

American Poetry since 1945

Edited by

ELEANOR SPENCER

First published 2017 by
PALGRAVE

Palgrave in the UK is an imprint of Macmillan Publishers Limited, registered in England, company number 785998, of 4 Crinan Street, London, N1 9XW.

Palgrave Macmillan in the US is a division of St Martin's Press LLC, 175 Fifth Avenue, New York, NY 10010.

Palgrave is a global imprint of the above companies and is represented throughout the world.

Palgrave® and Macmillan® are registered trademarks in the United States, the United Kingdom, Europe and other countries.

ISBN: 978–1–137–32446–7 hardback
ISBN: 978–1–137–32445–0 paperback

This book is printed on paper suitable for recycling and made from fully managed and sustained forest sources. Logging, pulping and manufacturing processes are expected to conform to the environmental regulations of the country of origin.

A catalogue record for this book is available from the British Library.

A catalog record for this book is available from the Library of Congress.

Printed and bound in the UK by The Lavenham Press Ltd, Suffolk.

Contents

Series Editor's Preface

Welcome to the latest series of New Casebooks.

Each volume now presents brand new essays specially written for university and other students. Like the original series, the new-look New Casebooks embrace a range of recent critical approaches to the debates and issues that characterize the current discussion of literature.

Each editor has been asked to commission a sequence of original essays which will introduce the reader to the innovative critical approaches to the text or texts being discussed in the collection. The intention is to illuminate the rich interchange between critical theory and critical practice that today underpins so much writing about literature.

Editors have also been asked to supply an introduction to each volume that sets the scene for the essays that follow, together with a list of further reading which will enable readers to follow up issues raised by the essays in the collection.

The purpose of this new-look series, then, is to provide students with fresh thinking about key texts and writers while encouraging them to extend their own ideas and responses to the texts they are studying.

Martin Coyle

Notes on Contributors

Linda Anderson is Professor of Modern American and English Literature at Newcastle University, and Director of the Newcastle Centre for the Literary Arts. She is the author of *Elizabeth Bishop: Lines of Connection* (Edinburgh University Press, 2013); and *Autobiography* (Routledge, 2002; 2010); and editor (with Jo Shapcott) of *Elizabeth Bishop: Poet of the Periphery* (Bloodaxe, 2002).

Steven Gould Axelrod is Distinguished Professor of English at the University of California, Riverside. He is the author of *Robert Lowell: Life and Art* (Princeton University Press, 1978); *Robert Lowell: A Reference Guide* (G. K. Hall, 1982); and *Sylvia Plath: The Wound and the Cure of Words* (Johns Hopkins University Press, 1990); and co-editor of the *New Anthology of American Poetry*, Volumes 1–3 (Rutgers University Press).

Paul Batchelor is a Lecturer and Director of Creative Writing in the Department of English Studies at Durham University. His first collection, *The Sinking Road* (Bloodaxe, 2008), was shortlisted for the Jerwood-Aldeburgh Best First Collection Prize and the Glen Dimplex Best First Collection Prize. He has also received an Eric Gregory Award and The *Times* Stephen Spender Prize for Translation. His poems and translations have appeared in *The Guardian*, *Poetry*, *Poetry Review*, *The Rialto*, *The Times* and *The Times Literary Supplement*.

Tracy Brain is Reader in English in the School of Humanities and Cultural Industries at Bath Spa University. She is the author of *The Other Sylvia Plath* (Pearson Education, 2001), and the editor (with Sally Bayley) of *Representing Sylvia Plath* (Cambridge University Press, 2011). She has also contributed to *The Cambridge Companion to Ted Hughes* (Cambridge University Press, 2011).

Stephen Burt is Professor of English at Harvard University. They are the author of several books of poetry and literary criticism, among them *Belmont* (Graywolf Press, 2013); *The Art of the Sonnet* (with David Mikics) (Belknap Press, 2011); *Close Calls with Nonsense* (Graywolf Press, 2009); and *The Forms of Youth: Twentieth-Century Poetry and Adolescence* (Columbia University Press, 2007). They are a regular contributor to *The New York Times Book Review*, *Poetry Review*, and *The Times Literary Supplement*, amongst others.

David Caplan is the Charles M. Weis Chair in English at Ohio Wesleyan University. He is the author of four books on poetry and poetry criticism, including *Questions of Possibility: Contemporary Poetry and Poetic Form* (Oxford University Press, 2004) and *Poetic Form: An Introduction* (Longman, 2006). His most recent book is *Rhyme's Challenge: Hip Hop, Poetry, and Contemporary Rhyming Culture* (Oxford University Press, 2014).

Wendy Martin is Professor of American Literature and American Studies at Claremont Graduate University. Her books include *An American Triptych: Anne Bradstreet, Emily Dickinson and Adrienne Rich* (University of North Carolina Press, 1984); *The Cambridge Introduction to Emily Dickinson* (Cambridge University Press, 2007); and (with Sharone Williams) *The Routledge Introduction to American Women Writers* (Routledge, 2016). Her edited collections of short stories include *We Are the Stories We Tell* (Pantheon, 1990), and *The Best of Times, The Worst of Times* (New York University Press, 2011).

Stephen Matterson is Professor of American Literature in the School of English at Trinity College, University of Dublin. His publications include *Berryman and Lowell: The Art of Losing* (Macmillan, 1988); a revised second edition of *Studying Poetry* (with Darryl Jones) (Bloomsbury Academic, 2010); *The Complete Poems of Walt Whitman* (Wordsworth, 2006); and *American Literature: The Essential Glossary* (Edward Arnold and Oxford University Press, 2003). He has also edited *Forever Young: The Changing Images of the United States* (with Philip Coleman) (Universitätsverlag, 2012); *Aberration in Modern and Contemporary Poetry* (with Lucy Collins) (McFarland, 2012), and *Rebound: The American Poetry Book* (with Michael Hinds) (Rodopi, 2004).

Lauren Morrison is a PhD student in the English Department at Claremont Graduate University. Her fields of specialization are nineteenth- and twentieth-century American literature. She is on the editorial staff of *Foothill: A Journal of Poetry*. She has contributed to the forthcoming *From the Gilded Age to the Progressive Era* and *Hollywood Heroines: The Most Influential Women in Film History*.

Lauri Ramey is Founding Director of the Center for Contemporary Poetry and Poetics, and Professor of African American Literature and Culture, American Studies, and Creative Writing at California State University, Los Angeles. Her books include *Slave Songs and the Birth of African American Poetry* (Palgrave Macmillan, 2010); *The Heritage Series* *of Black Poetry, 1962–1975* (Ashgate, 2008); *Black British Writing* (with R. Victoria Arana) (Palgrave Macmillan, 2009); *Every Goodbye Ain't Gone: Innovative Poetry by African Americans* (University of Alabama Press, 2006); and *What I Say: Innovative Writing by Black Poets in America* (University of Alabama Press, 2015) (both with Aldon Lynn Nielsen).

Stephen Regan is Professor in the Department of English Studies at Durham University, and Director of the Durham University Centre for Poetry and Poetics. He has a research and teaching specialism in Irish literature. His publications include *Philip Larkin* (Macmillan, 1992); *The Eagleton Reader* (Blackwell, 1998); *Irish Writing: An Anthology of Irish Literature in English 1789–1939* (Oxford University Press, 2004); *The Nineteenth-Century Novel: A Critical Reader* (Routledge, 2001); and an edition of George Moore's *Esther Waters* (Oxford University Press, 2012).

Eleanor Spencer teaches in the Department of English Studies at Durham University, where she is Vice-Principal at St Chad's College, and Digital Director of the Durham University Centre for Poetry and Poetics. She has contributed to *Kathleen Jamie: Essays and Poems on Her Work* (Edinburgh University Press, 2014), and *A Companion to Contemporary British and Irish Poetry, 1960–2010* (Wiley-Blackwell, forthcoming). Her current project is a monograph on the work of the British-American poet Anne Stevenson.

Rory Waterman is Lecturer in English and Creative Writing at Nottingham Trent University, where he leads the MA in Creative Writing. His collection *Tonight the Summer's Over* (Carcanet, 2013) was a Poetry Book Society Recommendation, and was shortlisted for the Seamus Heaney Prize. His critical books are *Belonging and Estrangement in the Poetry of Philip Larkin, R. S. Thomas and Charles Causley* (Ashgate, 2014); and *Poets of the Second World War* (Northcote House Publishers, 2015). He is a regular contributor to *The Times Literary Supplement*, and co-edits the arts magazine *New Walk*.

Acknowledgements

Excerpts from 'The Monument', 'Jeronimo's House', 'The Man-Moth', 'At the Fishhouses', 'Cape Breton', 'The Prodigal', 'Crusoe in England', and The End of March' from POEMS by Elizabeth Bishop. Copyright © 2011 by The Alice H. Methfessel Trust. Publisher's Note and compilation copyright © 2011 by Farrar, Straus and Giroux, LLC. Reprinted by permission of Farrar, Straus and Giroux, LLC.

Excerpts from 'As We Like It: Miss Moore and the Delight of Imitation', 'Efforts of Affection: A Memoir of Marianne Moor', 'The Sea and Its Shore', and 'In the Village' from PROSE by Elizabeth Bishop. Copyright © 2011 by The Alice H. Methfessel Trust. Editor's Note and compilation copyright © 2011 by Lloyd Schwartz. Reprinted by permission of Farrar, Straus and Giroux, LLC.

'Money Shot' from *Money Shot by Rae Armantrout*. Copyright © 2011 by Rae Armantrout. Reprinted with the permission of Wesleyan University Press.

Excerpt from 'Ativan' by Laura Kasischke. Copyright © 2012 by Laura Kasischke. Reprinted with the permission of Poetry Foundation.

Excerpt from 'The Day Lady Died' by Frank O'Hara. Copyright © 1964 by Frank O'Hara. Reprinted by permission of City Lights Books.

Chronology

1874 Birth of Robert Frost, Amy Lowell, Gertrude Stein.

1876 Publication of Mark Twain's novel *The Adventures of Tom Sawyer*. Colorado becomes the 38th state.

1878 Birth of Carl Sandburg.

1879 Birth of Wallace Stevens.

1880 The population of the United States passes fifty million.

1881 Publication of Henry James' *The Portrait of a Lady*.

1882 Birth of Mina Loy. Death of Ralph Waldo Emerson.

1883 Birth of William Carlos Williams. Racial segregation is legalized by a decision in the Civil Rights Cases. The Brooklyn Bridge is opened.

1884 Publication of Mark Twain's novel *The Adventures of Huckleberry Finn*.

1885 Birth of Ezra Pound.

1886 Birth of H.D. (Hilda Doolittle). Death of Emily Dickinson. The Statue of Liberty is erected on Bedloe's Island in the entrance to New York Harbor.

1887 Birth of Marianne Moore.

1888 Birth of T. S. Eliot.

1889 Birth of Claude McKay. North and South Dakota, Montana, and Washington join the United States.

1890 Publication of *Poems*, the first of six collections of Emily Dickinson's poetry. Idaho and Wyoming join the United States.

1892 Birth of Edna St Vincent Millay, Archibald MacLeish. Death of Walt Whitman; final edition of Whitman's *Leaves of Grass* published.

1894 Birth of e. e. cummings.

1896 Utah joins the United States.

1898 Publication of Charlotte Perkins Gilman's *Women and Economics*.

1899 Birth of Hart Crane, Allen Tate.

1900 Birth of Ivor Winters.

1901 Birth of Sterling Brown, Laura (Riding) Jackson.

1902 Birth of Langston Hughes, Ogden Nash. Publication of Edith Wharton's first full-length novel *The Valley of Decision*.

1903 Birth of Lorine Niedecker, Countee Cullen. Publication of W. E. B. Du Bois' collection of essays *The Souls of Black Folk*. The American Wright brothers make their first powered flight.

1904 Birth of Louis Zukofsky.
1905 Birth of Kenneth Rexroth, Robert Penn Warren.
1907 Birth of W. H. Auden. Oklahoma joins the United States. American cartoonist Bud Fisher creates Mutt and Jeff, the world's first daily comic strip, for the *San Francisco Chronicle.*
1908 Birth of Theodore Roethke. Publication of Ezra Pound's first collection, *A Lume Spento*, in Italy.
1909 W. E. B. Du Bois founds the National Association for the Advancement of Colored People (NAACP).
1910 Birth of Charles Olson.
1911 Birth of Elizabeth Bishop.
1912 Birth of John Cage. Publication of Edna St Vincent Millay's first collection, *Renascence.* New Mexico and Arizona join the United States. The RMS *Titanic* sinks in the Atlantic Ocean during her maiden voyage to New York, killing over 1500 passengers.
1913 Birth of Delmore Schwartz, May Swenson, Muriel Rukeyser. Publication of Robert Frost's *A Boy's Will*, Willa Cather's novel *O Pioneer.* The Armory Show (officially the International Exhibition of Modern Art) takes place in New York.
1914 Birth of John Berryman, Randall Jarrell. Publication of Robert Frost's *North of Boston.* Outbreak of World War I in Europe. The weekly journal *New Republic* is published for the first time. T. S. Eliot leaves the United States for Europe.
1916 Publication of H.D.'s first collection *Sea Garden.*
1917 The United States declares war on Germany. Birth of Robert Lowell, Gwendolyn Brooks. Publication of T. S. Eliot's *Prufrock and Other Observations.* The first Pulitzer Prizes are awarded for the best new US novel, play, history, and biography. French artist Marcel Duchamp submits a ceramic urinal to the Society of Independent Artists in New York, giving it the title *Fountain.*
1919 Birth of Lawrence Ferlinghetti. The Versailles Treaty.
1920 Birth of Barbara Guest. American Women are granted the right to vote. Prohibition begins. Publication of Ezra Pound's *Hugh Selwyn Mauberley*, Edith Wharton's novel *The Age of Innocence.*
1921 Birth of Richard Wilbur. Publication of Marianne Moore's first collection *Poems.*
1922 Birth of Jack Kerouac, Jackson Mac Low. Publication of T. S. Eliot's *The Waste Land* and William Carlos Williams' *Spring and All.*

1923 Birth of Denise Levertov, James Schuyler. Publication of Wallace Stevens' first collection *Harmonium*, e. e. cummings' first collection *Tulips and Chimneys*.

1924 Publication of Emily Dickinson's *Collected Poems* (first published edition) and André Breton's 'First Surrealist Manifesto'.

1925 Birth of Donald Justice, Kenneth Koch, Jack Spicer, Carolyn Kizer. Death of Amy Lowell. Publication of Ezra Pound's *A Draft of XVI Cantos*, F. Scott Fitzgerald's novel *The Great Gatsby*. Foundation of the weekly magazine *The New Yorker*. American artist Edward Hopper introduces a new style of urban realism with the painting *House by the Railroad*.

1926 Birth of A. R. Ammons, Robert Bly, Robert Creeley, Allen Ginsberg, James Merrill, Frank O'Hara, W. D. Snodgrass. Publication of Langston Hughes' *The Weary Blues*.

1927 Birth of John Ashbery, W. S. Merwin, James Wright. Release of the world's first motion picture with sound, *The Jazz Singer*.

1928 Birth of Donald Hall, Anne Sexton. *Steamboat Willie*, Disney's first animated cartoon with synchronized sound featuring Mickey Mouse, debuts in New York.

1929 Birth of Adrienne Rich, Thom Gunn. Wall Street crash. Publication of the 'Second Surrealist Manifesto', Ernest Hemingway's novel *A Farewell to Arms*. Opening of the Museum of Modern Art in New York.

1930 Birth of Gary Snyder. Publication of Hart Crane's *The Bridge* and T. S. Eliot's *Ash-Wednesday*. Experimental broadcast television begins in America.

1931 Publication of Ogden Nash's first collection *Hard Lines*. The Empire State Building opens in New York.

1932 Death of Hart Crane, birth of Sylvia Plath. Franklin D. Roosevelt announces New Deal. The French photographer Henri Cartier-Bresson has his first exhibition in the Julien Levy Gallery in New York.

1933 Adolf Hitler becomes Chancellor in Germany. Franklin D. Roosevelt becomes President of the United States. Prohibition is repealed.

1934 Birth of Mark Strand, Amiri Baraka (LeRoi Jones), Audre Lorde. The Dust Bowl (a period of drought and severe dust storms which damaged agriculture in the Great Plains) began.

1935 Publication of E .E. Cummings' *No Thanks* and *Tom*, Muriel Rukeyser's *Theory of Flight* and Wallace Stevens' *Ideas of Order*. The Federal Bureau of Investigation (FBI) is established with J. Edgar Hoover as its first director.

1936 Birth of Lucille Clifton. Publication of Margaret Mitchell's novel *Gone with the Wind*.

1937 Birth of Alicia Ostriker. Publication of Wallace Stevens' *The Man with the Blue Guitar*, John Steinbeck's novel *Of Mice and Men*. First issue of the *Kenyon Review*. Joseph Auslander named Consultant in Poetry.

1938 Birth of Charles Simic. Publication of Delmore Schwartz's *In Dreams Begin Responsibilities*.

1939 Birth of Frank Bidart. Death of Sigmund Freud. World War II begins in Europe. W. H. Auden and Christopher Isherwood emigrate to the United States, later becoming US citizens.

1940 Birth of Robert Pinsky.

1941 Birth of Billy Collins, Robert Hass, Lyn Hejinian. The bombing of Pearl Harbor, a United States naval base in Hawaii, precipitates the United States' entry into World War II.

1942 Birth of Marilyn Hacker, Sharon Olds. Publication of Langston Hughes' *Shakespeare in Harlem*, Wallace Stevens' *Parts of a World* and *Notes toward a Supreme Fiction*, Randall Jarrell's first collection *Blood for a Stranger*.

1943 Birth of Louise Glück, James Tate, Nikki Giovanni. Publication of T. S. Eliot's *Four Quartets*. Allen Tate named Consultant in Poetry.

1944 Robert Penn Warren named Consultant in Poetry.

1945 World War II ends in Europe following German surrender to Allied Powers. Adolf Hitler commits suicide. The United States drops atomic bombs on Hiroshima and Nagasaki killing 110,000. Japan surrenders to Allied Powers. The United Nations is founded. Publication of Gwendolyn Brooks' *A Street in Bronzeville* and Gertrude Stein's *Wars I Have Seen*. Tennessee Williams' play *The Glass Menagerie* is performed for the first time. Louise Bogan named Consultant in Poetry.

1946 Death of Gertrude Stein, Countee Cullen. Publication of Elizabeth Bishop's *North and South*, Robert Lowell's *Lord Weary's Castle*, James Merrill's *The Black Swan*, and William Carlos Williams' *Paterson*. Eugene O'Neill's play *The Iceman Cometh* is performed for the first time. Karl Shapiro named Consultant in Poetry.

1947 Birth of Rae Armantrout, Yusef Komunyakaa, Bob Perelman, Ai (Ai Ogawa). The CIA is established by the National Security Act. Tennessee Williams' play *A Streetcar Named Desire* is performed for the first time on Broadway, starring

Marlon Brando. Robert Lowell named Consultant in Poetry. American artist Jackson Pollock, a major figure in the abstract expressionist movement, develops the 'drip' technique with which he will become synonymous.

1948 Publication of Ezra Pound's *The Pisan Cantos*, Theodore Roethke's *The Lost Son and Other Poems*. The Berlin Blockade, the first major crisis of the Cold War, takes place in Berlin. Death of Claude McKay. Jack Kerouac coins the term 'the Beat Generation'. Leonie Adams named Consultant in Poetry.

1949 The United States joins NATO. Mao Zedong proclaims the foundation of the People's Republic of China. Arthur Miller's play *Death of a Salesman* is performed for the first time in New York. Elizabeth Bishop named Consultant in Poetry.

1950 Death of Edna St Vincent Millay. Birth of Jorie Graham, Dana Gioia, Joy Harjo. Publication of Charles Olsen's 'Projective Verse'. Start of the Korean War. Conrad Aiken named Consultant in Poetry.

1951 Publication of J. D. Salinger's first novel *The Catcher in the Rye*.

1952 Birth of Rita Dove. Publication of Robert Creeley's *Le Fou*, Robert Duncan's *Fragments of a Disordered Devotion*, Frank O'Hara's *A City Winter, and Other Poems*. Experimental American composer John Cage composes *4'33'*. William Carlos Williams named Consultant in Poetry.

1953 Arthur Miller's play *The Crucible* is first performed. Randall Jarrell named Consultant in Poetry.

1954 Birth of Sandra Cisneros, Louise Erdrich. The McCarthy Hearings begin. The United States Supreme Court rules unanimously that segregated schools are unconstitutional. American artist Jasper Johns paints the famous *Flag*.

1955 Death of Wallace Stevens. Publication of Elizabeth Bishop's *Poems: North and South – A Cold Spring*, Adrienne Rich's *The Diamond Cutters and Other Poems*. Rosa Parks refuses to give up her seat on a bus in Montgomery, Alabama.

1956 Publication of John Berryman's *Homage to Mistress Bradstreet*, Allen Ginsberg's *Howl and Other Poems*, Richard Wilbur's *Things of this World*. Black Mountain College closes. Lawrence Ferlinghetti is prosecuted and later acquitted for publishing Ginsberg's *Howl*.

1957 Publication of Denise Levertov's *Here and Now*, Wallace Stevens' *Opus Posthumous*, Jack Kerouac's novel *On the Road*. The Soviet Union launches Sputnik, the first artificial satellite.

1958 Publication of Theodore Roethke's *The Waking*, Truman Capote's novel *Breakfast at Tiffany's*. Robert Frost named Consultant in Poetry.

1959 Publication of Robert Lowell's *Life Studies*, Gary Snyder's *Riprap*, W. D. Snodgrass' *Heart's Needle*, William Burrough's novel *Naked Lunch*. Richard Eberhart named Consultant in Poetry.

1960 Publication of Sylvia Plath's *The Colossus*, Robert Duncan's *The Opening of the Field*, Randall Jarrell's *The Woman at the Washington Zoo*. The Nixon–Kennedy debate is the first televised United States presidential debate; 88% of American households now have television. Publication of Harper Lee's novel *To Kill a Mockingbird*.

1961 Death of H.D. (Hilda Doolittle) and Ernest Hemingway. Publication of Joseph Heller's novel *Catch-22*. Louis Untermeyer named Consultant in Poetry.

1962 Death of E .E. Cummings. Publication of John Ashbery's *The Tennis Court Oath*. Edward Albee's play *Who's Afraid of Virginia Woolf?* opens on Broadway. American artist Andy Warhol, a major figure in the Pop Art movement, shows *Campbell's Soup Cans* in the Ferus Gallery in Los Angeles.

1963 Death of Robert Frost, William Carlos Williams, Theodore Roethke, Sylvia Plath. Publication of Sylvia Plath's novel *The Bell Jar*, Betty Friedan's *The Feminine Mystique*. Assassination of President John F. Kennedy in Dallas, Texas. Howard Nemerov named Consultant in Poetry.

1964 Publication of John Berryman's *77 Dream Songs*, Robert Lowell's *For the Union Dead*, Saul Bellow's novel *Herzog*. The Civil Rights Act of 1964 outlaws major forms of discrimination against African Americans and women. Reed Whittemore named Consultant in Poetry.

1965 Death of T. S. Eliot, Randall Jarrell, Jack Spicer. Publication of Randall Jarrell's *The Lost World*. Assassination of activist Malcolm X in New York. Stephen Spender named Consultant in Poetry. The National Endowment for the Arts (NEA) is created by an Act of Congress. An exhibition in the Museum of Modern Art in New York titled *The Responsive Eye* shows a range of op art (visual art that uses optical illusions).

1966 Death of Mina Loy, Delmore Schwartz, Frank O'Hara. Birth of Sherman Alexie. Publication of Susan Sontag's first collection of essays, *Against Interpretation*. The feminist group the

National Organisation for Women (NOW) is founded. James Dickey named Consultant in Poetry.

1967 Death of Langston Hughes, Carl Sandburg. Publication of Anne Sexton's *Live or Die*. The Summer of Love in the Haight-Ashbury neighbourhood of San Francisco. The American artist Richard Estes, a major figure in the Photorealism movement, exhibits *Food Shop*.

1968 Death of Yvor Winters. Publication of Ezra Pound's last collection of cantos, *Drafts and Fragments of Cantos CX–CXVII*. Civil rights leader Dr Martin Luther King is assassinated in Memphis, Tennessee, sparking mass riots across the US. William Jay Smith named Consultant in Poetry.

1969 Publication of Philip Roth's novel *Portnoy's Complaint*, Kurt Vonnegut's novel *Slaughterhouse-Five*. American Astronaut Neil Armstrong becomes the first man to walk on the surface of the moon. The Woodstock Festival takes place in White Lake, New York. The Stonewall riots in New York mark the start of the modern gay liberation movement in the US.

1970 Death of Lorine Niedecker, Charles Olson. Publication of Maya Angelou's first novel *I Know Why the Caged Bird Sings*. The Public Broadcasting Service (PBS) is founded. William Stafford named Consultant in Poetry.

1971 Birth of Terrance Hayes. Death of Ogden Nash. Josephine Jacobsen named Consultant in Poetry.

1972 Death of Ezra Pound, Marianne Moore, John Berryman. Founding of United Graffiti Artists (UGA), a collective of *avant-garde* artists who exhibit graffiti in galleries such the Razor Gallery in New York.

1973 Death of W. H. Auden. Publication of Thomas Pynchon's novel *Gravity's Rainbow*, Erica Jong's *Fear of Flying*, Adrienne Rich's *Diving into the Wreck: Poems 1971–1972*. *Roe* v. *Wade* (landmark US Supreme Court case on abortion rights). Daniel Hoffman named Consultant in Poetry.

1974 Death of Anne Sexton. Resignation of US President Richard Nixon amidst Watergate Scandal. Stanley Kunitz named Consultant in Poetry.

1975 Publication of John Ashbery's *Self-Portrait in a Convex Mirror*. End of the Vietnam War.

1976 Publication of Elizabeth Bishop's *Geography II*. Celebration of the United States' bicentennial. Steve Jobs founds Apple Inc. Robert Hayden named Consultant in Poetry (the first African American to hold the post).

1977 Death of Robert Lowell, Elvis Presley.

1978 Death of Louis Zukofsky. Publication of Lyn Hejinian's *Writing is an Aid to Memory*, Audre Lorde's *The Black Unicorn*. Harvey Milk, the first openly gay public official, is assassinated in San Francisco. William Meredith named Consultant in Poetry.

1979 Death of Allen Tate, Elizabeth Bishop. White Night Riots; over 5000 demonstrators in San Francisco's gay community protest the lenient sentences of the Moscone and Milk assassin.

1980 Death of James Wright, Muriel Rukeyser, Robert Hayden. Publication of Jorie Graham's first collection *Hybrids of Plants and of Ghosts*. The US boycotts the Summer Olympics in Moscow. Launch of CNN, the first 24-hour cable TV news channel. John Lennon is assassinated outside the Dakota in New York.

1981 US President Ronald Reagan survives an assassination attempt. The Space Shuttle Columbia is the first flight of NASA's Space Shuttle Program. Launch of MTV, the first 24-hour cable TV network dedicated to airing music videos. Maxine Kumin named Consultant in Poetry.

1982 Death of Kenneth Rexroth, Archibald MacLeish. Publication of Alicia Ostriker's *A Woman Under the Surface*. Nearly one million demonstrators stage a peaceful protest against the nuclear arms race in New York's Central Park. Anthony Hecht named Consultant in Poetry.

1983 Publication of John Cage's *X: Writings '79–'82*.

1984 Publication of Robert Pinsky's verse translation *The Inferno of Dante*. Boycott of the Summer Olympics in Los Angeles by the Soviet Union and Eastern Bloc countries. Reed Whittemore and Robert Fitzgerald named Consultants in Poetry.

1985 The first .com domain name is registered heralding the birth of the internet. The title 'Consultant in Poetry' is changed to 'Poet Laureate' by an Act of Congress. Gwendolyn Brooks named Consultant in Poetry.

1986 Publication of Yusef Komunyakaa's *I Apologize for the Eyes in My Head*, Audre Lorde's *Our Dead Behind Us*. Robert Penn Warren named US Poet Laureate.

1987 Publication of Sandra Cisneros' *My Wicked, Wicked Ways*, Toni Morrison's novel *Beloved*. Wall Street stock market crash. Richard Wilbur named US Poet Laureate.

1988 Howard Nemerov named US Poet Laureate. American artist Jeff Joons, a major figure in the Neo-Pop Art movement, exhibits a sculpture titled 'Michael Jackson and Bubbles'.

1989 Death of Sterling Brown, May Swenson, Robert Penn Warren. Fall of the Berlin Wall.

1990 The Hubble Space Telescope is launched by NASA. Mark Strand named US Poet Laureate.

1991 Death of Laura Riding, James Schuyler. Collapse of the USSR. Operation Desert Storm; the US leads 34 coalition nations in an invasion of Iraq during the First Gulf War. Joseph Brodsky named US Poet Laureate.

1992 Death of Audre Lorde, John Cage. The Los Angeles riots (also known as the Rodney King riots). Mona Van Duyn named US Poet Laureate.

1993 The 'Don't ask, don't tell' policy prohibiting openly gay and bisexual armed forces personnel becomes law. Rita Dove named US Poet Laureate (the first African American woman to hold the post).

1995 Death of James Merrill. United States federal government shutdown over public funding. Robert Hass named US Poet Laureate.

1997 Death of Denise Levertov, Allen Ginsberg. Robert Pinsky named US Poet Laureate.

1998 US President Bill Clinton is impeached over allegations he had a sexual relationship with Monica Lewinsky, and later acquitted.

1999 Publication of Terrance Hayes' first collection *Muscular Music.*

2000 Death of Gwendolyn Brooks. Stanley Kunitz named US Poet Laureate.

2001 Death of A. R. Ammons. 9/11 terrorist attacks on the World Trade Center in New York and the Pentagon in Virginia. US and UK invasion of Afghanistan marks the start of the War on Terror. Billy Collins named US Poet Laureate.

2002 Death of Kenneth Koch.

2003 The United States, United Kingdom, Australia, and Poland invade Iraq. Todd Swift's electronic chapbook *100 Poets Against the War* is made available online, featuring the work of poets from around the world. Louise Glück named US Poet Laureate.

2004 Death of Donald Justice, Thom Gunn. The social networking site Facebook is launched. Ted Kooser named US Poet Laureate.

2005 Death of Robert Creeley.
2006 Death of Barbara Guest. The social networking service Twitter is created; the service has 100 million users by 2012. Donald Hall named US Poet Laureate.
2007 The late-2000s recession begins. Charles Simic named US Poet Laureate.
2008 Kay Ryan named US Poet Laureate.
2009 Death of W. D. Snodgrass. Publication of Rae Armantrout's *Versed*. Inauguration of Barack Obama, the first African American President of the United States.
2010 Death of Lucille Clifton, Ai (Ai Ogawa). W. S. Merwin named US Poet Laureate.
2011 The National September 11 Memorial on the site of the 9/11 attacks in 2001 is opened to the public. The last US troops are withdrawn from Iraq. United States debt-ceiling crisis. The 'Don't ask, don't tell' policy is repealed. Philip Levine named US Poet Laureate.
2012 Death of Adrienne Rich. Natasha Trethewey named US Poet Laureate.
2013 Barak Obama is inaugurated for his second term as President. Publication of Sharon Old's *Stag's Leap*. Edward Snowden leaks classified information about global surveillance by the United States National Security Agency (NSA).
2014 Death of Mark Strand, Carolyn Kizer. Restoration of full US diplomatic relations with Cuba. Charles Wright named US Poet Laureate.
2015 Death of James Tate. Publication of John Ashbery's twenty-sixth collection *Breezeway*. Juan Felipe Herrera named US Poet Laureate. Gay marriage is legalized in all 50 states.
2016 Donald Trump is named as the nominee of the Republican Party for President of the United States in the 2016 election. Hillary Clinton is named as the Democratic Party nominee, becoming the first ever female nominee of a major US political party.

'I hear America singing, the varied carols I hear': Introduction

Eleanor Spencer

In late 2011, a furiously articulate argument raged across the pages of *The New York Review of Books*. Helen Vendler, Arthur Kingsley Porter University Professor in the Department of English at Harvard University, and widely regarded as the leading critic of poetry in America, decried former American Poet Laureate Rita Dove's *The Penguin Anthology of 20th-Century American Poetry* for what she described as a politically motivated focus on 'multicultural inclusiveness' at the expense of coverage of canonical (that is, oft-anthologized and oft-taught) poets and poems – 'T.S. Eliot, Robert Frost, William Carlos Williams, Wallace Stevens, Marianne Moore, Hart Crane, Robert Lowell, John Berryman, Elizabeth Bishop (and some would include Ezra Pound).'[1] Dove's anthology, Vendler suggests, aims 'to shift the balance, introducing more black poets and giving them significant amounts of space, in some cases more space than is given to better-known authors'. 'These writers are', she wrote, 'included in some cases for their representative themes rather than their style.' Dove mounted a defence of her anthology in a later issue of the magazine, accusing Vendler of 'hubris', 'barely veiled racism', and 'an agenda beyond aesthetics'.[2] It was her intention, she asserted, only to 'choose significant poems of literary merit'.

Other prominent figures lent their voices and views to this fraught debate. Poet and novelist John Olson described Dove's anthology as a 'travesty', suggesting that the volume's 'exclusions are breathtaking'.[3] Similarly, the poet and literary critic Robert Archambeau wrote, 'as a scholar and critic, I find the representation of poetry here ... to be deeply flawed'.[4] Echoing Vendler, poet and musician Jeremy Bass wrote in his review of Dove's anthology in *The Nation* that the volume is 'at times more a cross section of cultural diversity than of literary achievement'.[5] Other notable figures came out in support of Dove, among them the poet Marguerite María Rivas who publicly wondered how Vendler could 'get it so wrong and be so out of touch with the ethos of contemporary American poetry'.[6]

It is both the privilege and the predicament of the anthologist to select those poets and those poems to be included, and, largely by default, those to be excluded. In her own volume, *The Anthology of Contemporary American Poetry* (1986), Vendler has made explicit her commitment to lasting aesthetic merit over socio-historical interest: 'I have had to leave out many poets whose aims were admirable but whose poems seemed thin (whatever their past historical effect).'[7] Dove has cast her net rather wider than other anthologists, and some 175 poets are represented within the volume, many of them likely to be unfamiliar even to American readers of poetry let alone readers outside the US. Vendler suggests that Dove regards 'selectivity' as 'elitism', and, indeed, Dove defiantly states in her rebuttal of Vendler's review, 'I am proud that no principle of selection emerges.'[8] There are, however, some peculiar lacunae in Dove's anthology. Sylvia Plath, Allen Ginsberg, and Sterling Brown are entirely absent (due to issues of copyright, Dove claims), and other well-known poets are glossed over seemingly rather hastily; Wallace Stevens, for example, is given six pages whereas the little known African American Modernist Melvin Tolson receives fourteen. That a number of well-known and well-regarded poets are either absent or arguably under-represented, whereas certain little-known poets are arguably over-represented, suggests that there *is* a tacit 'principle of selection' at work in this anthology, whether based primarily on aesthetics or ethics, to include those Dove claims have been historically 'sidelined from the mainstream's surging currents'.

That two 'establishment' figures as prominent as Vendler and Dove could disagree so completely as to how best to represent twentieth-century 'American poetry' is symptomatic of that diversity that Vendler describes in *The Anthology of Contemporary American Poetry* (1986):

> In England – a tiny country, agriculturally cultivated for centuries, architecturally and historically rich, uninvaded in battle since 1066, with a small, homogeneous educated class – a coherent poetry was possible for a number of centuries. In American – an enormous wilderness only recently settled, educationally and ethnically diverse, made and remade by waves of immigrants – poetry was bound to be diffuse, heterogeneous, and, vis-à-vis England, defensive.[9]

It is exactly this heterogeneity that Walt Whitman celebrates in his vision of harmonious, productive individualism, 'I Hear America Singing'. Each 'carpenter', 'mason', 'boatman', 'mother' and 'young wife' sings 'what belongs to him or her and to none else', yet these countless 'strong melodious songs' do not drown each other out in a competitive cacophony, but rather cohere in a joyful, soaring national anthem.[10] Despite Whitman's utopian vision, in reality these 'songs' are more difficult to reconcile. It may well be that the particular geography and history of America means that it is naïve or simplistic to talk of a single, coherent 'American poetry'; indeed, several critics have referred to 'American poetries' in the plural.[11]

This wrangle also raises important questions about the role of the anthology (and, no less, the obligation of the anthologist). Should anthologies be descriptive, including what is currently or historically most popular or considered most accomplished? Or should they be prescriptive, aiming to expand or revise the existing canon by introducing readers to little-known poets and poems who are arguably deserving of greater attention and acclaim? The ideal anthology would surely be, and do, both; using the work of well-known and well-regarded poets to provide a necessary point of entry, or a framework, through which readers can acquaint themselves with the work of lesser-known figures.

Like an anthology, an edited collection of essays must necessarily have a 'principle of selection', however explicit or oblique. Editing a volume of this nature entails a potentially fraught process of selection and rejection. Including one poet at the expense of another may be perceived as a deliberate act – or an unwitting exposé – of political, gender, or racial bias; or equally as a transparent effort to appear inclusive and egalitarian. This volume aims to introduce students of poetry and of American literature to the diverse body of work written by American poets or by poets in America after the Second World War. Many of the poets covered in this volume will be well known to readers, particularly those poets covered in Part One. These are those poets who are most frequently and widely taught on school and college syllabuses, both in the US and around the English-speaking world; John Berryman, Robert Lowell, Elizabeth Bishop, Adrienne Rich, John Ashbery, and Sylvia Plath. The essays on these poets do not aim simply to cement their status as stalwarts of the canon, but to situate these well-known poets within the wider terrain and traditions of twentieth-century American poetry; to examine the poetry from a fresh critical perspective; and, often, to unsettle or to complicate our perhaps too easy understanding of their work and import. It is, of course, the case that those prominent poets who had made their name in the interwar decades – Robert Frost, Wallace Stevens, William Carlos Williams, Ezra Pound, Marianne Moore, for example – were still writing and publishing significant work in the post-war years;

Williams' *Paterson* was published in five volumes from 1946 to 1958, Pound's *The Pisan Cantos* was published in 1948, and Moore's *Collected Poems* of 1951 earned her the National Book Award, the Pulitzer Prize, and the Bollingen Prize. It is fair to say, however, that these poets had, by and large, published the majority of their significant work prior to the start of the Second World War; indeed, Frost, Williams, and Pound published their first collections even before the start of the First World War. The generation covered in this collection, then, is that generation which came to prominence and acclaim in the years or decades following the Second World War. Plath, of course, died at the age of thirty in the early 1960s, and by 1980 only Ashbery and Rich survived. Rich died in 2012, having published her last collection, *Tonight No Poetry Will Serve: Poems 2007–2010*, in 2010. Ashbery published his most recent collection, *Breezeway*, in the first half of 2015, sixty-two years after the publication of his first collection, *Turandot and Other Poems*, in 1953.

Vendler asks of Dove's anthology, 'Which of Dove's 175 poets will have staying power, and which will seep back into the archives of sociology?' The answer to this question is, of course, only time will tell. It is, I would venture, as yet unclear who amongst the younger generation of poets will ultimately succeed the likes of Lowell, Bishop et al. in terms of stature in the 'American canon', but they may well be amongst those poets – as yet likely to be less familiar, even to American readers – covered in Parts Two and Three of this collection. These essays aim to give critical attention to those poets who are less widely known, though perhaps no less critically acclaimed. Many of these poets are several generations removed from Berryman, Lowell, Bishop and the like, and may in the near or far future come to occupy the canon and the public consciousness in much the same way as these famous forebears.

★

During the course of the Second World War, America suffered nearly 420,000 human fatalities. Worldwide, over sixty million people were killed, either in fighting, or as a result of war-related famine or disease. Approximately 3% of the world's total population (as calculated in 1940) died during this conflict.[12] In early August 1945, nearly three months after the surrender of Nazi Germany had ended World War II in Europe, America, having issued an unheeded call for Japan's unconditional surrender, dropped two atomic bombs – codenamed 'Little Boy' and 'Fat Man' – on the Japanese cities of Hiroshima and Nagasaki. These two bombings resulted in the deaths – either instantaneous or subsequent – of an estimated 185,000 people.[13] Six days after the bombing of Nagasaki, Japan announced its surrender to the Allies, marking the end of the Pacific War (which had begun with the bombing of the US naval base at Pearl Harbor in 1941), and of World War II.

Whilst contemporaneously fêted as a triumph of American military might and moral superiority, it is clear that this bloody conflict was, inevitably, to cast a darksome shadow over the second half of the twentieth century. In 1949, as the unspeakable atrocities of the Holocaust were revealed, the German sociologist and philosopher Theodor Adorno wrote his now famous (though oft misconstrued) dictum in the essay 'Cultural Criticism and Society'. Adorno writes that, in the aftermath of the Holocaust,

> Cultural criticism finds itself faced with the final stage of the dialective of culture and barbarism. To write poetry after Auschwitz is barbaric. And this corrodes even the knowledge of why it has become impossible to write poetry today. Absolute reification, which presupposed intellectual progress as one of its elements, is now preparing to absorb the mind entirely. Critical intelligence cannot be equal to this challenge as long as it confines itself to self-satisfied contemplation.[14]

Despite the apparent unequivocality of the phrase 'To write poetry after Auschwitz is barbaric,' when quoted out of context, Adorno was *not* advocating that poets should down their tools on principle in light of the human suffering of the Holocaust. Indeed, in a later essay he revisited and revised these lines, writing:

> I once said that after Auschwitz one could no longer write poetry, and that gave rise to a discussion I did not anticipate when I wrote those words ... I would readily concede that, just as I said that after Auschwitz one could not write poems – by which I meant to point to the hollowness of the resurrected culture of that time – it could equally well be said, on the other hand, that one must write poems, in keeping with Hegel's statement in his Aesthetics that as long as there is an awareness of suffering among human beings there must also be art as the objective form of that awareness.[15]

What Adorno was suggesting, then, was an engaged and aware poetics; a poetics that did not turn its back on the horrors of the Holocaust and did not unquestioningly set about re-establishing the culture in which, and from which, the Holocaust was permitted to occur. Poetry written in the aftermath of such an event, Adorno argues, has an ethical obligation that cannot be evaded, as well as an aesthetic function. This is not to say, of course, that all poetry written after World War II and the Holocaust must be explicitly 'about' conflict, genocide, and suffering. Poetry, and other art forms, may register the trials and traumas of war, and the shocking depravity of which humans are capable, obliquely rather than explicitly; indeed, many of the most affecting, disconcerting poems to be written in the midst of, or in the aftermath of earlier conflicts, are not obviously 'war poems'. Both T. S. Eliot's *The Waste Land*, and Mina Loy's 'Love Songs', for example, register not so much the physical wounds suffered by the soldier poets as the psychic damage inflicted on both individual and collective consciousness by World War I. During the decades following the war, America grew into a global superpower – a financial, industrial, military, and political behemoth. It demonstrated, and even increased, its reach through involvement in numerous other conflicts around the world, notable amongst them the Cold-War proxy wars in Korea (1950–1953) and Vietnam (1955–1975); the Gulf War (1990–1991); and the global 'War on Terror', launched in response to the 9/11 terrorist attacks on American soil. Amongst the generation of poets who came to prominence in the decades following the war, we see both the oblique registering of, and explicit engagement with, these conflicts and traumas.

Perhaps the most explicitly politically engaged poet and writer covered in this volume is Adrienne Rich. Rich's earliest work attracted several notable awards and honours, amongst them the Yale Series of Younger Poets Award, judged by W. H. Auden, for her first volume *A Change of World* (1951). Work from this early period demonstrated what Wendy Martin and Lauren Morrison describe in their essay, 'Adrienne Rich: Poetry and Social Change', as 'Rich's training in traditional poetic craft', her 'technical command', and her 'graceful and feminine use of language'. However, the poet was later to express intense ambivalence about this early work, writing that 'too many of the poems were, at best, facile and ungrounded imitations of other poets'. Her third collection, *Snapshots of a Daughter-in-Law* (1963), signalled Rich's changing priorities and preoccupations. As Martin and Morrison explain, 'Rich now call[ed] for a poetic tradition … centered on women and women's experience, initiating what [would] be a significant focus of her work for the rest of her career.' The volume was met with mixed reviews; whilst it received the Bess Hokin Prize from *Poetry Magazine*, it was also criticized for being simultaneously too personal and too political: 'I was seen as "bitter" and "personal"; and to be personal was to be disqualified, and that was very shaking because I'd really gone out on a limb,' Rich recalls. Rich's subsequent poetry reflects her growing politicization and her commitment to anti-war, civil rights, and feminist activism. In the late 1970s she wrote a number of socio-political essays, including the seminal 'Compulsory Heterosexuality and Lesbian Existence', in which she calls for a greater understanding and appreciation of lesbian experience, and posits that lesbianism should be understood as a 'continuum' encompassing a wide range of social, emotional, and sexual interactions between women.

The complex – even fraught – relationship between the 'personal' and the 'political' is nowhere more evident than in the work of the so-called 'Confessional' poets covered in this collection, John Berryman, Robert Lowell, and Sylvia Plath. Like Rich, these poets rebelled against the 'cult of impersonality' presided over by the Modernist poets T. S. Eliot and Ezra Pound and the influential New Critics, and forged a new poetics which documented and dramatized the autobiographical experiences of the poet with searing honesty (or, at least, gave a convincing 'performance' of doing just that).

In his 1919 essay 'Tradition and the Individual Talent', Eliot suggests that the poet must achieve 'a continual surrender of himself as he is at the moment to something which is more valuable', namely, the body of work produced by his forebears.[16] 'The progress of the artist', he asserts, 'is a continual self-sacrifice, a continual extinction of personality.' William Wordsworth's assertion that 'Poetry is the spontaneous overflow of powerful feelings [which] takes its origins from emotion recollected in tranquillity'[17] is dismissed by Eliot as 'an inexact formula'.[18] The poet's own 'powerful feelings' and emotions have no place in poetry, Eliot argues: 'Impressions and experiences which are important for the man may take no place in the poetry, and those which become important in the poetry may play quite a negligible part in the man, the personality.'[19] The culturally embedded stereotype of the tortured poet or artist, and the popularly professed relationship between personal suffering and creativity, are boldly deconstructed – dismantled, even – as Eliot decrees that 'the more perfect the artist, the more completely separate in him will be the man who suffers and the mind which creates; the more perfectly will the mind digest and transmute the passions which are its material.'[20] In 'A Retrospect' (1918), a manifesto for the fledgling Imagist movement, Pound set out a blueprint for a 'harder and saner' poetry, 'as much like granite as it can be', which, rejecting the 'emotional slither', 'rhetorical din, and luxurious riot' of much nineteenth-century writing, would instead derive its 'force' from 'its truth, [and] its interpretive power'.[21] This, together with Eliot's essay, would prove to be one of the foundational texts of a movement that would, following John

Crowe Ransom's 1941 volume of the same name, become known as 'The New Criticism'.

Adam Kirsch notes that so influential had New Criticism become that a young poet in the mid-twentieth century 'was faced with a body of poetry and criticism so authoritative that it took courage, and ingenuity, simply to avoid being crushed by it'.[22] In the late 1950s and early 1960s, however, poets such as Berryman, Lowell, Plath, Anne Sexton, and Randall Jarrell, were rebelling against the New Critical understanding of poetry, and in their work we see a calculated rejection of what Berryman called Eliot's 'amusing theory of the impersonality of the artist' in favour of a return to an earlier conception of the role; Walt Whitman's vision of the poet 'not as maker but as spiritual historian'.[23] These poets raised in the New Critical tradition, Lowell noted, had become 'terribly proficient at these forms', but now made a decisive 'breakthrough back into life', dismantling and discarding what they saw as the rigid confines of the reserved, academic, allusively obscurantist style of the Modernist poets.[24] Whereas the New Critics advocated the 'continual extinction of personality' within, and through, poetry, for these 'confessional' poets, the distance between 'the man who suffers' and 'the mind that creates' was collapsed so entirely that both Berryman and Lowell published poems that contained their home addresses.

The expression 'confessional' poetry was first coined by M. L. Rosenthal in his 1959 review of Lowell's *Life Studies*, 'Poetry as Confession'. Rosenthal suggested that for Lowell, the writing of poetry functioned as 'soul's therapy', a space in which to make 'the most naked kind of confession'. Whereas poets like Eliot and Pound employ what Rosenthal calls 'a certain indirection [that] masks the poet's actual face and psyche', he suggests that Lowell 'removes the mask' and that 'His speaker is unequivocally himself.'[25] As Steven Gould Axelrod reveals in his essay 'Robert Lowell: Protean Poet', Lowell's *Life Studies* 'struck at the time with a thunderbolt, and it still does'. The allusive, densely rhetorical style of the earlier collection *Lord Weary's Castle* was transformed, in *Life Studies*, into 'the language of a frail human being in a confusing social universe'. Lowell's fraught personal relationships, his burdensome familial inheritance, and his fragile mental health become his *materia poetica* in this collection, raising questions as to the potential ethical pitfalls of distilling art from life. These questions are more explicitly addressed in Lowell's later collection *The Dolphin*, in which he incorporates private letters from his former wife Elizabeth Hardwick into his poems, but also silently modifies those letters. Lowell's close friend Elizabeth Bishop chastised

Lowell, writing, 'Lizzie is not dead, etc. – but there is a "mixture of fact and fiction", and you have changed her letters ... One can use one's life as material, but these letters – aren't you violating a trust? ... *art just isn't worth that much*.' The poems seem to acknowledge a failure of ethical responsibility; indeed, in the final sonnet, the speaker half apologizes for 'not avoiding injury to others, / not avoiding injury to myself'.[26]

The infliction of 'injury', whether psychical or physical, accidental or deliberate, on the self or on others, is a dark preoccupation in much so-called 'confessional' poetry: the speaker of Plath's 'Lady Lazarus' conceives of suicide as an electrifying performance ('The big strip tease'), and Anne Sexton's 'Cinderella' nonchalantly describes a series of horrific self-mutilations ('her big toe got in the way so she simply / sliced it off and put on the slipper'). As Stephen Matterson reveals in his essay '"Whims & emergencies, discoveries, losses": The Poetry of John Berryman', this preoccupation verges on paranoia in Berryman's Dream Songs: 'In Song 29 [Berryman's Henry] lies in the dawn trying to recall whether he has murdered anyone in his drunken fits, counting his friends, and concluding with relief that "Nobody is ever missing."' Berryman is at pains to distance and differentiate himself from his persona Henry, even as their shared biographies (the suicide of the father, alcoholism, depression) suggest their sameness: 'Henry does resemble me, and I resemble Henry,' Berryman admits, 'but on the other hand I am not Henry. You know, I pay income tax; Henry pays no income tax. And bats come over and they stall in my hair – and fuck them, I'm not Henry; Henry doesn't have any bats.'[27] Berryman transcends gauche 'confession' in the myriad Dream Songs through what Matterson describes as 'the fluid exchange of identity between Henry and Berryman', achieved largely through 'a shifting of pronouns' and a suspension of 'the typographical conventions such as quotation marks which indicate distinctions between who is speaking'.

The so-called 'confessional' poets never regarded themselves as such, and Lowell, W. D. Snodgrass, and Berryman publicly expressed their dislike of the too-easy label. In a 1972 interview, Berryman said that he responded to Rosenthal's term with 'rage and contempt!', and added, 'The term doesn't mean anything. I understand the confessional to be a place where you go and talk with a priest. I personally haven't been to confession since I was twelve years old.'[28] Rosenthal later developed doubts about the usefulness of his coinage, reflecting that 'It was a term both helpful and too limited, and very possibly the conception of a confessional school has by now done a certain amount of damage.'[29] In the 1960s, others proffered alternative but hardly more 'helpful' terms, amongst them Al Alvarez ('extremist' poetry), Monroe Spears ('open' poetry), and Marjorie Perloff ('documentary' verse).[30] The term 'confessional' poetry has undoubtedly shaped and coloured the critical and popular reception and understanding of these poets' work. As Tracy Brain explores in her essay 'Sylvia Plath in the Early Twenty-First Century', fans and detractors alike have been, and indeed, still are, quick either to praise or to disparage Plath's poetry for what they read as its bold, unvarnished emotional honesty. Plath's suicide in 1963 at the age of thirty has led to her posthumous apotheosis as a cult figure; she is variously cast as a tortured genius, a feminist icon, a wronged wife, and the 'poster girl for teenage angst and suicide'.[31] Brain argues that the recent series of fifty-year anniversaries ('of the writing of the October poems of 1962; … of *The Bell Jar*'s original publication in January of 1963; … of Plath's death, on the eleventh day of the following month; [and] … of the discovery of the *Ariel* manuscript she left on her desk at that time') that were celebrated worldwide in late 2012 and early 2013 gave us an opportunity to read Plath's oeuvre in 'new ways'; 'putting her work in the context of writers she hasn't formerly been read alongside; looking attentively at her visual art; evaluating the ways she has been taken up by different cultures and causes; measuring her far-reaching influence; seeing her poems in dialogue with Ted Hughes' rather than in opposition to him; considering how politics, history and other contemporary concerns informed her literary production; and reappraising the generic boundaries under which her work has formerly been classified'. Looking not only at Plath's posthumous second collection *Ariel*, but also at her only novel *The Bell Jar*, published just a month before her death, Brain's essay reveals the previously overlooked 'enmeshed relationship between Plath's prose and poetry'. To reread a poem like 'Gulliver' alongside extracts from the novel is to read both texts anew; what distinguishes both is 'a rare combination of a poet's economy and a novelist's ability never to lose sight of the story she is telling'.

Elizabeth Bishop proffered her own alternative term for the work of her contemporaries: 'If I were a good critic and had a good brain', she wrote in a 1964 letter, 'I think I'd like to write a study of "The School of Anguish" – Lowell (by far the best), Roethke, and Berryman and their descendants like Anne Sexton and [Frederick] Siedel, more and more anguish and less and less poetry. Surely never in all the ages has poetry been so personal and confessional – and I don't think it is what I like, really[.]'[32] Whilst Bishop's childhood was marred by exactly the kind of 'anguish' and family trauma which has become the hallmark of the so-called 'confessional' poets, her poetry registers this experience only obliquely. Bishop's poetry might be helpfully understood as the negative image of the 'confessional' tendency; whereas many of her contemporaries look inwards, subjecting themselves to a painstaking – not to mention, painful – self-inventory and excoriation in verse, Bishop eschews the role of 'wounded surgeon' for the role of outward-looking traveller, observer, and inveterate 'foreigner'. Linda Anderson's essay 'Making and Making Do: The Poetry of Elizabeth Bishop' reveals that Bishop shared with her 'mentor' Marianne Moore a fascination with 'things': praising Moore's poetry she wrote, 'Why had no one ever written about things in this clear and dazzling way before?' As Anderson explores, Bishop conceived of the intricate processes of memory and imagination in strikingly spatial, physical terms: 'I have that continuous uncomfortable feeling of "things" in the head, like icebergs or rocks or awkwardly placed pieces of furniture ... And I can't help having the theory that if they are joggled around hard enough and long enough some kind of electricity will occur, just by friction.' In stark opposition to the 'confessional' poet's necessary centrality to his verse, Anderson suggests that Bishop seems to 'desire a form of artistic composition that eliminates the writer's conscious volition, shifting the perspective away from the controlling presence of the artist to an unconscious process'.

Just as the term 'confessional' poetry has both helped and hindered readers, other terms coined to corral and collect American poets together are similarly problematic, as Rory Waterman reveals in his essay, '"Singularly rich": Donald Allen's *The New American Poetry 1945–1960*'. Donald Allen's anthology, widely considered the single most influential anthology of the post-WWII period, and described by Mark Scroggins as the 'Bible of American counterpoetics', aimed to introduce a new generation of poets at that time largely unknown to the American reading public. Allen's volume positioned itself as a challenge and an antidote to the 'fairly traditional and largely formalist' anthologies that had come before, for example, *New Poets of England and America* (1957), edited by Donald Hall, Robert Pack, and Louis Simpson. There was, Allen thought, little that was 'New' about this earlier anthology, and his volume deliberately does not include a single poet previously included in *New Poets*. That these two anthologies, published only three years apart, both professing to offer a representative selection of the best 'New' American poetry, should have no overlap whatsoever is testament to the range and the diversity of poetry written in American in the decades after the end of World War II. Waterman reveals that Allen's neat portioning of his favoured poets into distinct generations and movements – 'the Black Mountain Poets, the San Francisco Renaissance, the Beats, the New York School' and 'fifth "group" of other poets not identified with a specific school or movement' – 'is a little too convenient.' Whilst this principle of organization may aid the unfamiliar reader lighting out in what Allen described as an 'almost completely uncharted' field, such rigid 'pigeonholing' of poets is bound to oversimplify the complex relationships between these poets' work, overemphasizing affinities whilst glossing over important divergences. As Waterman illustrates, 'some of the poets could really have been placed in two or more categories'. Gary Snyder, for example, who is included in Allen's miscellaneous fifth grouping, 'might equally have been in the San Francisco Renaissance section or among the Beats', and though Robert Duncan is presented in the Black Mountain section, 'he was also one of the most influential poets of the San Francisco Renaissance and it was there that he had come to prominence'. Despite the problematic nature of these groupings, though, Allen's anthology 'became the touchstone for a new set of approaches in American poetry', and succeeded in transforming many of the then largely unknown poets into now canonical figures.

One of the terms popularized by Allen's anthology was 'the New York School'. As Waterman explains, 'Allen says nothing about how his fourth group of poets are linked other than by geography: he just points out that some (John Ashbery, Kenneth Koch and Frank O'Hara) "migrated to New York in the early fifties", and associated with others (Edward Field, Barbara Guest and James Schuyler) who were already there, and leaves it at that.' Just as the likes of Berryman and Lowell denied the validity of the term 'confessional' poetry, Ashbery has similarly questioned the accuracy and usefulness of the term: 'as with all labels, it's inexact and can be really misleading', he warns. He suggests that the 'New York School' was little more than a marketing ploy, based on a happy accident of geography rather than any shared aesthetic ambition: 'This label was foisted on us by a man named John Bernard Myers, who ran the Tibor de Nagy Gallery ... I think the idea was that, since everybody was talking about the New York School of painting, if he created a New York School of poets that they would automatically be considered important because of the sound of the name. I don't think we ever were a school.'[33] Though, as Waterman notes, 'It seems customary for most artists aligned with any movement to deny it really exists,' Ashbery has clearly outlasted and transcended this initial 'alignment' with the ephemeral New York School. His twenty-sixth volume of poetry, *Breezeway*, was published in 2015, and the one-time *avant-garde enfant terrible* has, over the course of a six-decade-long poetic career, now become the grand old man of American poetry, winning almost every notable American poetry prize, serving for many years as a chancellor of the Academy of American Poets, and being named as Poet Laureate of New York State in 2001. As my own essay '"A work of art that the critic cannot even talk about": The Poetry of John Ashbery' suggests, he has both won admirers and alienated critics with 'a body of verse that seems not only to resist but also to mock ... analytical endeavors'. The 'madcap mixing and merging of the lexis, images, and reference points of "high" and "low" culture', that so confounds his detractors, makes this octogenarian poet the unlikely versifier for our digital age; indeed, in 2007 he was announced as mtvU's inaugural Poet Laureate.

Throughout Ashbery's sixty-year career he has exhibited what he has called a 'cuckoo instinct that makes me enjoy making my home in somebody else's nest'.[34] This 'cuckoo instinct' manifests itself in his adoption and adaptation of numerous fixed poetic forms (and particularly repetitional poetic forms), including the sonnet, the haiku, the haibun, the sestina, the villanelle, and the pantoum. For Ashbery, working with and within these forms is a means of 'getting into remoter areas of consciousness', and he describes how 'the really bizarre requirements' of these unusual forms function as a 'probing tool rather than as a form in the traditional sense'.

From the 1950s onwards, as America asserted its dominance on the world stage, many American poets turned their backs on fixed forms beloved of the New Critics, in favour of free verse. There developed a kind of binarism in thinking about fixed forms versus free verse, whereby fixed forms were associated with the patriarchy ('the dead, white males'), with the burden of (European) historical anteriority, and with social elitism and political conservatism, whereas free verse was considered demotic, democratic, and egalitarian. As the essays on Rich, Lowell, and Berryman reveal, we see a marked relaxation of style between their earliest volumes and their later work as they become more proficient at 'playing tennis with the net down', as Robert Frost would have it.[35] As such, the free verse that had previously been on the margins moved firmly into the mainstream. When free verse, associated with subversion of the status quo, *becomes* the status quo, how, then, might poets rebel? In the 1980s, a countermovement became apparent, as poets reclaimed and revived the fixed forms that had previously been rejected as modes of oppression. In his 1987 essay 'Notes on the New Formalism', Dana Gioia writes:

> While the overwhelming majority of new poetry published in the U.S. continues to be in "open" forms, for the first time in two generations there is a major revival of formal verse among young poets ... But the revival of rhyme and meter among some young poets creates an unprecedented situation in American poetry. The new formalists put free verse poets in the ironic and unprepared position of being the status quo. Free verse, the creation of an older literary revolution, is now the long-established, ruling orthodoxy; formal poetry the unexpected challenge.[36]

Just as Lowell in the late 1950s conceived of his use of free verse and personal subject matter as a bold 'breakthrough back into life', the New Formalists saw their revival of fixed forms as a similarly freeing, enlivening 'breakthrough'.[37] The work of the New Formalists – amongst them, Gioia, Marilyn Hacker, Mark Jarman, Charles Martin, and Phillis Levin – not only rehabilitated fixed forms in the minds of the American reading public, but also encouraged readers to appreciate that even free verse is not – and cannot ever be – entirely 'free': we are talking not about an absence of a set of rules, but rather about a *different* set of rules. Because free verse had, by the 1980s, become the poetic orthodoxy, no longer aesthetically or politically radical, both the use of free verse and the use of fixed forms had become largely politically neutralized.

This de-politicization of the question of form(lessness) was immensely freeing, theoretically making available to poets what David Caplan describes as 'the nearly countless forms and prosodies that the contemporary moment offers'. In addition, the dramatic rise in the number of creative writing programmes in the US from the 1990s onwards (in 1994 there were 64 M.F.A. programmes in creative writing; by 2014 that number had more than tripled to 229, with another 152 M.A. programmes) meant that aspiring poets were being schooled in the use of countless forms of which they might otherwise have been unaware.[38] However, in his essay 'The Art of Exclusion: Form and Prosody in American Poetry since 1970', Caplan suggests that 'In an era that presents such abundant poetic choices, too many exist for any poet to try, let alone master. To write a poem, then, is also *not* to pursue nearly countless options and opportunities.' Looking at poems by Robert Hass, Mark Strand, Rae Armantrout, Kenneth Goldbarth, and Donald Justice, amongst others, Caplan suggests that we must pay attention not only to what these poems are, but also to what they are *not*: 'in art', he argues, 'inclusion requires an equally powerful exclusion. No matter how generous, a poem must define what it is not.'

Gioia suggests that in the last two decades of the twentieth century the most pressing question with which American poets were faced was that of how to move beyond the stubborn residue of the Confessional heyday in the late 1950s and 1960s; what he calls 'the prolixity of the lyric; the bankruptcy of the confessional mode; the inability to establish a meaningful aesthetic for new poetic narrative'.[39] For these poets, fixed forms represent opportunities and possibilities for a renewed and revived lyric poetry, rather than restrictions or restraints. In his essay, 'The Great Divide? Post-confessional and Language Poetry', Paul Batchelor explores the various ways in which poets responded to 'the bankruptcy of the confessional mode'. We are, of course, already aware that 'confessional poetry' is 'a problematic label', and, as Batchelor notes, '"post-confessional poetry" risks adding a further layer of vagueness'. His essay reveals that 'the range of styles that can now be said to have derived something from confessionalism is vast, and would include the work of such diverse poets as Ai, Frank Bidart, Philip Levine, Sharon Olds, Adrienne Rich, and James Wright.' Some poets – C. K. Williams, Robert Pinsky and Louise Glück, amongst them – retained and reworked aspects of the 'confessional legacy', seeking to rehabilitate the textual function of the intimate lyric 'I'. Others – the Language Poets (or L=A=N=G=U=A=G=E Poets), amongst them Lyn Hejinian, Bob Perelman, and Rae Armantrout – rejected out of hand the premises of lyric poetry and the popular conception of the poem as a mode of self-expression. Just as the proponents of free verse set themselves up in aesthetic and political opposition to the formalists in the 1950s, the Language Poets similarly conceived of themselves as a radical countermovement. Charles Bernstein recalled, 'We shared a very strong dislike of the Official Verse Culture of that time, which seemed to favor poems so crippled by their formulas for personal epiphany that personal epiphany was shed at the starting line in favor of a highly mannered voicey voice "indicating" (like they used to say in Method Acting) rather than expressing the poet's feelings, the so-called feelings of the so-called poet.' Again, like the free versifiers, in time the Language Poets found themselves part of the mainstream they had previously attacked; as Batchelor notes, 'Language poetry is now widely taught in universities, many of its practitioners are tenured professors, and Rae Armantrout's *Versed* (2009) recently won the Pulitzer Prize: today's "Official Verse Culture", however it is defined, includes Language poetry.'

A significant number of the poets whose work might be included in anthologies of Language poetry are still writing in the second decade of the twenty-first century, and what we might think of as a second generation of Language Poets (or, at least, as poets influenced by Language poetry) – including Juliana Spahr, Kenneth Goldsmith, K. Silem Mohammad – has come to prominence in the last decade or so. In the final essay in this volume, 'Not Quite The End Of The World: American Poetry since 2000', Stephen Burt offers what is, essentially, a real-time survey of American poetry (or poetry in America, or poetry by Americans) after the millennium. Such a survey is, as Burt admits, a difficult task; 'To survey the American poetry of the two decades after [James] Merrill's death [in 1995] is to survey a bafflingly wide array of styles, schools, backgrounds, approaches to poetry, and definitions of "poetry". Their essay reveals an American poetry more diverse, more devolved, more decentralized than ever: 'Certainly we cannot say there is one current, one "mainstream" in American poetry now (if we ever could): nor can we say there is just one countertradition, one meaningful avant-garde,' they write. America's rich history as (largely) a nation of immigrants and settlers manifests itself in the 'lines of challenging poetry [which seem] to grow farther and farther from the formal repertoire of the European past.' African American, Native American, Asian American, Asian Pacific American, Arab American, Russian American, Hispanic and Latino American, Chicano, Hawai'ian, Irish American, and even European American poets, write poetry that proudly draws on, and often foregrounds, their 'polyglot backgrounds', but refuses to be constrained by naïve expectations of what 'Native American' or 'Chicano' poetry should sound like, or look like, or be concerned with.

It is one such 'naïve expectation' – namely 'that African American poetry is autobiographical, vernacular, unitary, and exclusively about the theme of oppression' – that Lauri Ramey challenges in her essay '"You Asked Me to Sing Then You Seemed Not to Hear": African American Poetry since 1945'. Ramey's essay reveals that African American poetry is subject to a complex set of expectations, foremost amongst them 'the peculiar criterion of authenticity'. It is exactly this burdensome white (mis)conception of black 'authenticity' that Terence Hayes challenges in 'Woofer' (2006), discussed in Burt's essay on poetry since the millennium: 'drums drummed upstairs from hi-fi woofers / because that's the closest I've ever come to anything / remotely ritualistic or African'. A white readership expects 'authenticity' from African American poets, yet may have little understanding that there are many different kinds of African American experience, all of them equally 'authentic'. A second expectation of African American poetry, Ramey suggests, is that it is traditional, more concerned with preserving historical modes than with experimentation. 'Literary criticism has', Ramey writes, 'typically ... regarded "black" and "avant-garde" writing as unrelated, even antithetical, bodies.' Whilst there are 'extensive studies of the innovators of white modernism and postmodernism', the long legacy of African American experimentalism has gone largely unremarked. Ramey's essay reveals 'a hidden canon' of formally and stylistically experimental verse, and illustrates that these poets draw 'on a variety of formally innovative trends associated with the historical avant-gardes ... blending them with African American references and racial signifiers'. Furthermore, there is a new generation of African American poets and practitioners – including mendi + keith obadike, giovanni singleton, and Julie Ezelle Patton – who are extending the tradition of oral and performance poetry by way of digital performance projects and conceptual online art and sound works. Ramey's essay explores to what extent it is helpful to think of African American poetry as a 'cohesive body of literature' (and, implicitly, whether an essay on 'African American Poetry since 1945' is a justified means of organization or a lazy ghettoization of otherwise diverse writers). Ramey suggests that 'Although this body of poetry is as diverse and varied as its individual creators, some common themes and threads often appear which justify its consideration as a literary tradition.' In a larger, more expansive collection of essays, it would have been possible to devote closer attention to individual African American poets – as, indeed, it would have been possible to offer more detailed coverage of a whole range of poets – male and female, black and white – who have, as things stand, not achieved the canonicity of the likes of Lowell, Bishop, Rich et al.

The advent of the internet has no less than revolutionized the way in which poets and presses engage (and are expected to engage) with their potential readership. Anyone – published poet or not – with a PC or smartphone and a WiFi connection can – in theory, at least – reach millions, if not billions, of readers on blogs, YouTube, and social media sites. The octogenarian Ashbery finds the prospect appealing: 'I'm not [on social media], but I wish I was ... Because it might offer new possibilities on the horizon.'[40] Given the sheer number of aspiring poets hoping for 'a big break', though, it is more likely that they will simply be lost in what Laura Kasischke describes in her poem 'The Internet' as 'This strange haze / made of information'. As Burt notes, 'to get noticed as a poet nowadays seems easier in one way (thanks to the Internet) but harder in others (thanks to the Internet, to the sheer size of the country, to the declining importance of older verbal arts, to the blaring news) than ever before'. Whilst there remains a certain degree of scepticism about the likely quality of new poetry self-published online, even the gatekeepers of Parnassus now acknowledge that much high quality and significant poetry is published, or at least first published, in e-zines.

Every year, *The Best American Poetry* produces a new volume showcasing the 'best' poems to be written in America or by Americans. Each year's volume is edited by a guest editor – usually an instantly recognizable 'name'; past editors include Ashbery (1988), Jorie Graham (1990), Rich (1996), Robert Creeley (2002), Lyn Hejinian (2004), Billy Collins (2006), and Terence Hayes (2014). The 2015 volume was edited by Sherman Alexie, who publicly stated his commitment to recognizing poetry published online: 'Rule #6: As part of the mission to represent the totality of American poetry, I will read as many Internet poems as I can find, whether published at popular sites or in obscure emagazines [*sic*] that have nine followers.'[41] Of the final selection, he writes, 'Approximately 15% of the poems were first published on the Internet.' The poems selected came from e-zines like *Able Muse*, *The Awl*, *Fence*, *Lemon Hound*, *Muzzle*, *PANK*, *The Rumpus*, *upstreet*, and *The Volta* to name but a few.[42] That 'Approximately 99% of the poets [included in the volume] are professors' suggests that even 'establishment' figures recognize the increasing role of the internet in finding and engaging a readership.

It was in the immediate and longer-term aftermath of the 9/11 terrorist attacks on the World Trade Center in New York, and the Pentagon in Virginia, that the potential of the internet for the dissemination of poetry became apparent. By February 2002, over 25,000 poems written in response to 9/11 had been published on the website *poems.com* alone. Three years later, the number of poems there had more than doubled.[43] The writing and sharing of poetry – regardless of its quality – functioned for many as a means to articulate and share a grief and confusion which seemed to exceed the expressive capacity of ordinary, everyday discourse. Dana Gioia suggests that 'the media may have provided information, but it was still left for poets to present language equal to the historical moment.'[44] This volume's historical coverage begins with the 'historical moment' of the end of World War II, in 1945; however, earlier traumas and losses continued, and continue, to preoccupy the imaginations of post-WWII poets. In his essay 'The Art of Losing: American Elegy since 1945', Stephen Regan explores the long shadow cast by the American Civil War over the work of Lowell, and suggests that, due to the prominent role played by the Lowell family in the Civil War, this particular trauma is of both political *and* personal significance to the poet. As Regan's essay reveals, 'In the aftermath of two world wars and the accompanying assault on religious belief, it became increasingly difficult for poets to perform the traditional elegiac rites of honouring the dead and consoling the living.' If, as Regan writes, many post-1945 American poets have wilfully renounced 'traditional elegiac codes and conventions, or else treat[ed] them ironically, while flagrantly disputing the comforting, consoling function of earlier poetry', then there are others, such as Anne Stevenson, Martín Espada, and Lucille Clifton who have found novel – but, crucially, authentic – ways in which to renovate and renew these traditions. It is those poets who have found ways to recover or revive the traditional codes and conventions, whether responding to deeply personal losses, or to high-profile national traumas, who have produced the most memorable and powerful poetry. Though American poets are ever driven by the Adamic impulse to 'make it new', it seems that in times of grief, there is a sense of strength and solace to be derived from the timeworn 'shared endeavor' of putting woe into words.

Notes

1. Helen Vendler, 'Are These the Poems to Remember?' (review of Rita Dove (ed.), *The Penguin Anthology of Twentieth-Century American Poetry*), *The New York Review of Books* (24 November 2011). Last accessed 17 August 2015. Available at: http://www.nybooks.com/articles/archives/2011/nov/24/are-these-poems-remember/
2. Rita Dove, 'Defending an Anthology', *The New York Review of Books* (22 December 2011). Last accessed 17 August 2015. Available at: http://www.nybooks.com/articles/archives/2011/dec/22/defending-anthology/
3. John Olson, 'Penguin's Flightless Anthology', *Tillalala Chronicles* (18 December 2011). Last accessed 17 August 2015. Available at: http://tillalala.blogspot.co.uk/2011/12/penguins-flightless-anthology.html
4. Robert Archambeau, 'What's the Matter with American Poetry? Rita Dove's Revisionist Canon', *Samizdat Blog* (29 October 2011). Last accessed 17 August 2015. Available at: http://samizdatblog.blogspot.co.uk/2011/10/whats-matter-with-american-poetry-rita.html
5. Jeremy Bass, 'Shelf Life: Rita Dove's Penguin Anthology of 20th Century Poetry', *The Nation* (2 November 2011). Last accessed 17 August 2015. Available at: http://www.thenation.com/article/164325/shelf-life#
6. Marguerite María Rivas, quoted in 'Poetry anthology sparks race row', *The Guardian* (22 December 2011). Last accessed 17 August 2015. Available at: http://www.theguardian.com/books/2011/dec/22/poetry-anthology-race-row
7. Helen Vendler, *The Anthology of Contemporary American Poetry* (London and New York: I. B. Tauris, 1986, 2003), p. 16.
8. See *The New York Review of Books* correspondence.
9. Helen Vendler, *The Anthology of Contemporary American Poetry*, p. 9.

10. Walt Whitman, *Complete Poems* (Ware, Hertfordshire: Wordsworth Editions, 2006), p. 12.
11. See Mike Chasar in *Everyday Reading: Poetry and Popular Culture in Modern America* (New York: Columbia University Press, 2012); Alan Golding in 'New, Newer, and Newest American Poetries', *Chicago Review*, 43.4 (Fall 1997): 7–21; and Hank Lazer in *Opposing Poetries: Part One* and *Part Two* (Evanston, IL: Northwestern University Press, 1996).
12. Figures taken from the website of The National WWII Museum, New Orleans. Last accessed 17 August 2015. Available at: www.nationalww2museum.org
13. Figures taken from the BBC online archive 'World War Two memories – written by the public, gathered by the BBC' (Fact File: Hiroshima and Nagasaki). Last accessed 17 August 2015. Available at: http://www.bbc.co.uk/history/ww2peopleswar/timeline/factfiles/nonflash/a6652262.shtml
14. Theodor W. Adorno, 'Cultural Criticism and Society' (1949), *Prisms* (1967) (Boston: MIT Press, 1983), p. 34.
15. Theodor Adorno, 'Lecture Fourteen (15 July 1965)', *Metaphysics: Concept and Problems* (Cambridge: Polity Press, 2000), p. 110.
16. T. S. Eliot, 'Tradition and the Individual Talent', in Frank Kermode (ed.), *Selected Prose of T. S. Eliot* (London: Faber and Faber, 1975), p. 40.
17. William Wordsworth, 'From Preface to Lyrical Ballads', in M. H. Abrams (ed.), *The Norton Anthology of English Literature*, Vol. 2 (New York: W. W. Norton), p. 151.
18. T. S. Eliot, 'Tradition and the Individual Talent', p. 43.
19. T. S. Eliot, 'Tradition and the Individual Talent', p. 42.
20. T. S. Eliot, 'Tradition and the Individual Talent', p. 41.
21. Ezra Pound, 'A Retrospect', *Pavannes and Divagations* (1918), rpt. in *Toward the Open Field: Poets on the Art of Poetry, 1800–1950*, ed. Melissa Kwasny (Middletown, CT: Wesleyan University Press, 2004), p. 256.
22. Adam Kirsch, *The Wounded Surgeon: Confession and Transformation in Six American Poets* (New York: W. W. Norton, 2005) p. xii.
23. Adam Kirsch, *The Wounded Surgeon: Confession and Transformation in Six American Poets*, p. xiv.
24. Robert Lowell, 'The Art of Poetry, No. 3' (Interview with Frederick Seidel), *The Paris Review*, 25 (Winter/Spring 1961). Last accessed 17 August 2015. Available at: http://www.theparisreview.org/interviews/4664/the-art-of-poetry-no-3-robert-lowell
25. M. L. Rosenthal, 'Poetry as Confession', *The Nation* (19 September 1959), rpt. M. L. Rosenthal, *Our Life in Poetry: Selected Essays and Reviews* (New York: Persea Books, 1991), pp. 109–112.
26. Robert Lowell, *Collected Poems*, ed. Frank Bidart and David Gewanter (London: Faber and Faber, 2003), p. 708.
27. John Plotz et al., 'An Interview with John Berryman', in Harry Thomas (ed.), *Berryman's Understanding: Reflections on the Poetry of John Berryman* (Boston, MA: Northeastern University Press, 1988).
28. Peter A. Stitt, 'John Berryman, The Art of Poetry No. 16', *The Paris Review*, 53 (Winter 1972). Last accessed 17 August 2015.

Available at: http://www.theparisreview.org/interviews/4052/the-art-of-poetry-no-16-john-berryman

29. M. L. Rosenthal, *The New Poets: American and British Poetry Since World War II* (New York: Oxford University Press, 1967), p. 25.
30. See Steven K. Hoffman, 'Impersonal Personalism: The Making of a Confessional Poetic', *ELH*, 45 (Winter 1978), p. 687 (note 4).
31. Kathryn Williams, quoted in Chris Mugan, 'Kathryn Williams explores the works and influences of Sylvia Plath in a new light', *The Independent* (22 May 2015). Last accessed 17 August 2015. Available at: http://www.independent.co.uk/arts-entertainment/music/features/kathryn-williams-explores-the-works-and-influences-of-sylvia-plath-in-a-new-light-10267891.html
32. Elizabeth Bishop, 1964 letter to Anne Stevenson, quoted in Brett C. Millier, *Elizabeth Bishop: Life and the Memory of It* (Berkeley, CA: University of California Press, 1993), p. 361.
33. Peter Stitt, 'The art of poetry XXXIII: John Ashbery', *The Paris Review*, 90 (Winter 1983). Last accessed 17 August 2015. Available at: http://www.theparisreview.org/interviews/3014/the-art-of-poetry-no-33-john-ashbery
34. David Lehman, 'The Shield of a Greeting: The Function of Irony in John Ashbery's Poetry', in David Lehman (ed.), *Beyond Amazement: New Essays on John Ashbery* (Ithaca, NY: Cornell University Press, 1980), p. 111.
35. Robert Frost, quoted in Deidre J. Fagan (ed.), *Critical Companion to Robert Frost: A Literary Reference to His Life and Work* (New York: Facts on File, 2007), p. 75.
36. Dana Gioia, 'Notes on the New Formalism', *The Hudson Review*, 40 (Autumn 1987): 395.
37. Robert Lowell, 'The Art of Poetry, No. 3'.
38. Cecilia Capuzzi Simon, 'Why Writers Love to Hate the M.F.A.', *The New York Times* (9 April 2015). Last accessed 17 August 2015. Available at: http://www.nytimes.com/2015/04/12/education/edlife/12edl-12mfa.html?_r=0
39. Dana Gioia, 'Notes on the New Formalism', p. 408.
40. Adam Fitzgerald, 'John Ashbery' (Interview), *Interview* (April 2015). Last accessed 17 August 2015. Available at: http://www.interviewmagazine.com/culture/john-ashbery/
41. Sherman Alexie, 'Sherman Alexie Speaks Out on *The Best American Poetry 2015*' (7 September 2015), *The Best American Poetry Blog*. Last accessed 17 September 2015. Available at: http://blog.bestamericanpoetry.com/the_best_american_poetry/2015/09/like-most-every-poet-i-have-viewed-the-publication-of-each-years-best-american-poetry-with-happiness-i-love-that-poem-je-1.html
42. Sherman Alexie (ed.), *The Best American Poetry 2015* (New York: Scribner Poetry, 2015), pp. 204–206.
43. Philip Metres, 'Beyond Grief and Grievance: The poetry of 9/11 and its aftermath', *Poetry Foundation* (7 September 2011). Last accessed 17 August 2015. Available at: http://www.poetryfoundation.org/article/242580

44. Dana Gioia, '"All I Have Is a Voice": September 11th and American Poetry.' *Disappearing Ink: Poetry at the End of Print Culture* (Saint Paul, MN: Greywolf Press, 2004), p. 166.

Further Reading

Altieri, Charles, *Self and Sensibility in Contemporary American Poetry* (New York: Cambridge University Press, 1984).

Ashton, Jennifer (ed.), *The Cambridge Companion to American Poetry Since 1945* (Cambridge: Cambridge University Press, 2013).

Blasing, Mutlu Konuk, *Politics and Form in Postmodern Poetry: O'Hara, Bishop, Ashbery, and Merrill* (Cambridge and New York: Cambridge University Press, 1995).

Breslin, James E. B., *From Modern to Contemporary: American Poetry 1945–1965* (Chicago, IL: University of Chicago Press, 1985).

Burt, Stephen (ed.), *The Cambridge History of American Poetry* (New York: Cambridge University Press, 2014).

Fredman, Stephen, *A Concise Companion to Twentieth-Century American Poetry* (Malden: Wiley-Blackwell, 2005).

Gioia, Dana, 'Notes on the New Formalism', *The Hudson Review*, 40 (Autumn 1987): 395–408.

Harbach, Chad, *MFA vs NYC: The Two Cultures of American Fiction* (New York: n+1 / Faber and Faber, 2014).

Kalaidjian, Walter, *The Cambridge Companion to Modern American Poetry* (Cambridge: Cambridge University Press, 2015).

Kirsch, Adam, *The Wounded Surgeon: Confession and Transformation in Six American Poets* (New York: W. W. Norton, 2005).

Longenbach, James, *Modern Poetry after Modernism* (New York and Oxford: Oxford University Press, 1997).

McGurl, Mark, *The Programme Era: Postwar Fiction and the Rise of Creative Writing* (Cambridge, MA: Harvard University Press, 2009).

Pearce, Roy H., *The Continuity of American Poetry* (New Haven, CT: Princeton, 1977).

Rosenbaum, Susan B., *Professing Sincerity: Modern Lyric Poetry, Commercial Culture, and the Crisis in Reading* (Charlottesville, VA: University of Virginia Press, 2007).

Travisano, Thomas, *Midcentury Quartet: Bishop, Lowell, Jarrell, Berryman, and the Making of the Postmodern Aesthetic* (Charlottesville, VA: University Press of Virginia, 1999).

Vendler, Helen, *The Anthology of Contemporary American Poetry* (London and New York: I. B. Tauris, 1986, 2003).

Von Hallberg, Robert, *American Poetry and Culture 1945–1980* (Cambridge, MA: Harvard University Press, 1985).

Part I
Poets

1

'Whims & emergencies, discoveries, losses': The Poetry of John Berryman

Stephen Matterson

For a time, John Berryman's place in the literary history of the twentieth century seemed assured. He was the author of the popular and critically acclaimed sequence *The Dream Songs* (1969), credited with playing a pivotal role in his generation's revival of the personal element in American poetry, and his work stimulated a critical engagement that placed him prominently alongside his most important contemporaries, Theodore Roethke, Robert Lowell, Elizabeth Bishop, and Randall Jarrell. He was the subject of significant biographical studies, and his work demonstrably drew a wide readership; one that in the 1970s and 1980s placed *The Dream Songs* on the promotional lists of book clubs, a position occupied alongside Robert Frost's *Collected Poems*. Berryman's success seemed to be of a particular moment in the 1960s and 1970s, but it was both hard-earned and the result of a long poetic development, beginning with his publishing poetry in the 1940s. Like his contemporaries he made radical shifts in his style during the 1950s, and emerged as a major figure because of that.

Berryman was born in the small town of McAlester, in the recently elected state of Oklahoma, in 1914. His parents were Martha and John Smith, and he was named John Allyn Smith. In 1925 the family – that is, the parents and the two children, John and his younger brother Robert Jefferson – moved to Tampa, Florida. In Oklahoma their father had worked as a banker, though in Florida he and Martha became involved in the property market during a boom. The major and in some respects defining moment of Berryman's life and poetry occurred in June 1926, when his father committed suicide by shooting himself. As with most suicides, the contexts are complex. There were problems in the Smith marriage, with divorce being discussed, and the family had financial problems as the property boom ended abruptly. Whatever the reasons, the act haunted Berryman for his whole life; it is no exaggeration to say that *The Dream Songs* are mostly concerned with its consequences, which include an ongoing and potentially corrosive self-examination. One fairly immediate consequence was the very name 'John Berryman', acquired when his widowed mother remarried, and the family moved to New York.

As a student, Berryman proved illustrious. His undergraduate work at Columbia was crowned by a scholarship at the University of Cambridge that he held in 1936–37. He taught and researched at Harvard and at Princeton before taking up a position at the University of Minnesota in Minneapolis in 1955. Although he took frequent trips away, he was based there until his death by suicide in January 1972, at the age of fifty-seven. By then he was not only an internationally acclaimed poet but also a distinguished professor in the Humanities, an authority on subjects as varied as textual editing, Shakespeare, Stephen Crane, and New Testament studies; an erudite, lively, and committed scholar. His academic reputation, however, should not conceal what was an often tumultuous private life. Heavy drinking from the 1940s onwards eventually became alcoholism, and numerous sexual affairs damaged his first two marriages and seriously threatened his third. In her memoir of their life together Berryman's first wife, Eileen Simpson, wrote of her decision to leave him. The reasons were not only 'drinking and bad sex', as Berryman himself had put it: 'it was more his need to live in turbulence – if it wasn't drinking and women, it was the way he worked, on *Lear*, *Crane*, and *Bradstreet* – that finally forced me to make my decision.'[1]

Although some of Berryman's poetry appeared in *Five Young American Poets* in 1940, his first published collection was a pamphlet in 1942, bearing the somewhat laconic title *Poems*. His first book-length collection, *The Dispossessed*, was published in 1948. This included most of the pamphlet poems, and indeed, covered work first written in the late 1930s. Although it is an uneven collection, *The Dispossessed* is fascinating in showing radically different kinds of poetic development. Many of the poems are very much of their time, and tend mainly to show Berryman's gifted absorption of others, notably Yeats and Auden. Yeats particularly engaged him; as he recalled in a 1965 essay; 'I began work in verse-making as a burning, trivial disciple of . . . Yeats . . . whom I didn't so much wish to resemble as to *be*.'[2] These poems are orderly, formally achieved, and often rather impersonal. A recurrent theme is poetry's power to preserve, to freeze time, and to speak to us across the ages. The book's opening poem, 'Winter Landscape', is a fine example of this. Alluding obliquely to Brueghel's painting 'Hunters in the Snow', Berryman meditates on art's ability to transcend time, to provide an enduring record of a scene when all around it has been 'irrecoverably lost'.[3] The poem's sinuous twenty-five lines comprise one sentence, ensuring that the reader experiences the recall of the moment without a pause. The tone is detached, impersonal and authoritative, even touching on the magisterial; just the kind of tone Auden had used for his poem on another Brueghel painting, 'Musée des Beaux Arts'. There's also more than a nod to Yeats' 'Sailing to Byzantium'. Yet alongside this strand of poems, there are competing kinds of poetic voice, radically different in terms of form, tone, and theme. With hindsight we can say with certainty that these prefigure Berryman's major achievements in the coming years, *Homage to Mistress Bradstreet* and *The Dream Songs*. Yet even in 1948, works such as 'The Ball Poem' and many of those appearing in the last two sections of *The Dispossessed*, testified to a developing alternative poetic, a different voice.

This developing poetic has three main characteristics: a flexible use of poetic personae; a verbal economy that typically includes fractured syntax; and a more improvised poetic form. Berryman spoke several times about 'The Ball Poem' as pivotal to his development as a poet. The poem is exactly the same length as 'Winter Landscape' but is not presented in stanzas. In it an observer records a boy's loss of the ball with which he has been playing (it bounces over the harbour wall). The speaker sympathetically records the loss and identifies with the child, but is ambivalently both within and without the narrative. This fluid manipulation of identity through pronouns anticipates much that will come in Berryman's work, especially the shifting character of Henry in *The Dream Songs*. Berryman commented on 'The Ball Poem' as a 'discovery', a realization that

> a commitment of identity can be 'reserved,' so to speak, with an ambiguous pronoun. The poet himself is both left out and put in; the boy does and does not become him and we are confronted with a process which is at once a process of life and a process of art. A pronoun may seem a small matter, but she matters, he matters, it matters, they matter.[4]

The poem's thematic difference from 'Winter Landscape' is equally striking. Rather than being a preserver, the poet is now an explorer of lost things, claiming ambivalent empathy with those who lose, and equating knowledge of loss with maturity and growth; the 'epistemology of loss', as Berryman calls it in the poem.[5] This theme is developed further in the sequence titled 'The Nervous Songs', consisting of nine songs in character and two coda poems. The songs give a foretaste of *The Dream Songs*, in their consistent use of three six-line stanzas, and in the sympathetic rendering of the marginalized and dispossessed. While they lack the managed tonal shifts that are a key element of the Dream Songs, and the fluid use of performing selves, they still stand out as radically different from other poems in *The Dispossessed*. This is partly in the uncertain syntax, in the staccato-like phrases, and in the heavy use of caesura, all appropriate for speakers in crisis, for whom language is at its limits. Berryman was to become inordinately attached to syntactic inversion, to the way it jolts the reader through defamiliarization, renewing and refreshing language. He had been drawn to this technique for a long time; in a 1936 letter to his mother he approvingly cites the passage from Virginia Woolf's *Mrs Dalloway* beginning 'A thing there was that mattered.'[6] Robert Lowell recalled Berryman in the 1940s; 'John could quote with vibrance to all lengths, even prose, even late Shakespeare, to show me what could be done with disrupted and mended syntax. This was the start of his real style.'[7] Lowell's elegy for Berryman recalls their discussing *The Winter's Tale*, 'Leontes' jealousy / in Shakespeare's broken syntax.'[8] This disrupted syntax links with another Berryman characteristic, the use of the ampersand, growing steadily over the pages of *The Dispossessed*. This punctuation gives an air of immediacy, jauntiness and the suggestion of improvisation to the poems, as well as creating a link to the seventeenth-century poetry that Berryman loved so much.

We now know that Berryman held a covert poetic resource in developing *The Dispossessed* and moving beyond it. In 1947, during and after an extra-marital affair, Berryman had composed a sonnet sequence of more than a hundred poems on the illicit relationship. Clearly, his poetic imagination is increasingly drawn to possibilities of lyric sequence, to the long narrative poem consisting of individual sections, in the manner of Sidney's *Astrophil and Stella* and Shakespeare's *Sonnets*. But Berryman's sonnets are also deeply personal, by far the most revealing poetry he had written so far; his sense of the sequence as private clearly encouraged the candour evident in them. By the time they were published (in a slightly revised format) in 1967, Berryman's work had undergone a transformation, both in his use of the long poem and in the use of highly personal material. *Homage to Mistress Bradstreet* (1953) was, like his *Sonnets*, a major achievement, hailed by its reviewers as something genuinely new in American poetry. Invoking America's first published poet, Berryman engages with Anne Bradstreet and her Puritanism in 57 stanzas, and conducts a dialogue with her in a kind of historical short-circuit. *Bradstreet* is a scholarly poem (Berryman intensively researched colonial America for several years for it); it is also impatient, quirky, and obliquely autobiographical. In fact, Berryman scarcely refers to Bradstreet's poetry at all, and is dismissive in the two brief mentions given to it. He was similarly curt when he described her as a 'boring high-minded Puritan woman who may have been our first American poet but is not a good one'[9].

Bradstreet's importance is dual. It is a major work in its own right, and it pioneered a trail that would lead to *The Dream Songs*. Its qualities can be overlooked precisely because of the Songs, where they are magnified and intensified, but this should not distract us from their actuality. There is the eight-line stanza form which, Berryman claimed, he had modified from Yeats via the seventeenth-century poet Abraham Cowley. This gave him, he felt, a new flexibility, a refreshing sense of freedom from the management of a single tone or mode of expression; 'flexible and grave, intense and quiet, able to deal with matter both high and low'.[10] This flexibility extends to identity itself, as Berryman weaves in and out of the poem, at times speaking for Bradstreet, at times representing her from a mid-twentieth-century perspective. There is also dramatic narrative. This is not exactly the kind of narrative rejected by the high modernists, in favour of the fragmented submerged narrative of *The Waste Land*. Berryman's narrative is intense and although oblique is not obscure, allusive, or mythographic. 'When I finally woke up to the fact that I was involved in a long poem, one of my first thoughts was: Narrative. Let's have narrative, and at least one dominant personality, and no fragmentation – in short, let's have something spectacularly NOT *The Waste Land*, the best long poem of the age.'[11] *Bradstreet*'s language is quirky, solemn, irreverent, but above all it has a bold, extraordinary liveliness scarcely evident in Berryman's published poetry until then. These are very much the effects that are magnified, intensified and made more extreme in *The Dream Songs*. The flexibility of persona is extended to a whole cast of characters; the submerged autobiography now comes at times to the surface, and the three-stanza format allows Berryman even more tonal range.

Berryman began writing Dream Songs around 1955, and they started then to appear in magazines and journals. The first collection, *77 Dream Songs*, was published in 1964, and they were completed with *His Toy, His Dream, His Rest* in 1968; a one-volume edition appeared in 1969. Altogether there are three hundred and eighty-five Songs; all are numbered and some have titles. He never quite relinquished the form or the idiom; he wrote a few Songs after 1968, including several just prior to his death. Taken together, the Songs are among the most acclaimed poetry collections of the twentieth century, and led to Berryman receiving numerous awards; these included the so-called 'triple crown'; the National Book Award, the Pulitzer Prize, and the Bollingen Prize. The numbering of the Songs and their division into seven books suggests much more of a sequence than is actually apparent. The books vary enormously in size, and while there is some sense of chronological sequence there is no very strict adherence to this. Some Songs are clearly sequential in their treatment of a subject or scene: two obvious examples are 78–91, dealing with the death and return of the protagonist Henry, and 146–156 on the death of Berryman's friend the poet Delmore Schwartz. There is also a large overarching trajectory involving Henry's grief and puzzlement over his father's suicide, which culminates in the final song's attempt to move beyond this emotional storm and look to the future represented by his daughter's birth. But the real delight and power of the Songs do not arise from sequence. They come from the invention of Henry, from the Songs' wide emotional range, from the presence of different voices, from their panoramic representation of a life and of a generation, and above all from the reader's engagement with their tonal and stylistic shifts.

The Songs have an air of improvisation, an articulate and charged responsiveness to the moment, a genuinely fresh and original voice in poetry. In this sense they represent a work continually in progress, taking the reader in unexpected directions, providing few certainties. Berryman guides us to this through one of his epigraphs to *77 Dream Songs*, quoting Olive Schreiner's phrase 'But there is another method.' It appears in the preface to her 1883 novel *The Story of an African Farm*:

> Human life may be painted according to two methods. There is the stage method [in which] each character is duly marshalled at first, and ticketed; we know with an immutable certainty that at the right crises each one will reappear and act his part, and, when the curtain falls, all will stand before it bowing. There is a sense of satisfaction in this, and of completeness. But there is another method – the method of the life we all lead. Here nothing can be prophesied. There is a strange coming and going of feet. Men appear, act and re-act upon each other, and pass away. When the crisis comes the man who would fit it does not return. When the curtain falls no one is ready. When the footlights are brightest they are blown out; and what the name of the play is no one knows. If there sits a spectator who knows, he sits so high that the players in the gaslight cannot hear his breathing.[12]

The performance metaphor here is very telling. In one sense, Henry is making up his performance (and is being made up) as he goes along.

He must find in each moment the resources needed for his survival, and neither he nor the reader is able to predict where anything is leading. In fact the concept of surviving is essential to the Songs. One of Berryman's friends, the critic Daniel Hughes, described them as 'spells for survival'; a compelling designation that gains force when Berryman's commendation of poetry as a kind of magic is recalled.[13] In his biography of Stephen Crane, Berryman emphasized the evolution of poetry from the primitive:

> A savage dreams, is frightened by the dream, and goes to the medicine man to have it explained. The medicine man can make up anything, anything will reassure the savage, so long as the manner of his delivery is impressive; so he chants, perhaps he stamps his foot, people like rhythm, what he says becomes rhythmical, people like to hear things *again*, and what he says begins to rhyme. Poetry begins – as a practical matter, for *use*.[14]

As well as numerous specified adversities and adversaries, Henry must negotiate a means of accommodating himself to his past, to the demands of the present, to his own waywardness and shifting moods. Berryman's notebook description of the Songs as a 'survival epic' illuminates this; they both describe the survival and make it possible, one of the many connections between Berryman and the other middle generation poets. Where other epics may have to do with heroism, with creation, with glory, Berryman's is about just getting through with whatever is needed to do this: Henry 'arose, benign, & performed'.[15] When Berryman invokes Achilles he does not enter the poem as the great tragic warrior, but as someone with 'plights & gripes' resembling those of Henry, a sulking figure in his tent refusing to emerge and join in. Although this seems impudently anti-heroic, it is more of an invocation of a more complex, multidimensional form of heroism. Sulking or withdrawal might work at times to see you through a crisis. It is exactly what 'Huffy Henry' is doing in the first Dream Song: 'unappeasable Henry sulked'.[16]

A survival epic needs to begin with a fall, and although the nature of the fall is unspecified, this is what the Songs do.

> All the world like a woolen lover
> once did seem on Henry's side.
> Then came a departure.[17]

In some ways it is 'The Ball Poem' over again, as Henry careers from the comforting certainties and securities of childhood to an adulthood of loss and insecurity, and this first Song has a similar shifting of pronouns. But much more is at stake now, and the Songs will subsequently and repeatedly brood on the nature of this 'fall', eventually citing the suicide of the father as the point of origin for the fragmentation and despair that Henry feels: 'Thereafter nothing fell out as it might or ought.'[18] The suicide is the cause of multiple losses, of Henry's wayward behaviour, instability, and mental shifts, someone thrown off course.

The shift of pronouns is now more significant than in 'The Ball Poem'. Here 'I' and 'Henry' begin as divergent, different voices; 'I see his point'; 'I don't see how Henry, pried / open for all the world to see, survived.'[19] But by line fifteen the first person is changing from the narrator's voice into that of Henry himself, and Henry speaks the line 'Once in a sycamore I was glad'. The shift is not readily apparent, because Berryman has here suspended the typographical conventions such as quotation marks which indicate distinctions between who is speaking. This comes to be a key feature of the Songs. The intent is not simply to confuse; it indicates the fluid exchange of identity between Henry and Berryman. At times they are distinct, as are other characters who enter the poem, but at times the voices appear to merge. A good example is the progression of Song 235. The poem focuses on the death of Ernest Hemingway, and begins 'Tears Henry shed for poor old Hemingway'.[20] Stanza 2 begins with the line 'Save us from shotguns & fathers' suicides.' The plural is apposite in encompassing Henry's father's suicide, the suicide of Hemingway's father, and the fact that Hemingway, another suicide, was also a father. But it also moves towards a universal, including of course Berryman, so that by the poem's ending, the voices of Berryman and of Henry have once more merged:

> Mercy! My father; do not pull the trigger
> or all my life I'll suffer from your anger
> killing what you began.[21]

The persona of Henry is assumed for the poem, a performing self who functions as one of Berryman's own resources for survival. The penultimate Song shows the persona being dropped, as Henry confronts his father's suicide more directly than ever before, standing above his grave 'with rage' on an 'awful pilgrimage'. He imagines descending into the grave and tearing open the coffin,

> & then Henry
> will heft the axe once more, his final card,
> and fell it on the start.[22]

Although the Song's pronouns are jumbled, 'I' and 'Henry' are separating. Henry the improvised persona invented for the sequence is now leaving it, or rather, is being left behind in it as Berryman reclaims the first-person voice. In the final Song, Henry has become an analogy rather than a voice; 'My house is older than Henry.'[23]

It is important, though, not to exaggerate the narrative arc of the Dream Songs; this is in no way a programmed sequence. Berryman wrote the last one long before he had completed the book, and the majority of the Songs have little or no reference to the father's suicide, even when they may be said to be exploring its effects. They may be read in any order, and if they form a sequence at all, it is mazy, zig-zagged, and always likely to go off in a variety of directions and digressions. In the spirit of Schreiner's 'method' the Songs are improvised, considering and reacting to events in the world and in Berryman's life, combining memory, dream, and speculation with a whole range of attitudes and emotions. This inclusion of the personal was a pointed rejection of New Critical ideas about poetry and those of T. S. Eliot in particular. In a 1968 interview Berryman spoke of his 'strong disagreement with Eliot's line – the impersonality of poetry ... I'm very much against that; it seems to me on the contrary that poetry comes out of personality.'[24] Also new in the Songs is Berryman's manipulation of shifting tones and poetic styles. His earlier work was generally characterized by the maintenance of a serious tone and a heightened poetic diction, maintained even where the syntax may become contorted. But now his polyphonic poetic allows singing right across the scale. This is heightened by his use of the nineteenth-century US minstrel tradition, to which he drew attention in his introductory note to the one-volume edition of the Songs:

> The poem ... is essentially about an imaginary character (not the poet, not me) named Henry, a white American in early middle age sometimes in blackface, who has suffered an irreversible loss and talks about himself sometimes in the first person, sometimes in the third, sometimes even in the second; he has a friend, never named, who addresses him as Mr Bones and variants thereof.[25]

Generally, in the shows Bones and Tambo (named for the musical instruments they carried; castanets made of bones and a tambourine) were the 'end' men, engaging with each other through an interlocutor and providing the punch-line or oblique observations on the action. Berryman's minstrelsy is far less formally stylized, significant primarily for giving licence to the performance of a wide emotional and linguistic range. It also means that at times Tambo acts variously as Henry's conscience, a guide, and Job's comforter.

The broad emotional and linguistic range is evident throughout the Songs. It represents Henry's wandering mind, a complex shifting between his emotional state, and the multiplicity of meanings generated by experience. This last is important in reminding us of the 'Dream' element of the Songs; of the need to interpret dreams, to approach them in the way that Henry does (diverging from Freud), as 'a panorama / of the whole mental life'.[26] Presenting 'the whole mental life' might mean recording the mind's shifts, as in Song 331. It begins with Henry's measured, even solemn, reflection on his mortality:

> This is the third. What have I more to say
> except that I hope in my dying hour
> nobody will be ashamed of me[27]

By line seven he is distracted by his surroundings, with the near bathetic: 'There's a lot of hair in Ireland, much of it red.' But this banality is then absorbed into the ongoing if jaunty meditation about death, leading to reflections on the late works of Yeats, Beethoven, and Goya. This linguistic accommodation is seen brilliantly in the much anthologized Song 4. Here Henry lusts after a fellow diner in a restaurant:

> Filling her compact & delicious body
> with chicken páprika, she glanced at me
> twice.[28]

While enjoying the poem's robust vulgarity, Berryman is reminding us of the sexual urges that drive love poetry, no matter how decorous, genteel, courtly, and dignified the language: Helen Vendler calls this song a 'joyous blasphemy of traditional love poetry'.[29]

The incorporation of the comic into the Songs' fabric (their 'chortle sin') should not camouflage their tragic and highly serious elements.[30] In part they are elegiac as Berryman reflects on the deaths of literary figures and friends during the period of their composition. The ten Songs, 'one solid block of agony', for Schwartz are among the most accomplished and moving in the collection, which includes reflections on the deaths of Frost, Hemingway, Stevens, Faulkner, Jarrell, Roethke, and Plath among others; to the extent that Christopher Ricks thought of *The Dream Songs* as a twentieth-century *In Memoriam*.[31]

While Henry considers his life to have been derailed by his father's suicide, it is important to see that his own actions and addictions are both consequences of the suicide and serve to exacerbate those consequences, generating what threatens to become a vicious and destructive cycle.

> Hunger was constitutional with him,
> women, cigarettes, liquor, need need need
> until he went to pieces.[32]

Writing comes from these 'pieces', and the conflation of writing with these addictions recurs in the Songs. In particular, Henry's alcoholism leads to further dislocations, erratic behaviour, guilt, shame, and depression. Typical effects of alcoholism, such as insomnia, depression, and loss of memory through blackouts recur as characteristics of Henry's life, lost in 'A maze of drink'.[33] In Song 29 he lies in the dawn trying to recall whether he has murdered anyone in his drunken fits, counting his friends and concluding with relief that 'Nobody is ever missing.'[34]

Henry's alcoholism is of course also Berryman's. Although he had been alcoholic for a long time, probably since the late 1940s, in the mid- to late 1960s this reached a crisis point, when he was drinking two bottles of whisky a day. He had also been taking large numbers of prescription drugs and was smoking up to five packs of cigarettes daily.[35] He initially sought treatment for his condition in 1969, and this continued into the early 1970s, with residential spells at rehabilitation centres. He lightly fictionalized his experiences of group therapy for his posthumously published unfinished novel, *Recovery* (1973), which illuminates some key aspects of the Dream Songs. At one point Berryman's autobiographical figure, Alan Severance, reflects on how alcoholism makes him a spectator of his own life rather than an actor in it, controlled by the desire for alcohol: '[I] found myself wondering whether I would turn off right towards the University and the bus home or whether I would just continue *right on* to the Circle and up right one block to the main bar I use there, and have a few. *Wondering*. My whole fate depending on pure chance.'[36]

In some ways Berryman's work after the Dream Songs may be seen, in the light of his recovery from alcoholism, as attempts to reclaim a self, another form of recovery. It is notable that the autobiographical poems in the first part of *Love & Fame* (1970) focus on the period of his life as an undergraduate; a period of promise and early achievement, before marriage, before the heavy drinking of the mid-1940s. While the poems lack the potent energies of the Songs, they have an impressive lyric authority, and there is a sense of sequence to the collection as Berryman recalls aspects of his life and then expresses a newly regained religious faith in Part Four's 'Eleven Addresses to the Lord'. It is as though Berryman wants to consider an alternative fate, an alternative to the life he led after 1947. In 'Message' he writes that *Love & Fame* is 'not an autobiography-in-verse', 'not my life', which is 'occluded & lost':

> That consisted of lectures on St Paul,
> scrimmages with women, singular moments
> of getting certain things absolutely right.
> Laziness, liquor, bad dreams.
>
> That consisted of three wives & many friends,
> whims & emergencies, discoveries, losses.[37]

The collection's fresh lyricism is one path out of the style of *Bradstreet* and Dream Songs, but Berryman agonized over this return to short poems. For the first time he had started to send poems out to friends for their comments, and even after publication he had serious doubts about the quality of the work. Saul Bellow, a friend of Berryman since they were colleagues at Princeton in the early 1950s, recalls Berryman giving him a copy of *Love & Fame* and then striking out several of the poems, scribbling 'Crap!' and 'Disgusting!' in the margins.[38] The unevenness of the post-Dream Songs work was even more evident in the posthumously published *Delusions, Etc. of John Berryman*. To some, such as Bellow, it seemed that Berryman had given so much to his poetry that by this point there was simply nothing left. This is something of a harsh judgement of *Delusions, Etc.* While uneven, there are some high points, notably 'Beethoven Triumphant'. This complex meditation on the composer incorporates Berryman's lifelong love of music and, as one critic has shown, reminds us how pervasive musical allusion is in Berryman's overall work.[39] The book also continues to express the new-found Christian belief initiated with *Love & Fame*.

Perhaps inevitably, critical perception of Berryman has tended to centre on the Dream Songs, and has consequently labelled him as part of what M. L. Rosenthal dubbed the 'confessional' movement. In an interview Berryman angrily rejected this labelling and its implicitly limited representation of his work, but he did play a leading role in his generation's breakaway from the New-Critically sanctioned objective, impersonal short lyric.[40] His critical reputation has wavered. Tellingly he was scarcely mentioned in Blackwell's *A Companion to Twentieth Century Poetry* but a number of recent studies indicate a resurgence of interest, and, perhaps more significantly, have engaged in different ways with wider aspects of Berryman's work.[41]

When Bellow told the story of Berryman deleting poems from *Love & Fame*, he mentioned that Berryman ('shakily') wrote next to one of them, 'This is certainly one of the truest things I've been gifted with.'[42] The poem was 'Surprise Me', one of the 'Eleven Addresses to the Lord', which opens:

> Surprise me on some ordinary day
> with a blessing gratuitous. Even I've done good
> beyond their expectations. What count we then
> upon Your bounty?[43]

Some of Berryman's finest work is in this moving meditative sequence when, having reviewed his life, he moves towards a dedication of himself to God. Number 8 of the Addresses was read at his funeral, with its final stanza:

> Ease in their passing my beloved friends,
> all others too I have cared for in a travelling life,
> anyone anywhere indeed. Lift up
> sober toward truth a scared self-estimate.[44]

In truth, Berryman's self-estimation was the ongoing work of his poetry, and at his finest he brings zest and vigour to this scrutiny. As he states in Dream Song 283, he is 'in love with life / which has produced this wreck'.

Notes

1. Eileen Simpson, *Poets in their Youth* (New York: Random House, 1982), p. 233.
2. John Berryman, *The Freedom of the Poet* (New York: Farrar, Straus and Giroux, 1976), p. 323.
3. John Berryman, in Charles Thornbury (ed.), *Collected Poems* (London: Faber and Faber, 1990), p. 11.
4. John Berryman, *Freedom of the Poet*, pp. 326–7.
5. John Berryman, in Charles Thornbury (ed.), *Collected Poems*, p. 11.
6. John Berryman, in Richard J. Kelly (ed.), *We Dream of Honour: John Berryman's Letters to His Mother* (New York: W. W. Norton, 1988), p. 55.
7. Robert Lowell, in Robert Giroux (ed.), *Collected Prose* (London: Faber and Faber, 1987), p. 112.
8. Robert Lowell, in Frank Bidart and David Gewanter (eds), *Collected Poems* (New York: Farrar, Straus and Giroux, 2003), p. 738.

9. John Berryman, *Freedom of the Poet*, p. 328.
10. John Berryman, *Freedom of the Poet*, p. 328.
11. John Berryman, *Freedom of the Poet*, p. 327.
12. Olive Schreiner, in Joseph Bristow (ed.), *The Story of an African Farm* (Oxford: Oxford University Press, 2008), p. 7.
13. Daniel Hughes, 'The Dream Songs: Spells for Survival', *Southern Review*, 2(1) (1966): 5–17.
14. John Berryman, *Stephen Crane*, p. 272. Quoted in Charles Thornbury, 'Introduction', *Collected Poems*, p. liii.
15. John Berryman, *The Dream Songs* (London: Faber and Faber, 1990), p. 151.
16. John Berryman, *The Dream Songs*, p. 3.
17. John Berryman, *The Dream Songs*, p. 3.
18. John Berryman, *The Dream Songs*, p. 3.
19. John Berryman, *The Dream Songs*, p. 3.
20. John Berryman, *The Dream Songs*, p. 254.
21. John Berryman, *The Dream Songs*, p. 254.
22. John Berryman, *The Dream Songs*, p. 406.
23. John Berryman, *The Dream Songs*, p. 407.
24. John Plotz et al., 'An Interview with John Berryman', in Harry Thomas (ed.), *Berryman's Understanding: Reflections on the Poetry of John Berryman* (Boston, MA: Northeastern University Press, 1988), p. 7.
25. John Berryman, *The Dream Songs*, p. vi.
26. John Berryman, *The Dream Songs*, p. 349.
27. John Berryman, *The Dream Songs*, p. 353.
28. John Berryman, *The Dream Songs*, p. 6.
29. Helen Vendler, *The Given and the Made* (London: Faber and Faber, 1995), p. 37.
30. John Berryman, *The Dream Songs*, p. 64.
31. Christopher Ricks, 'Recent American Poetry', *Massachusetts Review*, 11(2) (1970): 336.
32. John Berryman, *The Dream Songs*, p. 333.
33. John Berryman, *The Dream Songs*, p. 361.
34. John Berryman, *The Dream Songs*, p. 33.
35. See John Haffenden, *The Life of John Berryman* (London: Routledge and Kegan Paul, 1982), p. 375.
36. John Berryman, *Recovery* (London: Faber and Faber, 1973), p. 33. Italics in original.
37. John Berryman, *Collected Poems*, p. 201.
38. Saul Bellow, 'Foreword' to Berryman, *Recovery*, p. xiii. After the American edition received poor reviews, Berryman omitted several poems and made various revisions for the 1971 English edition.
39. See Maria Johnston, 'Berryman's Music', in Philip Coleman and Philip McGowan (eds), *After Thirty Falls: New Essays on John Berryman* (Amsterdam and New York: Rodopi Press, 2007), pp. 191–208.
40. See Peter Stitt, 'The Art of Poetry', in Thomas (ed.), *Berryman's Understanding*, p. 21.

41. See, for instance, Philip Coleman's *John Berryman's Public Vision* (Dublin: University College Dublin Press, 2014); Brendan Cooper's *Dark Airs: John Berryman and the Spiritual Politics of Cold War American Poetry* (New York: Peter Lang, 2009); Tom Rogers' *God of Rescue: John Berryman and Christianity* (New York: Peter Lang, 2011); and the essays, mostly by younger scholars, in *After Thirty Falls: New Essays on John Berryman*, edited by Philip Coleman and Philip McGowan (2007).
42. Saul Bellow, 'Foreword,' *Recovery*, p. xiii.
43. John Berryman, *Collected Poems*, p. 220.
44. John Berryman, *Collected Poems*, p. 220.

Further Reading

Berryman, John, *Recovery* (London: Faber and Faber, 1973).

Berryman, John, *The Freedom of the Poet* (New York: Farrar, Straus and Giroux, 1976).

Berryman, John, *We Dream of Honour: John Berryman's Letters to His Mother*, ed. Richard J. Kelly (New York: W. W. Norton, 1988).

Berryman, John, *Collected Poems*, ed. Charles Thornbury (London: Faber and Faber, 1990).

Berryman, John, *The Dream Songs* (London: Faber and Faber, 1990).

Coleman, Philip, *John Berryman's Public Vision* (Dublin: University College Dublin Press, 2014).

Coleman, Philip and Philip McGowan (eds), *After Thirty Falls: New Essays on John Berryman* (Amsterdam and New York: Rodopi Press, 2007).

Cooper, Brendan, *Dark Airs: John Berryman and the Spiritual Politics of Cold War American Poetry* (New York: Peter Lang, 2009).

Haffenden, John, *The Life of John Berryman* (London: Routledge and Kegan Paul, 1982).

Lowell, Robert, *Collected Prose*, ed. Robert Giroux (London: Faber and Faber, 1987).

Lowell, Robert, *Collected Poems*, ed. Frank Bidart and David Gewanter (New York: Farrar, Straus and Giroux, 2003).

Ricks, Christopher, 'Recent American Poetry', *Massachusetts Review*, 11(2) (1970): 313–36.

Rogers, Tom, *God of Rescue: John Berryman and Christianity* (New York: Peter Lang, 2011).

Schreiner, Olive, *The Story of an African Farm*, ed. Joseph Bristow (Oxford: Oxford University Press, 2008).

Simpson, Eileen, *Poets in their Youth* (New York: Random House, 1982).

Thomas, Harry (ed.), *Berryman's Understanding: Reflections on the Poetry of John Berryman* (Boston, MA: Northeastern University Press, 1988).

Vendler, Helen, *The Given and the Made* (London: Faber and Faber, 1995).

2

Robert Lowell: Protean Poet

Steven Gould Axelrod

Robert Lowell, a poet of remarkable verbal skills, intellectual gifts, and personal wounds, dominated American poetry from the 1940s through the 1970s. His work as a public poet, a 'confessional' poet, and a meditative poet is remembered today as a central, if sometimes controversial, contribution to the literary history of post-war America. He helped define his era, and his achievement has had rippling effects on poetry ever since.

Lowell transformed English-language poetry at several different points in his career. He first made his mark with his two initial volumes of poetry, *Land of Unlikeness* (1944) and *Lord Weary's Castle* (1946). These volumes seemed to Allen Tate and Randall Jarrell to portend a new style of poetry – traditional in form, complex in style, critical in social perspective, and, according to Jarrell, 'post-modern' in ethos.[1] *Lord Weary's Castle*, in particular, was a turning point: it could be seen as one kind of culmination of the modernist project or, conversely, as an effort to discover a successor poetics.

Lowell then transformed himself and poetry again, thirteen years later, with *Life Studies* (1959). This volume inspired the critical term 'confessional poetry', and it endures as a landmark of that poetic movement.[2] Along with contemporaneous collections by Allen Ginsberg and W. D. Snodgrass, *Life Studies* posed a vital alternative to T. S. Eliot's 'Impersonal theory of poetry', which had dominated poetic practice up to that point.[3] The volume demonstrated a decisive turn away from Lowell's previous style of density, citationality, and prophetic fervour. It installed instead a revolutionary personal poetics, in which self-disclosure was contained and shaped by irony and by Lowell's hallmark verbal sophistication. This volume established the autobiographical voice as one side in a poetic debate with language-centred poetry that continued for at least the next half-century.

In a similar way, *The Old Glory* (1965) seemed to have the potential to transform American historical drama; and *For the Union Dead*

(1964), *Near the Ocean* (1967), *Notebook* (1970), and *History* (1973) offered to transform historical poetry. Nevertheless, Lowell's late meditative work – exemplified in *Notebook, History, For Lizzie and Harriet* (1973), *The Dolphin* (1973), and *Day by Day* (1977) – struck some influential critics as aesthetically (not to mention ethically) flawed. Scholars have debated his position in poetic history ever since, but his impact has never died, and it notably revived in the twenty-first century with the posthumous publication of his *Collected Poems* (2003), his *Letters* (2005), and his complete correspondence with Elizabeth Bishop in *Words in Air* (2008). These volumes have brought Lowell's intriguing and often stunning words back to the forefront of poetic and cultural awareness.

*

Robert Traill Spence Lowell IV was born in Boston, the only child of Robert Traill Spence Lowell III and Charlotte Winslow Lowell. Among his ancestors and family members were Puritan patriarchs Edward Winslow and Josiah Winslow, poets James Russell Lowell and Amy Lowell, astronomer Percival Lowell, and Harvard president Abbott Lawrence Lowell. These antecedents may have been illustrious in some sense, but many of them were also deeply flawed. Josiah Winslow had pursued the genocidal Prince Philip's War against Native Americans. Abbott Lawrence Lowell had been a useful cog in the machine that controversially sent Italian anarchists Sacco and Vanzetti to their deaths in 1927. On a lower level of infraction, Percival Lowell had discovered 'canals' on Mars, and James Russell Lowell seemed to Robert Lowell to have been 'pedestalled for oblivion'.[4] Lowell considered his forebears more of a burden than a point of pride. Moreover, he grew up in a collateral branch of the family, consumed by social pretentions and downwardly spiralling financial realities, and torn by his parents' disputes. Lowell grew up deeply ambivalent about his family, his country, and himself; three topics that became central to his poetic art.

Lowell studied at St Mark's School, where his brutish demeanour won him the nickname 'Cal', meant to evoke the mad Roman tyrant, Caligula, as well as Shakespeare's beast-man, Caliban. He then studied at Harvard from 1935 to 1937, where he received little recognition for his early attempts at writing poetry. After a violent altercation with his father – recalled in his poems 'Rebellion', 'Anne Dick 1. 1936', 'Father', and 'Mother and Father 1', he left home, camped out for a summer on the lawn of the poet Allen Tate, and transferred that autumn, at Tate's suggestion, to Kenyon College, where he studied from 1937 to 1940.[5] At Kenyon, he began to find himself. He studied with the poet John Crowe Ransom, befriended fellow students and writers Randall Jarrell and Peter Taylor, and published poems in the student magazine, *Hika*. Lowell graduated *summa cum laude* in Classics. After graduating, he married the brilliant fiction writer Jean Stafford, converted to Roman Catholicism, and did a year of graduate study at Louisiana State University with two cutting-edge New Critics, Cleanth Brooks and Robert Penn Warren.

Lowell then returned for a year's stay at the home of Tate and his wife, the novelist Caroline Gordon. There he wrote the religious and political poems that appeared in his first book, *Land of Unlikeness* (1944), a volume marked by its intense rhetoricity. In 1943 Lowell was inducted into the army. Although he had previously attempted to enlist, he now refused the draft, releasing a public letter to President Roosevelt objecting to the bombing of German cities and the demand for Germany's unconditional surrender. Sentenced to a year in prison, he served five and a half months, emerging (as he later said) 'educated – not as they wished *re*-educated'.[6]

Two years after his release from prison Lowell published his first widely circulated volume, *Lord Weary's Castle* (1946), which included heavily revised versions of ten poems from *Land of Unlikeness* along with thirty-two new poems. *Lord Weary's Castle* won the Pulitzer Prize and received glowing reviews by many prestigious poetry reviewers, including the above-referenced Jarrell along with John Berryman, Louise Bogan, Babette Deutsch, Richard Eberhart, Leslie Fiedler, R. W. Flint, Selden Rodman, and Peter Viereck[7] The awards and reviews established Lowell as the leading poet of his generation. In *Lord Weary's Castle*, the poet's dense rhetoric brought specific objects and events to life, and his linguistic and citational complexity was on full display.

In Jarrell's career-making review, he wrote that *Lord Weary's Castle* concerns a 'conflict of opposites' between everything that blinds or binds and everything that grows or changes.[8] This conflict informs the poems in numerous ways. The tension manifests itself in such poems as 'Colloquy in Black Rock' and 'Where the Rainbow Ends' as a clash between a capitalist, warlike social structure and the possibility of Christian salvation. In 'Colloquy in Black Rock', for example, the 'mud' of secular culture ultimately flies from the wings of the 'blue kingfisher' that dives 'in fire' on the speaker's heart.[9] The conflict between stasis and change in 'At the Indian Killer's Grave' and 'Concord' appears as a historical opposition between exploitation and genocide, on the one side, and Christian pacifism, on the other.

In 'At the Indian Killer's Grave', for example, the narrator imagines the Indian King Philip condemning his Puritan killers for having hurled 'anathemas at nature and the land', and then finds sudden relief in a vision of Mary and Jesus.[10] The tension in 'Rebellion' and 'In the Cage' arises in the form of a psychic battle between violence and remorse. In 'Rebellion', the speaker laments that as he sought to 'contract' the world of pain, his aggression towards his father caused it to 'spread' instead.[11] In this volume the dense, vivid, and allusive language produces moments of wrenching intensity along with occasions of exaltation.

The art of *Lord Weary's Castle* is perhaps best seen in the volume's long centrepiece, 'The Quaker Graveyard in Nantucket'. This poem laments all that our nineteenth-century forebears lost 'in the mad scramble of their lives'; and it mourns present-day losses as well, in imagery that echoes and alters that of *Moby-Dick*: 'The bones cry for the blood of the white whale.'[12] 'The Quaker Graveyard in Nantucket', like 'At the Indian Killer's Grave', proffers Jesus and Mary as sources of redemption. But it is the enduring angst of the narrating subject – even more than his quest for transcendence – that dominates the discourse. At the end of 'The Quaker Graveyard', the speaker contemplates a world where predatory 'combers lumbered to the kill' as soon as 'God formed man from the sea's slime'; this is a lonely place to be, where human beings remain unsheltered and unguided as 'the Lord survives the rainbow of His will'.[13]

Attaining a peak of imaginative power, *Lord Weary's Castle* culminates one strain of poetic modernism, generated by New Critical techniques of focalizing tensions in the text. Moreover, the volume participates in a tradition of eschatological critique that we can trace back through such modernists as Eliot, Pound, and Yeats to the very foundations of English-language literature. At the same time, however, the volume struggles to cast off traditional schemata, and to develop new ways of articulating an emerging postmodern condition.

★

By mid-century the style that Lowell forged in *Lord Weary's Castle* no longer struck him as a viable way forward. During this period he encountered a series of life-changing alterations. He lost his Roman Catholic faith; he divorced Jean Stafford and married the critic and novelist Elizabeth Hardwick; his parents died, leaving him a legacy of both money and guilt; and his always-unsettled psychic condition coalesced into a regular series of harrowing bipolar episodes that necessitated periodic institutionalizations. Moreover, he no longer valued the very stylistic choices that had brought him fame. Looking back at his career some years later, he asserted that his strength had not been in mining a single vein of silver, but in recognizing when a vein had petered out and in finding a new one. He invoked the examples of Eliot and Picasso, who worked 'in one surprising style for some years, then surprised with another'.[14]

In *The Mills of the Kavanaughs* (1951) he tried adapting his style of verbal condensation to narrative poems, but with only middling success. Perhaps he was hoping to cross the dense, elliptical textures of Hart Crane, Allen Tate, and Dylan Thomas with the storytelling of Robert Frost. Several of the resulting poems – for example, 'Mother Marie Therese' and 'Falling Asleep Over the Aeneid' – were compelling, and some of the others were strong enough; but none moved him far enough along the new path he sought. Feeling creatively blocked, and perhaps embodying the exhaustion of the modernist project, he reduced himself to virtual silence. He toured Europe with Elizabeth Hardwick, taught at the University of Iowa and several other American universities, started a family (his daughter Harriet Lowell was born in 1957), and spent time in psychiatric hospitals, when his now-diagnosed bipolar disorder flared up. But he could write very little that satisfied him. He drafted a brilliant prose memoir of his childhood, but then found it too painful to revise and publish. He published only a small handful of poems. Without the comfort of hindsight, which would have told him he was in transition to a new surprising style, he experienced this period as 'six or seven years' ineptitude – a slack of eternity'.[15] He worried that he was 'finished'.

In the summer of 1957 Lowell was settled in Boston and desperate to be writing poetry again. He found his old poems 'incomprehensible' when he read them in public.[16] He looked to other contemporary practices for inspiration. Ginsberg had turned his reading of 'Howl' into living theatre. Although Lowell didn't want to turn his own poems into a staged performance, he did want to understand them and to have them be understood by others. He read with admiration the painful yet graceful divorce poems his former student W. D. Snodgrass was then composing (which would appear in *Heart's Needle* in 1959). He also was studying the poetry of his friend Elizabeth Bishop and of his new mentor William Carlos Williams.[17] He carried Bishop's 'The Armadillo' around in his wallet, paid visits to Williams to drink whiskey and discuss poetics, and engaged in a vital literary correspondence with both of them. All of these poets, in very different ways, propelled Lowell to invent a new style that was 'as pliant as conversation', a 'heightened conversation'.[18] The poems in this style would centre on personal experience and familial memory rather than on cultural or religious prophecy. They would translate the visual art of family portraits or a photograph album into the medium of poetry, and they would have the human richness, observation, and irony of good fiction – of Flaubert's novels or Chekhov's short stories.[19]

In late summer of 1957 Lowell drafted the amazing 'Skunk Hour'. Within a year – and in the midst of another episode of mania, depression, and recovery – he completed the rest of the poems that make up the 'Life Studies' sequence in *Life Studies* (1959). The sequence begins with gentle yet sardonic memory poems about Lowell's grandparents, his Uncle Devereux and great-aunt Sarah, his fractious and desperate parents, and always Robert Lowell himself, beginning at five and a half and growing a little older in every passing poem. Eventually the inherently elegiac poems become explicit elegies. 'Commander Lowell' mourns the death of Lowell's father, but in a series of stingingly ironic scenes that turn the elegiac tradition upside down: '"Anchors aweigh," Daddy boomed in his bathtub'.[20] 'Sailing Home from Rapallo' recalls Lowell's return from Rapallo, where his mother had died, accompanied by her body: 'Mother travelled first-class in the hold.'[21] These death poems, subtitled with death dates in the early 1950s, unexpectedly give voice to the years of virtual silence, Lowell's 'slack of eternity'.

The sequence eventually moves to a period very close to the present day. 'Waking in the Blue' evokes Lowell's stay in a 'house for the "mentally ill"'.[22] The sequence implies that a family history like Lowell's, one of cultural privilege and emotional deprivation, leads indirectly to psychosis. The disability portrayed is Lowell's own, but it is more than his: it exposes the chaos hidden within every image of wholeness. The final four poems loop back to remembered events from Lowell's adult life, culminating in the event that must have closely preceded his admission to the mental hospital – a voyeuristic episode that Lowell claimed was inspired by Walt Whitman, perhaps to complicate the autobiographical interpretation that the volume everywhere encourages. The poem is 'Skunk Hour', one of Lowell's signature texts.

'Skunk Hour' takes place in a village modelled on Castine, Maine, where Lowell and Hardwick owned a summer cottage, inherited from his aunt. The first four stanzas portray a community in decline, peopled by figures of loss and compulsion, much as in an Edwin Arlington Robinson poem: an heiress 'in her dotage'; a 'summer millionaire' who has been 'lost' to bankruptcy, imprisonment, or death; a gay decorator hoping to marry a woman of wealth.[23] Each of these characters produces a specular image of the condition of late capitalism and of the isolated, anguished speaker himself. Lowell explained that 'Sterility howls through the scenery. ... Then all comes alive in stanzas V and VI.'[24] In those stanzas, the speaker portrays himself driving to lover's lane, watching for 'love-cars'. 'Nobody's here –,' he observes, 'only skunks'. Lowell later commented, 'This is the dark night. I hoped my readers would remember John of the Cross' poem. My night is not gracious, but secular, puritan, and agnostic. An existentialist night. Somewhere in my mind was a passage from Sartre or Camus about reaching some point of final darkness where the one free act is suicide.'[25] The speaker's final vision of the skunks restores a shaky sense of humour and sociality, seemingly halting his slide into oblivion. Lowell explained: 'Out of this comes the march and affirmation, an ambiguous one, of my skunks in the last two stanzas. The skunks are both quixotic and barbarously absurd, hence the tone of amusement and defiance.'[26] The poem's devastating portrait of a dysfunctional subjectivity and social structure – rendered in a style combining conversational features with skewed poetic rhythms, rhymes, and resonances – has the power to shake up one's vision of the world and to transform one's sense of what a poem can do.

When *Life Studies* was published in 1959 it created a sensation. It brought the narrative drive of autobiography and the ethos of self-disclosure into verse in a startling way. Moreover, the poems possessed verbal qualities that were aesthetically exciting: dynamic juxtapositions of ironic distance and interior revelation, absorbing narrativity, and a highlighted verbal fabric. The volume offended a few well-placed reviewers, but such reviewers as Al Alvarez, Louise Bogan, Donald Davie, G. S. Fraser, John Hollander, Alfred Kazin, Frank Kermode, Stanley Kunitz, M. L. Rosenthal, and Stephen Spender praised it lavishly. Lowell himself thought the volume a 'breakthrough back into life'.[27] James Longenbach has shown that Lowell's practice in *Life Studies* and especially thereafter continued to include elements inherited from his modernist precursors.[28] But no change or 'breakthrough' is absolute. The new practice always to some degree absorbs and builds on the previous practice. Nevertheless, *Life Studies* struck at the time with a thunderbolt, and it still does.[29] The 'Life Studies' sequence begins by representing Lowell as a young boy silently observing familial conflicts and deaths; it concludes by portraying him as an adult encountering his own marital difficulties, accumulating losses, and finally the breakdown of mind and spirit. The seemingly self-certain rhetoric of *Lord Weary's Castle* became, in *Life Studies*, the language of a frail human being in a confusing social universe. Lowell remade himself as a poet, and he fostered the remaking of poetry.

★

Following the publication of *Life Studies*, Robert Lowell and Elizabeth Hardwick moved from Boston to New York, where they both assumed new lives as prominent literary intellectuals. In the 1960s Lowell published four major volumes of poetry and had two plays produced. Yet if Lowell wanted to celebrate his poetic rebirth, he also intended to reinvent himself again. He felt that after *Life Studies*, 'continuous autobiography was impossible'.[30] He sought to return now from the personal to the commons – to the literary and public spheres. In *Imitations* (1961), for example, he composed an anthology of European poems in free translation or Drydenesque imitation – a mammoth extension of the six 'imitations' scattered through *Lord Weary's Castle*. Lowell's translations in *Imitations* opened new perspectives on the anthologized poems, while the volume itself amounted to something more than an anthology. It was a sequence with 'a basically symmetrical structure in which the central section is the crux' (as Stephen Yenser argued) and a 'confrontation' or 'symbiosis' between Lowell's voice and the voices of the imitated poets (as Donald Carne-Ross suggested).[31]

In *For the Union Dead* (1964), *Near the Ocean* (1967), and *Notebook 1967–68* (1969), Lowell readdressed the larger national and international issues that had played such an important role in *Lord Weary's Castle*. The perspective now was not religious but secular and anxious. Lowell still maintained the 'realism about my life' that had been achieved in *Life Studies*, but the new poems were more intricately organized, and they explicitly alluded to the nightmare of Cold War history.[32] For example, the speaker of 'Fall 1961' laments, in reference to nuclear warfare, 'A father's no shield / for his child.'[33] In all of these poems, the world is a dangerous place, and the individual is unsheltered before it. Lowell's plays of this decade also did political work. The dramatic trilogy, *The Old Glory* (first performed in 1964 and published in 1965), transformed classic tales by Nathaniel Hawthorne and Herman Melville into parables of enduring American investments in authoritarianism, imperialism, and white supremacy. The last of the three plays, 'Benito Cereno', revises its predecessor text in a particularly powerful way. *Prometheus Bound* (first performed and published in 1967) questions patriarchy and war by viewing Aeschylus' ancient drama through the lens of Vietnam War era politics.

The title poem of *For the Union Dead*, another of Lowell's signature poems, meditates on the place of racism, war, and greed in American culture.[34] It is an elegy for the first Union Army regiment composed of free African American soldiers – though commanded by a white Boston Brahmin, Robert Gould Shaw. In a sense, it's a continuation of Lowell's line of family elegies, because Shaw was married to one of Lowell's ancestors. Moreover, the poem secularizes the Christian-prophetic mode Lowell established in *Lord Weary's Castle*, and it combines that prophetic mode with the intimist or 'confessional' mode he pioneered in *Life Studies*. Reading the poem in public for the first time, Lowell explained, 'It is about childhood memories, the evisceration of our modern cities, civil rights, nuclear warfare, and more particularly Colonel Robert Shaw and his Negro regiment, the Massachusetts Fifty-fourth. I brought in early personal memories because I wanted to avoid the fixed, brazen tone of the set-piece and official ode.'[35] The poem depicts Augustus St Gaudens' 1897 bas-relief of the heroic Union Army soldiers, which looks out on noisy, traffic-jammed Boylston Street from a corner of Boston Common; it describes the sculpture as being 'out of bounds' now, since passers-by and drivers in cars generally ignore it. The poem concludes, 'a savage servility slides by on grease'. Responding to this poem, Richard Poirier called Lowell 'our truest historian'.[36]

In a similar vein, 'Waking Early Sunday Morning', published in *Near the Ocean*, combines personal self-reflection with historicist observation. It laments an indifferent cosmos and a global politics of violence and war. Written as the Vietnam War escalated, the poem condemns American foreign policy for producing 'small war on the heels of small / war – until the end of time'.[37] Lowell wrote the poem in the aftermath of his controversial public refusal to attend a White House Festival of the Arts. In his letter of refusal to President Lyndon Johnson, dated 3 June 1965, Lowell had written: 'We are in danger of imperceptibly becoming an explosive and suddenly chauvinistic nation. … At this anguished, delicate and perhaps determining moment, I feel I am serving you and our country best by not taking part in the White House Festival of the Arts.'[38] Lowell later observed that this single public act 'brought more publicity than [all my] poems, and I felt miscast, felt burdened to write on the great theme, private though almost "global".'[39] Miscast or not, the episode produced another of his signature poems, a high point in his practice of private–public poetry.

While Lowell was consciously inserting his writing into the political life of his nation, he was actively involving himself in politics as well. When he publicly declined President Johnson's invitation, the President's 'roar in the Oval Office could be heard all the way into the East Wing'.[40] Lowell subsequently joined Allen Ginsberg, Denise Levertov, Norman Mailer, and thousands of other protestors in the 1967 March on the Pentagon, and he acted as a senior advisor to antiwar Senator Eugene McCarthy in the 1968 presidential primaries. Lowell reflected on such activities in a flurry of political essays and in poems included in his next volume, *Notebook 1967–68* (1969). This book, a diary-like collection of unrhymed sonnets patterned around the seasonal cycle, focuses on the year's political events as well as historical, literary, and personal topics. Lowell then continued writing his sonnet-like poems, publishing a 'revised and expanded edition' of the book, now titled simply *Notebook*, in 1970.

★

As the 1970s proceeded, Lowell shifted back again from the public sphere to his personal experience. Perhaps he was hurt by the lukewarm critical response to *Notebook 1967–68* and *Notebook*; and he must have been consumed by the turbulence of his private life. In 1970 he moved, without Elizabeth Hardwick, to England in order to teach at Essex University. Living in England, he began an intimate relationship with the fiction writer and essayist Caroline Blackwood, had a son with her (Robert Sheridan Lowell), and then married her after divorcing Hardwick. As these life-changing events occurred, he continued to produce unrhymed sonnets, revising them with the help of poet Frank Bidart, and finally publishing another revised and expanded version in two new volumes, *History* and *For Lizzie and Harriet* (both in 1973). He also published a brand new sonnet sequence called *The Dolphin* (1973), which conflated his love for Blackwood, imaged as an iconic 'dolphin' and erotic mermaid, with a meditation on his lifelong artistic quest.

The Dolphin is often stylistically muddy, perhaps as an artistic choice or perhaps because Lowell wrote it while sedated on the antidepressant Thorazine. Moreover, the volume violated the privacy and legal rights of Elizabeth Hardwick by versifying her eloquent personal correspondence to him, without her permission. Despite its artistic and ethical issues, *The Dolphin* is often quite beautiful, and it earned Lowell a second Pulitzer Prize. Nevertheless, the volume received mixed reviews and lost him, on ethical grounds, the friendship of Adrienne Rich.[41] The volume's final quasi-sonnet, called simply 'Dolphin', demonstrates what the sequence achieves at its best.[42] Meditating on the ambiguous relationship of embodied experience to textual production, the speaker accuses himself of plotting (in a double sense) 'too freely' with his life. A final line, separated from the others by a space and adding to the standard fourteen-line format of the other poems, proclaims with a mixture of pride and shame: 'my eyes have seen what my hand did'. That is to say, the poet's eyes saw first what his hand later wrote down, but also that his eyes saw and affirmed the inscribed words that the hand produced. The failures and triumphs of Lowell's writing had never been so explicit as they became in this poem and sequence.

Suffering from congestive heart failure and responding to the increasing dysfunction of his marriage to Blackwood, Lowell ultimately moved back to the United States and to Hardwick. He published one final book of poems, *Day by Day* (1977), a moving account of the complicated conditions of his existence and a continued exploration of his final great theme: the aesthetics of poems that are at once an affirmative autobiographical utterance and a complexly imagined making. The volume concludes with a poem called 'Epilogue', Lowell's culminating *ars poetica*.[43] The poem reflects on the complex role memories of personal experience played in this poet's creative life.

The poet-speaker of 'Epilogue' denounces the 'threadbare art of my eye' and argues that the artist's vision is not properly '*a lens*' but rather '*trembles to caress the light*'. Perhaps one might interpret this as the poet's critique of his involvement with an epistemological project at the expense of formal experiment and verbal play – that is, his retention of a strong representational purpose instead of initiating a full, and perhaps more *avant-garde*, engagement with language itself. The critique intensifies: the poet accuses his writing of being 'heightened' from life yet 'paralyzed' by fact, failing to achieve either a satisfying referentiality or a challenging a-referentiality. The argument then turns on the word 'Yet'. From that point onward, the poem assumes a tentative form of self-defence. It asks, 'why not say what happened?' This question has often been taken as rhetorical. The implied answer would then be, 'Yes, one can and should say what happened.' Viewing the question that way opens a can of worms. How can one 'say what happened', when saying involves the mediation of words whereas 'what happened' resides in the irretrievable, multi-dimensional world of objects and events. There is an unbridgeable gap between a happening and what Nietzsche called the 'constraints' or 'prison house' of language.[44] But if one understands this question as real rather than rhetorical, the trouble diminishes. Saying what happened becomes an aesthetic aim to be considered – a problematic rather than a given.

The next line elaborates on that problematic: we cannot achieve accuracy per se, but we can 'pray' for the 'grace' of accuracy. More than factuality, what is sought is a spiritual state that is both within and outside of what can be proven. The imperative is to give each 'figure' of reality its 'living' name, which may be subtly different from its literal name. Reality is thus portrayed as always already figurative in human mentation; and the quest for 'grace' re-invokes the supernatural aura of Lowell's earliest work. The poem does not answer the question of art's relationship to life but raises that question anew, in a simple way that derives from a complicated understanding.

Several days after the publication of *Day by Day*, Lowell died of heart failure in a New York taxicab, en route home to Hardwick in New York from a visit with Blackwood in Ireland. Lowell died as he lived and wrote, traversing an unsettled world – 'lost', as he once wrote of Ulysses, 'in the uproarious rudeness of a great wind'.[45] Yet the restlessness that marked his poetic career seemed to have given way to a kind of peace. He understood the stakes of his drive to generate 'living' names more clearly at the end than he had at the beginning. From his early prophetic words to his later personal and public ones to his last meditative ones, Lowell made himself an innovative, dependably fascinating figure in American poetry. He brought modernism to one sort of climax, then challenged and changed mid-century poetry, and finally impacted, in multiple ways, the poetry of the future. From almost the beginning of his career to the very end, he wrote texts that have become landmarks, including 'The Quaker Graveyard in Nantucket', 'Skunk Hour', 'For the Union Dead', 'Waking Early Sunday Morning', and 'Epilogue'. Lowell once ruefully observed, 'My art, like many others, fails.'[46] Yet his living names endure.

Notes

This essay was developed with the support of a research grant from the Polish National Science Center (UMO-2012/07/B/HS2/01590) for the study of Robert Lowell's autobiographical prose, and a research grant from the University of California, Riverside. I thank Professor Grzegorz Kosc of the University of Lodz for reading this essay and providing a helpful correction.

1. Randall Jarrell, 'From the Kingdom of Necessity' (review of *Lord Weary's Castle*), *Nation*, 164 (11 January 1947): 75–7; rpt. in Steven Gould Axelrod (ed.), *The Critical Response to Robert Lowell* (Westport, CT: Greenwood Press, 1999), pp. 30–7.

2. The idea, if not the exact phrase, originated in M. L. Rosenthal, 'Poetry as Confession', *Nation*, 189 (19 September 1959): 154–5; rpt. in Axelrod, *The Critical Response to Robert Lowell*, pp. 64–8. See also M. L. Rosenthal, 'Robert Lowell and the Poetry of Confession', *The Modern Poets* (New York: Oxford University Press, 1960), pp. 225–37.
3. T. S. Eliot, 'Tradition and the Individual Talent' (1919); rpt. in *Selected Prose of T. S. Eliot*, ed. Frank Kermode (New York: Harcourt Brace Jovanovich / Farrar, Straus and Giroux, 1975), p. 40.
4. Robert Lowell, *Collected Prose*, ed. Robert Giroux (New York: Farrar Straus and Giroux, 1987; London: Faber, 1987), p. 276.
5. Robert Lowell, *Collected Poems*, ed. Frank Bidart and David Gewanter (New York: Farrar, Straus and Giroux, 2003), pp. 32, 509, 510, 511.
6. Robert Lowell, *Collected Prose*, p. 279.
7. See Steven Gould Axelrod and Helen Deese, *Robert Lowell: A Reference Guide* (Boston, MA: G. K. Hall, 1982) for bibliographical information and abstracts of all reviews Lowell received in his lifetime.
8. Randall Jarrell, 'From the Kingdom of Necessity', p. 75; rpt. in Axelrod, *The Critical Response to Robert Lowell*, p. 30.
9. Robert Lowell, *Collected Poems*, p. 11.
10. Robert Lowell, *Collected Poems*, p. 57.
11. Robert Lowell, *Collected Poems*, p. 32.
12. Robert Lowell, *Collected Poems*, pp. 15, 17.
13. Robert Lowell, *Collected Poems*, p. 18.
14. Robert Lowell, *Collected Prose*, p. 269.
15. Robert Lowell, *Collected Prose*, p. 269.
16. Robert Lowell, *Collected Prose*, p. 284.
17. See Steven Gould Axelrod, *Robert Lowell: Life and Art* (Princeton, NJ: Princeton University Press, 1978), pp. 84–101; and Robert Lowell and Elizabeth Bishop, *Words in Air: The Complete Correspondence*, ed. Thomas Travisano with Saskia Hamilton (New York: Farrar, Straus and Giroux, 2008), pp. 127–267.
18. Robert Lowell, *Collected Prose*, p. 284. See also *Collected Prose*, p. 227; and Jeffrey Meyers (ed.), *Robert Lowell: Interviews and Memoirs* (Ann Arbor, MI: University of Michigan Press, 1988), p. 79.
19. Jeffrey Meyers, p. 88.
20. Robert Lowell, *Collected Poems*, p. 173.
21. Robert Lowell, *Collected Poems*, p. 179.
22. Robert Lowell, *Collected Poems*, p. 183.
23. Robert Lowell, *Collected Poems*, pp. 191–2.
24. Robert Lowell, *Collected Prose*, p. 226.
25. Robert Lowell, *Collected Prose*, p. 226.
26. Robert Lowell, *Collected Prose*, p. 226.
27. Robert Lowell, *Collected Prose*, p. 244.
28. James Longenbach, *Modern Poetry after Modernism* (New York and Oxford: Oxford University Press, 1997), pp. 5–7, 9–14, 16–21.

29. Sylvia Plath, for example, spoke of 'the new breakthrough that came with, say, Robert Lowell's *Life Studies*, this intense breakthrough into very serious, very personal, emotional experience which I feel has been partly taboo' ('Sylvia Plath', *The Poet Speaks*, ed. Peter Orr (London: Routledge & Kegan Paul, 1966), 1: 67–8.
30. Robert Lowell, *Collected Prose*, p. 269.
31. Stephen Yenser, *Circle to Circle: The Poetry of Robert Lowell* (Berkeley, CA: University of California Press, 1975), p. 167. Donald Carne-Ross, 'The Two Voices of Translation', in Thomas Parkinson (ed.), *Robert Lowell: A Collection of Critical Essays* (Englewood Cliffs, NJ: Prentice Hall, 1968), pp. 153, 160.
32. Robert Lowell, *Collected Prose*, p. 269.
33. Robert Lowell, *Collected Poems*, p. 329.
34. Robert Lowell, *Collected Poems*, pp. 376–8.
35. Lowell manuscripts, Houghton Library, Harvard University.
36. Richard Poirier, 'Our Truest Historian', *New York Herald Tribune Book Week* (11 October 1964): 1.
37. Robert Lowell, *Collected Poems*, pp. 383–6.
38. Robert Lowell, *Collected Prose*, p. 371.
39. Robert Lowell, *Collected Prose*, p. 270.
40. Eric Goldman, *The Tragedy of Lyndon Johnson* (New York: Knopf, 1969), p. 429.
41. For Rich's public response, see her scathing review of *History*, *For Lizzie and Harriet*, and *The Dolphin* in her column, 'Carydid', in *American Poetry Review*, 2 (September–October 1973), pp. 42–3; rpt. in Axelrod, *Critical Response*, pp. 185–7.
42. Robert Lowell, *Collected Poems*, p. 708.
43. Robert Lowell, *Collected Poems*, p. 838.
44. Friedrich Nietzsche, *The Will to Power*, trans. Walter Kaufmann and R. J. Hollingdale (New York: Vintage, 1968), p. 283.
45. Robert Lowell, *Collected Poems*, p. 715.
46. Robert Lowell, *Collected Prose*, p. 289.

Further Reading

Axelrod, Steven Gould, *Robert Lowell: Life and Art* (Princeton, NJ: Princeton University Press, 1978).

Axelrod, Steven Gould (ed.), *The Critical Response to Robert Lowell* (Westport, CT: Greenwood Press, 1999).

Axelrod, Steven Gould and Helen Deese, *Robert Lowell: A Reference Guide* (Boston, MA: G. K. Hall, 1982).

Bishop, Elizabeth and Robert Lowell, *Words in Air: The Complete Correspondence*, ed. Thomas Travisano with Saskia Hamilton (New York: Farrar, Straus and Giroux, 2008).

Hamilton, Ian, *Robert Lowell: A Biography* (New York: Random House, 1982).

Lowell, Robert, *Collected Prose*, ed. Robert Giroux (New York: Farrar Straus and Giroux, 1987; London: Faber, 1987).

Lowell, Robert, *Collected Poems*, ed. Frank Bidart and David Gewanter (New York: Farrar, Straus and Giroux, 2003).

Lowell, Robert, *Letters*, ed. Saskia Hamilton (New York: Farrar, Straus and Giroux, 2005).

Mariani, Paul, *Lost Puritan: A Life of Robert Lowell* (New York: W. W. Norton, 1994).

Meyers, Jeffrey (ed.), *Robert Lowell: Interviews and Memoirs* (Ann Arbor, MI: University of Michigan Press, 1988).

Parkinson, Thomas (ed.), *Robert Lowell: A Collection of Critical Essays* (Englewood Cliffs, NJ: Prentice Hall, 1968).

Rosenthal, M. L., *The Modern Poets* (New York: Oxford University Press, 1960).

Yenser, Stephen, *Circle to Circle: The Poetry of Robert Lowell* (Berkeley, CA: University of California Press, 1975).

3

Making and Making Do: The Poetry of Elizabeth Bishop

Linda Anderson

1

In 1934, Elizabeth Bishop, recently graduated from Vassar College, visited Cuttyhunk Island, off the coast of Massachusetts. As with her visit to Newfoundland two years before, she seems to have enjoyed the sense of limits the island imposed and its lessons about exigency and improvisation. The 'Cuttyhunk' notebook is one of Bishop's earliest travel diaries but even here, while she is observing and recording, she is also aware of the possible connections and analogies with poetry:

> Mr Van Wuthenaur wanted to 'simplify life' all the time – that's the fascination of an island ... On an island you live all the time in this Robinson Crusoe atmosphere; making this do for that, and contriving and inventing ... a poem should be made about making things in a pinch – & how it looks sad when the emergency is over ... The idea of making things do – of using things in an unthought of way because it's necessary – has a lot more to it.[1]

Brett Millier believes that this early four-page notebook yielded phrases and ideas that Bishop incorporated into 'a half-dozen later poems': 'Crusoe in England' is obviously one poem whose inception we could trace back to this early writing, but Millier detects resonances and images in others including 'At the Fishhouses' and 'The Map'.[2] If Bishop seems to have admired how island dwellers could learn to 'make do', using whatever materials were to hand, her own method as a writer similarly seems to have meant drawing on accidental encounters and stray materials from her various travels. However, the part played by the notebooks themselves should not be underestimated nor their role in hoarding the ideas and images that would be of use years, or even decades, later. In many ways Bishop was an 'archival' writer for whom the accumulations of writings which were incidental took on their own resonances over time, and provided a key to what became her major theme: time or memory itself.

In 1935, as an apprentice writer, Bishop started on her story 'The Sea and Its Shore' during a visit to France; she worked on it intermittently for the next three years, experimenting with ideas that were to preoccupy her throughout her life: the interaction of sea and shore and their ability to represent fluctuating boundaries; and temporary, notional, or makeshift shelters or dwellings. Her protagonist, Edwin Boomer, whose initials (E.B.) indicate their shared lineage, is the first of the vagrant characters who populate her work: his job seems to be to comb the shore for fragments of paper which, as they blow about, have 'no discernible goal', though their favourite motion seems to be 'an oblique one, slipping sidewise'.[3] This seems like an early evocation of Bishop's own preferred trajectory for her writing. Boomer's emphasis on the material life of print and writing is also of interest, reflecting Bishop's own highly visual response to her craft: for instance, she observed the relation of waves to handwriting in her notebooks, and wondered at the effect of holding writing up to a mirror.[4] She also seems to have had, as part of her modernist or surrealist inheritance, an ongoing interest in ephemeral writing like newspaper cuttings, mail order catalogues, and labels of all kinds.

At this time, in the 1930s and the early 1940s, Bishop was both indebted to Marianne Moore who took on a mentoring role in relation to Bishop – perhaps in too conscientious a manner for Bishop's liking – and exercised by the differences between them. Bishop's attempts at prose in these early years provided one point of tension in their relationship. Moore disliked the 'cleverness' of these pieces, which included 'In Prison' as well as 'The Sea and Its Shore', and which, for her, suffered from 'tentativeness and interiorizing'.[5] Bishop, for her part, expressed the belief that she was working out her own theory combining Edgar Allan Poe's ideas with those of seventeenth-century prose.[6] The influence of the literary critic M. W. Croll, and his essay 'The Baroque style in Prose', which she had quoted in her student essay on Gerard Manley Hopkins, has been widely commented on by critics, and Croll's idea of Baroque prose as portraying 'not a thought but a mind thinking' has been seen as the key to the development of her poetic voice,[7] which makes use of extended observations, interrupted by emotion or self-questioning, in order to represent 'the mind thinking'.[8] Yet, the letter with its reference to Poe as well as to Croll, suggests she was also preoccupied with metaphor and the restraint Poe advocated in its use: in his essay 'The Poetic Principle', Poe had explicitly dissociated the 'Truth' of poetry from a self-conscious 'efflorescence of language' and argued that poetry was, in effect, 'the exact converse of the poetical'.[9] In Bishop's essay on 'Miss Moore and Edgar Allan Poe' (1948) she quoted approvingly from another of Poe's essays 'The Philosophy of Composition'[10] about the need to avoid 'the excess of the suggested meaning', and then drew a parallel with Moore's restrained use of metaphor: 'It is one of the qualities that gives her poetry its steady aura of both reserve and having possibly more meanings, in reserve.'[11] Holding in reserve – different from the modesty often ascribed to her – became, of course, one of Bishop's own key poetic strategies.

Bishop valued Moore for her observations and emphasis on 'things': 'Why had no one ever written about things in this clear and dazzling way before?' Bishop lamented in her unpublished memoir of Moore, 'Efforts of Affection'.[12] Moore's approach, influenced by her study of biology at Bryn Mawr, was often forensic in its detail, and she could literally place botanical and biological specimens under the microscope before writing about them. Objects, singly or within her personal collection, provided an interiority for Moore, a 'continually inward movement', that engendered an excess or surplus of meanings, which could be held back or alluded to without obvious symbolic intent.[13] As this letter to Moore reveals, however, Bishop struggled with how to generate the necessary connection or 'friction' that would allow her significant 'things' to signify:

> I have that continuous uncomfortable feeling of 'things' in the head, like icebergs or rocks or awkwardly placed pieces of furniture. It's as if all the nouns were there but the verbs were lacking – if you know what I mean. And I can't help having the theory that if they are joggled around hard enough and long enough some kind of electricity will occur, just by friction.[14]

That she could suggest geographical spaciousness and distance, setting it alongside her interior 'furniture', however 'awkwardly placed', takes this into a different realm from the kind of containment and compacting of images that characterizes Moore's poetry, and hints at the solution Bishop eventually found by using journeys, oblique narratives and the resonances of memory.

The year before she wrote this letter, Bishop had explored in her poem 'The Monument', the positioning of a wooden box-like construction that disorientates the viewer's sense of perspective with its invocation of sky, sea and distance:

> 'Why does that strange sea make no sound?
> Is it because we're far away?
> Where are we? Are we in Asia Minor,
> Or in Mongolia?'[15]

These questions seem to echo those raised later in 'Questions of Travel' where again an interjected speaking voice questions the relationship between the imagining of distant places and their reality.[16] In 'The Monument' the 'crated scenery' is roughly assembled, and yet it seems to want 'to be a monument, to cherish something'. In the end the monumental nature of the wooden structure can only be thought of as provisional or in process, something which is inevitably exposed to the actions of nature and time – 'the strong sunlight, the wind from the sea / all the conditions of its existence'[17] – and open to the future:

> It is the beginning of a painting,
> a piece of sculpture, or poem, or monument,
> and all of wood. Watch it closely.[18]

The extent to which interiors might fail to be self-contained, sealed off from the action of change and decomposition (or recomposition), is a dilemma that finds its way into Bishop's writing in various forms. In her poem 'Jerónimo's House', written at roughly the same time as 'The Monument', in the late 1930s, the dwelling is again temporary, and both clapboards and crates suggest a flimsiness, whatever their aesthetic or spiritual potential, which offers little in the way of permanence or shelter:

> My house, my fairy
>   palace, is
> of perishable
>   clapboards with
> three rooms in all,
>   my gray wasps' nest
> of chewed-up paper
>   glued with spit.[19]

Moore's poem 'The Paper Nautilus', written only slightly after 'Jerónimo's House', and sharing with Bishop's poem the imagery of the wasp's nest, imagines a structure that intricately folds inside and outside together, 'a dull / white outside and smooth-edged inner surface' and which, for all its emphasis on the mutual freedom of mother and offspring, also imagines the relationship as permanently engraved in stone:

like the lines in the mane of
a Parthenon horse,
round which the arms had
wound themselves as if they knew love
is the only fortress
strong enough to trust to.[20]

The classical imagery Moore uses seems to enshrine an idea of eternity. When Bishop imagined a fort or fortress, as she did in 'Paris 7AM', it is revealing of their differences that Bishop makes comparisons with the dissolving structures of a snow-fort and a sand-fort, before imagining their survival as not eternally 'white', as for Moore, but 'grayed and yellowed' with decay.[21]

Bishop's 'Monument' probably refers, as Bonnie Costello argues, to a 'frottage' in Max Ernst's *Histoire Naturelle*, a book Bishop had studied on her first trip to France in 1933.[22] Frottage introduces materiality in its literal tracing of wooden floorboards, even as it allows the imagination or the unconscious free scope. Bishop was knowledgeable about contemporary art, sharing ideas and reading with her friend from Vassar, Margaret Miller, who helped to research the groundbreaking exhibition 'Fantastic Art, Dada and Surrealism' at the Museum of Modern Art in 1936, and was also engaged with a later one about collage in 1948, which featured the work of Max Ernst, amongst other artists such as Georges Braque, Pablo Picasso, and Juan Gris.[23] Gris particularly intrigued Bishop with his use of *papier collé*, a technique in some ways similar to frottage, which employed printed matter as part of the 'real' surface of a work, reducing the 'monumental space' of his pictures to a 'flat surface'.[24] Bishop's early poem 'The Man-Moth' takes as its inspiration a misprint in the *New York Times*, and thus suggests her openness at this time to the use of chance as promoted by the surrealists, and to the surface itself as meaningful without reference to some other hidden 'depth' which it symbolizes or represents. The figure of the Man-Moth also seems to be related to Edward Boomer's observations about papers and flight in 'The Sea and the Shore', and his drunken vision of letters (or misprints) which seem to 'fly from the pages'.[25] Ultimately, Bishop's Man-Moth, aspiring and plangent, cannot escape the canvas he belongs to, and his interiority is called up in terms of the signifying media – photography and painting – rather than what they represent, as he crawls across the 'façades' or surfaces:

> Up the façades,
> his shadow dragging like a photographer's cloth behind him,
> he climbs fearfully, thinking that this time he will manage
> to push his small head through that round clean opening
> and be forced through, as from a tube, in black scrolls on the light.[26]

In her book *Deep Skin* in which she explores Bishop's relationship with visual art, Peggy Samuels refers to the discussions that Margaret Miller and Bishop had about collage.[27] Miller's own notes in relation to the 1948 exhibition promote the importance of collage in modern art, arguing that it has been 'the means through which the artist incorporates reality in the picture without imitating it'.[28] Samuels herself describes collage as 'an art form that solves the problem of disconnection' by being able to bring 'disparate registers of experience and of representation into extensive relation with one another'.[29] Bishop's problems about how 'things' could signify and the need for some action ('verbs') or 'friction' to make it happen, as she wrote to Moore, and her interest in eliding 'deep' or symbolic meaning in a signifying surface, seem to come together in a thoughtful meditation in her notebook in 1935, which assembles a 'collage' of objects of her own, seemingly triggered by her reading of a mail order catalogue. Bishop begins first of all by trying to pinpoint the strange effect created by the catalogue, with its combination of text and image, and wishing for an object which could, like this, 'produce these ghosts, distortions, funeral engraved nightmares of itself – with prices and writing underneath'.[30] Then, in a passage which curiously recalls Virginia Woolf in her diary in 1919 wishing for 'some deep old desk, or capacious hold-all, in which one flings a mass of odds & ends without looking them through' and which 'after a year or two' would have 'sorted itself & refined itself & coalesced',[31] Bishop goes on in her notes to wish for a 'junk-room, store-room or attic' where

> I could keep and had kept, all my life the odds and ends that took my fancy. The buffalo robe with moth-eaten scalloped red-flounced edges, my aunt's doll with the limp neck, buttons, china, towels stolen from hotels, stones, pieces of wood, beach toys, old hats, some of my relations cast-off clothes, liquor labels, tin-foil, bottles of medicine to smell,

bottles of colored water – things which please by their neatness, such as small lined blank books, blocks of solder – *Everything and Anything*: If one had such a place to throw things into, like a sort of extra brain, and a chair in the middle of it to go and sit on once in a while, it might be a great help – particularly as it all decayed and fell together and took on a general odor.

Both Woolf and Bishop seem to desire a form of artistic composition that eliminates the writer's conscious volition, shifting the perspective away from the controlling presence of the artist to an unconscious process. In 'The Monument' Bishop imagines her 'artist-prince' as receptive rather than powerful and in the passage above as well, her role – even though she imagines herself as enthroned in the midst of things – is passive. In 1949 Bishop revealingly wrote to Robert Lowell that she felt that she had 'written more poetry by *not* writing it than writing it'.[32] In effect she looked to letters with their disjunctive narratives, and their status as a form of writing she did not equate with 'work', as well as the provisional nature of drafts, to mitigate the finality or monumentality in relation to writing that she both distrusted and struggled with.[33] In 1963 she encouraged fellow poet Robert Lowell to go on sending her his rough copies, writing to him: 'No – I like these "messy copies" – much better than final ones – a correction makes it "breathe", after all – or turn over, or blink.'[34] Imagining creative space as a 'junk-room, store-room or attic' in her notebook entry above, Bishop is also imagining a place that is both ancillary and informal. At the same time her lovingly described list of objects – which seem to resonate with her own past – are also subject to the action of time as change or decay. If Bishop was puzzled about connection, and about the energy that might animate things without overt use of metaphor or symbol, then time became for her the answer, a process that could infuse and enfold, turning a spatially conceived list or collage into something densely suggestive. Bishop's notorious slowness, the numbers of drafts she worked through in order to arrive at a finished poem, the interpolation of years and even decades into the process of composition, quite literally, introduced time into her writing. The extent to which she was returning across time, using old phrases and perceptions laid down before, suggests the way her writing required a creative 'storeroom' or 'attic', an intervening process, which might change her descriptions and her intently visualized objects and places, into something else.

2

Bishop took the inspiration for one of her most lauded and influential poems 'At the Fishhouses' from a trip she made to Nova Scotia in 1946, her first return to this significant landscape of her childhood for almost ten years. She begins the poem with the evocation of age, both in the 'old man', an almost archetypal figure, and the description of physical objects; 'an ancient wooden capstan', the 'black old knife', and even the moss growing on the 'shoreward walls' of the 'small old buildings'.[35] Yet the poem really concentrates on the 'iridescent' surface, the scene as presence, before in a bold and unprecedented move in terms of positioning and register, it imagines the 'unbearable' depths of the sea: 'Cold dark deep and absolutely clear, / the clear grey icy water'. In the famous ending of the poem, time itself becomes the subject, the knowledge of the deep or the deepest knowledge conceived not as being *in* flux but *as* flux:

> It is like what we imagine knowledge to be:
> dark, salt, clear, moving, utterly free,
> drawn from the cold hard mouth
> of the world, derived from the rocky breasts
> forever, flowing and drawn, and since
> our knowledge is historical, flowing, and flown.

Bishop at this time was experimenting with both narrative and different uses of time in her poems, though she never attempted this kind of metaphysical speculation and 'depth' again. In 'Cape Breton', a poem that is roughly contemporary, the possibility of narrative briefly emerges when 'a small bus comes along', 'packed with people', and a man then gets off, 'carrying a baby'.[36] We follow his journey a little way before he disappears into a landscape, which throughout, has refused meaning or penetration behind its obscurely veiled surface:

> Whatever the landscape had of meaning appears to have been bandoned,
> unless the road is holding it back, in the interior,
> where we cannot see[.]

In 'The Prodigal', another poem from the same period, Bishop defers the inevitable narrative of return, already determined by her choice of story or vehicle for her poem, dwelling instead on the present, the period of procrastination and its subjective dynamics:

> Carrying a bucket along a slimy board,
> he felt the bats' uncertain staggering flight,

his shuddering insights, beyond his control,
touching him. But it took him a long time
finally to make up his mind to go home.[37]

Bishop's imaginative return home to the traumatic scene of her early childhood, and the mining of her own memories for her writing, was able to happen in a sustained way after she had settled in Brazil in 1952, a place she arrived in almost by accident, and continued to stay more or less continually for the next fifteen years, thanks to her relationship with the cultured heiress, Lota de Macedo Soares. At the beginning of their relationship, Lota was constructing a house in Petropolis, on her share of the family estate, some fifty miles from Rio de Janeiro in the mountains, and though in its finished form it was to be a noted example of modernist architecture, the process of construction seems to have involved a period of living in fairly primitive conditions. Bishop wrote to Lowell about the 'oil-lamps, no floors – just cement covered with dogs' footprints', and how, as cook, she was confronted with 'the raw materials, all unshelled, unblanched, un-skinned, or un-dead', noting, 'I can cook goat now – with wine sauce.'[38] Bishop seems to have found this improvised living, as in her early sojourn on Cuttyhunk, creative, and it is possible that it is the shock of cooking goat here, as well as a degree of inventiveness in how they were living, that eventually found their way into her poem 'Crusoe in England', and helped to form Crusoe's memories of island life and, particularly, of being haunted by the sounds and smells of goats.

Bishop's first writing after she settled in Brazil was in prose, and her use of this form perhaps demonstrates her need to explore, not a new relation to place, but to time. In the masterpiece she wrote in Brazil, 'In the Village', Bishop was able to return to the traumatic memories of her mother's breakdown when she was just six, and her mother's subsequent institutionalization. After the events recorded in the story, Bishop, shockingly, never saw her mother again, nor was she talked about within the family, even though she lived for another eighteen years. However, Bishop is not simply recalling her childhood in the story, but also representing the complex process of remembering, with its belatedness and disjunctions between events, understanding and affect. The story begins with a preliminary paragraph, unlocated in time, and with a sound – a scream – conflated with its echo as a form of endless repetition, less heard as sound within time than engraved in memory: 'The scream hangs like that, unheard, in memory – in the past, in the present, and those years between.'[39] The story negotiates different times. From the child's point of view, the present and immediate perceptions predominate. However, the objects noticed by the child are also characterized by strangeness, distance, and otherness, which hint at other times of sadness and loss. As her aunt and her grandmother unpack her mother's trunk of possessions which have been transported from a Boston the child cannot remember, her perception lights on the scent 'from somewhere else'; postcards from 'another world … the world of sad brown perfume, and morning' (sounding inevitably like 'mourning'), and 'broken china' which her grandmother says, 'breaks her heart'.[40] Eventually the child absconds with another object, one of the embroidery tools, 'a little ivory stick with a sharp point', suggestive of her own painful piercing by memory: 'To keep it forever I bury it under the bleeding heart by the crab-apple tree, but it is never found again.'[41] This act of interment represents, as much as it conceals, a loss that is itself deeply buried.

In turning to a later poem, 'Crusoe in England', published in her remarkable collection *Geography III*, we are also turning to a poem described by Millier as 'as close as Elizabeth came to a verse autobiography'[42] and by Joanne Feit Diehl as one resembling 'In the Village' in that it is a 'narrative of contiguity and metonymic relations', using a 'digressive' rather than a 'metaphoric' style.[43] Bishop finally completed 'Crusoe in England' in 1971, after she had left Brazil, and after the tragic death of Lota. Like many of her later poems, however, it was worked on and anticipated over many years, and, as we have seen, may well have had its roots in observations recorded as far back as 1934, in one of her earliest notebooks. Bishop announced to Robert Lowell in 1964 that she was working into the early hours on 'a poem about Robinson Crusoe'[44] and signalled to her editor at *The New Yorker*, Howard Moss, in 1965 that she'd soon be sending 'a long poem' entitled 'Crusoe at Home', and had been rereading the novel, finding it both 'morally appalling' and 'fascinating'.[45] That Bishop, after tantalizing Moss with it for many years, eventually rewrote the poem after Lota's death, may help to account for its bleak conclusion, and the removal of the word 'home' from its title: the poem ends up challenging any settled notion of location in terms of time and space. Crusoe, having been 'rescued', looks back at his experience on the island, replete with its fifty-two 'dead' volcanoes, one for each week of the year, and presenting him, having lost his own standards of measurement, with confusions about his own size and the proportion and scale of objects around him:

I'd think that if they were the size
I thought volcanoes should be, then I had
become a giant;

I couldn't bear to think what size
the goats and turtles were[.][46]

Bishop, faced with the imminent loss of her home in Brazil, had already explored in a series of three prose-poems, 'Rainy Season; Sun-Tropics', the connection between displacement, and the ability to relate and harmonize inner and outer worlds. The ungainly creatures she describes or briefly inhabits – a giant toad, a strayed crab and a giant snail – are also strangely out of scale, at odds with their own bodies, and their habitat; both her giant toad and giant snail experience themselves as 'too big', and dwell on the idea of 'pity', entreating compassion for themselves from the reader.[47] For Crusoe, his need for pity is so bound up with the resounding term 'solitude' he so tellingly forgets, that pity becomes 'self-pity', and its pit or 'crater' of despair becomes, through repetition, part of his attempt to create a sense of home:

What's wrong about self-pity, anyway?
With my legs dangling down familiarly
over a crater's edge, I told myself
'Pity should begin at home.' So the more
pity I felt, the more I felt at home.[48]

As Paul Muldoon has noted, the word 'crater' turns up in another context in another contemporary poem, '12 O'Clock News', where Bishop talks in parallel about war reporting and her desk and writing process, without us being quite sure which is a metaphor for which.[49] The 'ash heaps' of volcanoes in 'Crusoe in England', described as having 'parched throats' that were 'hot to touch', could also contain an allusion to smoking which always seems to have accompanied writing for Bishop, a habit she shared with Lowell to whom, in 1949, she sent an ashtray that 'will really hold the cigarette while you write or scratch your head'.[50] To draw attention to a possible analogy between the writing process and the geography of Crusoe's island is suggestive in terms of the way the Crusoe story operated as part of Bishop's mythology of writing and of the writer's life from the earliest days of her career. It is also the case that Bishop is working out in this poem not just how Crusoe, 'making things in a pinch' creates a 'home-made' world on his island out of the available materials and his own, beleaguered, and sometimes violent, imaginings, but how memory provides the thread, the connective energy. It is important that throughout the poem Crusoe is remembering and there is a liveliness to his looking back to his island, the place of necessity and invention, which does not apply to his more comfortable present. Back in England, the objects that helped form his inner world have lost their meaning, have become 'uninteresting lumber':

The knife there on the shelf –
it reeked of meaning, like a crucifix.
It lived. How many years did I
beg it, implore it, not to break?
I knew each nick and scratch by heart,
the bluish blade, the broken tip,
the lines of wood-grain on the handle …
Now it won't look at me at all.
The living soul has dribbled away.
My eyes rest on it and pass on.[51]

The knife he treasured no longer reflects an intimate relationship with his past. The sense of depletion, ultimately a diminution of his own internal world, seems related to the death of Friday, a fact withheld until the end of the poem and the more powerful for being inadequately represented. In another late poem, her famous 'One Art', also published in *Geography III*, the objects Bishop lists increase in scale and momentousness – keys, her mother's watch, houses, and continents – but ultimately are substitutes for an inexpressible loss, the 'disaster' which her 'art' attempts to keep at bay, but which comes back with a crushing inevitability at the end. This poem, like 'Crusoe in England', struggles to convert the bitterness of loss into resignation.

Yet, in other poems in *Geography III* Bishop can also employ memory to arrive at a more benign sense of recuperation and return where the linking made possible through the passage of time allows her to find a meaning for her ruined objects, her ruined world. 'The End of March', written by Bishop in 1974, and using the shoreline as its setting, takes its structure from a walk and a return journey along the same route after she fails to reach her 'dream house'. The discovery of the string in the poem – possibly a kite string – seems to carry some submerged meaning, a ghostly presence, never fully recovered:

a thick white snarl, man-size, awash,
rising on every wave, a sodden ghost,
falling back, sodden, giving up the ghost …
A kite-string? – But no kite.[52]

Coming back, however, the kite is no longer thought of as simply lost, or dead, but imagined as having been in movement before:

On the way back our faces froze on the other side.
The sun came out for just a minute.
For just a minute, set in their bezels of sand,
the drab, damp, scattered stones
were multi-coloured,
and all those high enough threw out long shadows,
individual shadows, then pulled them in again.
They could have been teasing the lion sun,
except that now he was behind them
a sun who'd walked the beach the last low tide,
making those big, majestic paw-prints,
who perhaps had batted a kite out of the sky to play with.

The figure of the lion is an animation of the sun, with a likeness based on colour, and is benignly playful, its other associations – suggested in that initial description of its 'snarl' – suspended. The tense – that use of the conditional – is important; it is also of course, the time of imagination and writing.

On one level Bishop's late poems are poems of memory. It is as if she found her subject matter when she was in Brazil and then later was able not only to rework the material she had accumulated over years in her notebooks and in her memory, but also to incorporate the meaning of the passage of time into them. Bishop's later poems seem often to be both complete and open. The 'makeshift' – the chance to use what was to hand and write in the provisional way that she found so releasing in letters and notebooks – has combined with the ability to contemplate the process. In their ability to lead her back to where the poems began, and to include within themselves something of the history of their own potential and making, these late poems also give Bishop a way, not of transcending loss, but of containing its ambivalences – 'half groan, half acceptance' – within their final form.[53]

Notes

1. Quoted in Brett Millier, *Elizabeth Bishop: Life and the Memory of It* (Berkeley and Los Angeles: University of California Press, 1993), p. 62.
2. Brett Millier, *Elizabeth Bishop: Life and the Memory of It*, p. 63.
3. Elizabeth Bishop, *Prose: Centenary Edition* (London: Chatto and Windus, 2011), p. 13.
4. See Linda Anderson, *Elizabeth Bishop: Lines of Connection* (Edinburgh: Edinburgh University Press, 2013), p. 58.
5. Marianne Moore, in Bonnie Costello (ed.), *Selected Letters* (New York and Harmondsworth: Penguin Books, 1997), p. 391.

6. Elizabeth Bishop, in Robert Giroux (ed.), *One Art: The Selected Letters* (London: Chatto and Windus, 1994), p. 73.
7. See Thomas Travisano, *Elizabeth Bishop: Her Development* (Charlottesville, VA: University Press of Virginia, 1988), pp. 71–2; Susan McCabe, *Elizabeth Bishop: Her Poetics of Loss* (Philadephia, PA: The Pennsylvania State University Press, 1994), pp. 93–4; Jamie McKendrick, 'Bishop's Birds', in Linda Anderson and Jo Shapcott (eds), *Elizabeth Bishop: Poet of the Periphery* (Tarset: Bloodaxe Books, 2002), p. 139.
8. See Barbara Page, 'Stops, Starts and Dreamy Divagations', in Anderson and Shapcott (eds), *Elizabeth Bishop: Poet and the Periphery*, pp. 20–1.
9. Edgar Allan Poe, 'The Poetic Principle' (1850), in *Edgar Allan Poe: Essays and Reviews* (New York: Library of America, 1984), p. 76.
10. It may not be irrelevant that Poe's essay contains a reference to *Robinson Crusoe*: 'It appears evident, then, that there is a distinct limit, as regards length, to all works of literary art – the limit of a single sitting – and that, although in certain classes of prose composition, such as "Robinson Crusoe" (demanding no unity), this limit may be advantageously overpassed, it can never properly be overpassed in a poem.'
11. Elizabeth Bishop, *Prose: Centenary Edition*, p. 256.
12. Elizabeth Bishop, *Prose: Centenary Edition*, p. 118.
13. Susan Stewart, *On Longing: Narratives of the Miniature, the Gigantic, the Souvenir, the Collection* (Durham, NC: Duke University Press, 1993), p. 162
14. Elizabeth Bishop, in Robert Giroux (ed.), *One Art: The Selected Letters*, p. 94.
15. Elizabeth Bishop, *Poems: Centenary Edition*, p. 25.
16. Elizabeth Bishop, *Poems: Centenary Edition*, p. 92.
17. Elizabeth Bishop, *Poems: Centenary Edition*, p. 26.
18. Elizabeth Bishop, *Poems: Centenary Edition*, p. 27.
19. Elizabeth Bishop, *Poems: Centenary Edition*, p. 35.
20. Marianne Moore, *Complete Poems* (New York and London: Penguin, 1994), p. 121.
21. Elizabeth Bishop, *Poems: Centenary Edition*, p. 28.
22. Bonnie Costello, *Elizabeth Bishop: Questions of Mastery* (Cambridge, MA: Harvard University Press), pp. 221–2.
23. See Linda Anderson, *Elizabeth Bishop: Lines of Connection*, p. 35.
24. See Daniel-Henry Kahnweiler, *Juan Gris: His Life and Work* (London: Lund Humphries, 1947), p. 86. Bishop knew this book and referred to it enthusiastically in a letter to Robert Lowell in 1948. See *Words in Air: The Complete Correspondence between Elizabeth Bishop and Robert Lowell* (London: Faber and Faber, 2008), p. 43.
25. Elizabeth Bishop, *Prose: Centenary Edition*, p. 13.
26. Elizabeth Bishop, *Poems: Centenary Edition*, p. 16.
27. Peggy Samuels, *Deep Skin: Elizabeth Bishop and Visual Art* (New York: Cornell University Press, 2010), p. 103.

28. MoMA Press Release ('Large Retrospective Exhibition of Collages by Modern Europeans and Americans'), 1948. Available at: http://www.moma.org/pdfs/docs/press_archives/1271/releases/MOMA_1946-1948_0146_1948-09-17_48917-36.pdf?2010 (last accessed on 1 September 2015).
29. Peggy Samuels, *Deep Skin*, p. 102
30. Quoted in Linda Anderson, *Elizabeth Bishop: Lines of Connection*, pp. 52–53.
31. Virginia Woolf, in Anne Oliver Bell (ed.), *The Diary of Virginia Woolf* (I), 5 vols (Harmondsworth: Penguin, 1983), p. 266.
32. Elizabeth Bishop and Robert Lowell, *Words in Air*, p. 81.
33. Elizabeth Bishop, in Robert Giroux (ed.), *One Art: The Selected Letters*, p. 273.
34. Elizabeth Bishop and Robert Lowell, *Words in Air*, p. 483.
35. Elizabeth Bishop, *Poems: Centenary Edition*, p. 63.
36. Elizabeth Bishop, *Poems: Centenary Edition*, p. 65.
37. Elizabeth Bishop, *Poems: Centenary Edition*, p. 69.
38. Elizabeth Bishop and Robert Lowell, *Words in Air*, p. 134 (21 March 1952).
39. Elizabeth Bishop, *Prose: Centenary Edition*, p. 62.
40. Elizabeth Bishop, *Prose: Centenary Edition*, p. 65.
41. Elizabeth Bishop, *Prose: Centenary Edition*, p. 66.
42. Brett Millier, *Elizabeth Bishop: Life and the Memory of It*, p. 447.
43. Joanne Feit Diehl, 'Bishop's Sexual Politics', in Marilyn May Lombardi (ed.), *Elizabeth Bishop: The Geography of Gender* (Charlottesville and London: University Press of Virginia, 1993), p. 43.
44. Elizabeth Bishop and Robert Lowell, *Words in Air*, p. 552.
45. Joelle Biele (ed.), *Elizabeth Bishop and The New Yorker* (New York: Farrar, Straus and Giroux, 2011), p. 273.
46. Elizabeth Bishop, *Poems: Centenary Edition*, p. 182.
47. Elizabeth Bishop, *Poems: Centenary Edition*, pp. 163–4.
48. Elizabeth Bishop, *Poems: Centenary Edition*, p. 183.
49. Paul Muldoon, *The End of the Poem: Oxford Lectures in Poetry* (London: Faber and Faber, 2006), p. 102.
50. Elizabeth Bishop and Robert Lowell, *Words in Air*, p. 84 (31 January 1949).
51. Elizabeth Bishop, *Poems: Centenary Edition*, p. 186.
52. Elizabeth Bishop, *Poems: Centenary Edition*, p. 199.
53. Elizabeth Bishop, *Poems: Centenary Edition*, p. 192.

Further Reading

Anderson, Linda, *Elizabeth Bishop: Lines of Connection* (Edinburgh: Edinburgh University Press, 2013).

Anderson, Linda and Jo Shapcott (eds), *Elizabeth Bishop: Poet of the Periphery* (Tarset: Bloodaxe Books, 2002).

Biele, Joelle (ed.), *Elizabeth Bishop and The New Yorker* (New York: Farrar, Straus and Giroux, 2011).

Bishop, Elizabeth, in Robert Giroux (ed.), *One Art: The Selected Letters* (London: Chatto and Windus, 1994).

Bishop, Elizabeth, *Poems: Centenary Edition* (London: Chatto and Windus, 2011).

Bishop, Elizabeth, *Prose: Centenary Edition* (London: Chatto and Windus, 2011).

Bishop, Elizabeth and Robert Lowell, *Words in Air: The Complete Correspondence between Elizabeth Bishop and Robert Lowell* (London: Faber and Faber, 2008).

Costello, Bonnie, *Elizabeth Bishop: Questions of Mastery* (Cambridge, MA: Harvard University Press).

Lombardi, Marilyn May (ed.), *Elizabeth Bishop: The Geography of Gender* (Charlottesville and London: University Press of Virginia, 1993).

Millier, Brett, *Elizabeth Bishop: Life and the Memory of It* (Berkeley and Los Angeles: University of California Press, 1993).

Samuels, Peggy, *Deep Skin: Elizabeth Bishop and Visual Art* (New York: Cornell University Press, 2010).

4

Adrienne Rich: Poetry and Social Change

Wendy Martin and Lauren Morrison

Adrienne Rich was committed to the transformative power of poetry, and she remained a forceful agitator on behalf of the rights of women and the oppressed throughout her career. Her journey begins with Women's Liberation, but her activism is not bound to gender or sexuality. Indeed, Rich was committed to raising her readers' awareness to all forms of oppression, inequality, and political aggression.

Over the course of her life, Rich was a passionate advocate for a radical political transformation. Insisting that poetry could produce significant social change, she emphasized the importance of freedom and equality, which would transcend gender, nationality, and class. In response to accusations that poetry has no serious impact on political realities, Rich responds that 'poetry is either inadequate, even immoral, in the face of human suffering, or it is unprofitable, hence useless. Either way, poets are advised to hang our heads or fold our tents. Yet, in fact, throughout the world, transfusions of poetic language can and do quite literally keep bodies and souls together, and more.'[1]

As a young girl, Rich learned to compose poems in complex forms and meters. Her father, Arnold Rich, a pathologist at Johns Hopkins University, taught his daughter Greek and Latin and introduced her to Tennyson, Arnold, Longfellow, and Pater. Her earliest poetry reflects her demanding childhood education. She continued to study poetry at Radcliffe College where she read the male poets taught to undergraduates then – 'Frost, Dylan Thomas, Donne, Auden, MacNeice, Stevens, and Yeats.'[2] During her final year at Radcliffe, her first collection of poetry, *A Change of World*, was selected for the Yale Series of Younger Poets Award by W. H. Auden who memorably praised her poems as 'neatly and modestly dressed'. He went on to say in his Introduction to this collection that these poems 'speak quietly but do not mumble, respect their elders but are not cowed by them, and do not tell fibs'.[3] While the content of *A Change of World* focuses on Rich's experiences and concerns as an undergraduate, her form displays her technical command as seen in 'The Kursaal at Interlaken':

> The air is bright with after-images.
> The lanterns and the twinkling glasses dwindle,
> The waltzes and the croupiers' voices crumble,
> The evening folds like a kaleidoscope.
> Against the splinters of a reeling landscape
> This image still pursues us into time:
> Jungfrau, the legendary virgin spire,
> Consumes the mind with mingled snow and fire.[4]

While the formal elements in these poems underscore Rich's training in traditional poetic craft, *A Change of World* is also marked by a distinctly modernist conception of art and the creative mind. Rich presents the artist's mind divided from base corporeal experience. 'At a Bach Concert' presents this dualism: 'A too-compassionate art is half an art. / Only such proud restraining purity / Restores the else-betrayed, too-human heart.'[5]

In 1955, Rich published *Diamond Cutters, and Other Poems* for which she received the Ridgely Torrence Memorial Award of the Poetry Society of America. *Diamond Cutters* has been lauded for its graceful and feminine use of language and the further maturation of her technical artistry. Later in her career, Rich expressed ambivalence towards this volume. In the foreword to her *Collected Early Poems: 1950–1970* (1993), she writes of the temptation to remove any poems representing *Diamond Cutters* from her retrospective anthology: '[*Diamond Cutters*] received much praise; but too many of the poems were, at best, facile and ungrounded imitations of other poets.'[6] Though Rich discredits this work for lacking an authentic voice, *Diamond Cutters* showcases the aesthetic beauty and polished style of Rich's earliest writings and intimates her growing awareness of disparities between her education and her experience:

> let me be
> Always a connoisseur of your perfection.
> Stay where the spaces of the gallery
> Flow calm between your pose and my inspection,
> Lest one imperfect gesture make demands
> As troubling as the touch of human hands.[7]

Here Rich begins to question the separation of aesthetic experience from bodily reality. She questions the assumption that the object's perceived perfection requires its removal from natural surroundings. The sterile gallery space allows for calm observation, but lacks human touch – a loss of connection that is troubling for Rich; however, in her effort to distance herself from what she has been taught, she paradoxically continues to use highly rhymed and technically precise forms to express her doubts.

With this second collection, the strict dualism in *A Change of World* becomes unstable – foreshadowing Rich's ultimate renunciation of aesthetic abstraction and her growing commitment to poetry with a powerful political dimension. For Rich, art and politics are no longer divided.

In the years immediately following her graduation from Radcliffe and her marriage to Alfred Conrad in 1953, Rich struggled with the conflict between her desire to produce creative work and her circumscribed position as a woman, wife, and mother. Retrospectively, Rich saw herself embedded in a historical moment: 'these were the fifties, and in reaction to the earlier wave of feminism, middle-class women were making careers of domestic perfection, working to send their husbands through professional schools, then retiring to have large families'.[8] By 1959, Rich had given birth to three sons; experiencing the conflict between her needs as an individual and her traditional domestic role, she described herself as having lost her sense of control. Self-determination and confidence were replaced with the sensation that she was drifting 'on a current which called itself my destiny'.[9] Rich acutely felt the pressure to act the part of an accomplished housewife, and the demands of marriage and motherhood had a paralysing effect on her ability to write. Although she continued to receive awards and honorary appointments during an eight-year hiatus from publishing, Rich did not publish her next volume of poems, *Snapshots of a Daughter-in-Law*, until 1963.

Snapshots was well-received – winning such honours as the Bess Hokin Prize from *Poetry Magazine*. In this collection, Rich begins a major transition from writing poems of personal significance to a broader understanding of the political importance of her poetry. Rich now calls for a poetic tradition that is centred on women and women's experience, initiating what will be a significant focus of her work for the rest of her career. *Snapshots* details her resentment and despair at the traditional social values that thwart women's potential, and invokes Mary Wollstonecraft, Simone de Beauvoir, and other independent, exceptional women to inspire a counter narrative in which women are valued for more than their domestic and decorative functions.

In *Snapshots*, Rich sheds formal constraints both in style and content and begins to write in ways that reflect her perspective as a woman. Later, she observed that in *Snapshots* she actively created a female voice in contrast to her earlier poems in which she 'had tried very much *not* to identify myself as a female poet'.[10] The title poem weaves together fragments of the past, including quotations from Mary Wollstonecraft, Denis Diderot, William Shakespeare and many others, to assemble an historical context for the reader. Rich laments that women who claim their selfhood and reject male expectations are rewarded with 'solitary confinement, / tear gas, attrition shelling. / Few applicants for that honor'.[11] In this collection, Rich expresses the anger and emotional alienation she has experienced as a result of her domestic confinement. And she foregrounds these emotions both for herself and for her reader to process: conscious attention to these experiences makes possible a thorough examination of the limiting expectations and constraints imposed on women, both historically and in the present.

Snapshots of a Daughter-in-Law marks a stylistic shift for Rich: the sonorous delicacy of her more traditional earlier poetry is superseded by abrupt and jarring language. Rich uses this break with traditional poetic form to reflect on the isolation of men and women in marriage, observing that the sharp division of masculine and feminine roles estranges both partners from essential aspects of their common humanity. In 'The Knight' Rich penetrates the man's armour to reveal 'a lump of bitter jelly' where we expect a virile hero. She asks 'Who will unhorse this rider / and free him from between / the walls of iron, the emblems / crushing his chest with their weight?'[12] While Rich writes to liberate women from confining domestic roles, she is also interested in how men's roles lead to immature and disconnected lives. For Rich, patriarchy is a dynamic system which can be disrupted by personal responsibility and awareness.

During the decade of the 1960s, Rich committed herself to political activism in both her personal life and her writing. She moved with her family to New York City in 1966, taught at several universities, and became active in the civil rights and anti-war movements. By the end of the 1960s, her poetry addresses civil rights both domestically and abroad and mourns victims of the Vietnam and Algerian wars. Condemning the indiscriminate and depersonalized exercise of power by bureaucrats, her sorrow and anger are palpable:

The radiotelescope flings its nets
at random; a child is crying,
not from hunger, not from pain,
more likely impotence. The generals are sweltering

in the room with a thousand eyes.
Red-hot lights flash off and on
inside air-conditioned skulls.[13]

Writing in the shadow of the decade's violent unrest, *Necessities of Life: Poems, 1962–66* (1966) and *Leaflets* (1969) reveal Rich's commitment to creating poetry that is relevant to her contemporary political moment and is charged with the capacity to transform readers and reality. In *Leaflets* the poet reveals her intentions outright – 'I want to choose words that even you / would have to be changed by.'[14]

As she expands her poetic vision to embrace political change, Rich continues to challenge the formal limitations of her work. 'Picnic', with its lines dispersed on the page like 'the chicken bones scattered / for the fox we'll never see', reflects her personal transformation and her decision to compose her poems in a freer style.[15] In such examples, we see Rich's willingness to relinquish the security of rhyme and the standard poetic line and confront the darker dimension of life; no longer does she rely on formal structures to hold charged emotions in check.

Exploring unfamiliar and open-ended poetic forms Rich experiments with the ghazal, a form of Arabic verse, in the third section of *Leaflets*. The poems in 'Ghazals: Homage to Ghalib' capture the dislocation created by the social and political unrest of the 1960s and the disjointed experience in a destabilized world. Consisting of five couplets, the ghazal enables Rich to portray emotional and social flux and to create a collage of contradictory images, exposing fractures in the political landscape: 'each couplet [is] autonomous and independent of the others. The continuity and unity flow from the associations and images playing back and forth among the couplets in any single *ghazal*.'[16] As Rich moves away from established Western forms towards alternative poetic patterns and free verse, she simultaneously affirms the active integration of art and politics.

In *The Will to Change: Poems 1968–70* (1971), Rich further establishes her voice as a political poet as well as a woman poet. Insisting that the effects of systemic disenfranchisement are both far-reaching and extremely personal, her poetry is suffused with sorrow and a pointed anger as she recounts the restrictions placed on women by patriarchal institutions. This collection was written during a time of significant change in Rich's own life. In 1970, Rich decided to end her marriage and that same year her husband committed suicide. Sadness, and a sense of loss and uncertainty, pervade her poetry at this time; these feelings of disintegration and desolation are embodied in the disjointed stanzas of 'Shooting Script':

> Now to give up the temptations of the projector; to see instead the
> web of cracks filtering across the plaster.
>
> To read there the map of the future, the roads radiating from the
> initial split, the filaments thrown out from that impasse.
>
> To read the instructions on your palm; to find there how the
> lifeline, broken, keeps its direction.
>
> To reread the etched rays of the bullet-hole left years ago in the
> glass; to know in every distortion of the light what fracture is.
>
> To put the prism in your pocket, the thin glass lens, the map
> of the inner city, the little book with gridded pages.
>
> To pull yourself up by your own roots; to eat the last meal in your old
> neighborhood.[17]

In spite of this rupture in her life, Rich's poems remain infused with hope. Out of the complexities and confusion of her past, 'The web of cracks' and the 'filaments thrown out from that impasse' herald the poet's determination to find and make meaning in the face of uncertainty and to create a new life. For Rich, denial and avoidance stunt growth: only intentional, critical exploration of personal and political traumas can lead to life-affirming change.

In *Diving into the Wreck: Poems 1971–72* (1973), often considered to be her finest collection of poetry, Rich filters basic experiences through a female-centred consciousness. This rewriting and relearning of love, motherhood, and relationships is imperative, as it allows women to transcend local and social boundaries imposed on them by traditional cultural values. Rich's conception of feminism is complex and requires the participation of all women; she is not interested in a single definition of what it means to be a woman, which would be a mere re-enactment of patriarchal determinism. Instead, Rich celebrates diverse expressions of womanhood.

In the title poem, 'Diving into the Wreck', Rich imagines herself as a diver sounding the recesses of a shipwreck. This exploration takes her through the cultural as well as her personal past. The journey is difficult, but Rich assures us that it is not to be avoided: the poet descends 'here alone', 'I put on / the body-armor of black rubber', 'I go down, / Rung after rung.'[18] She must submerge herself in order to move beyond 'the wreck and not the story of the wreck / the thing itself and not the myth'.[19] The poet is energized as she recuperates power from her past and seeks community with other women. *Diving into the Wreck* won the National Book Award in 1974; however, Rich accepted the award with her two fellow nominees, Audre Lorde and Alice Walker, and she read a statement prepared by all three on behalf of 'all the women whose voices have gone and still go unheard in a patriarchal world, and in the name of those who, like us, have been tolerated as token women in this culture … We believe that we can enrich ourselves more in supporting and giving to each other than by competing against each other.'[20]

Women's ability to name and determine their own experience was a central demand of the feminist movement of the 1970s. In an essay written in 1971 that uses the title of the last play written by Henrik Ibsen, 'When We Dead Awaken: Writing as Re-Vision', Rich addresses the need for women to rethink and challenge their silence and impotence. This re-vision is 'the act of looking back, of seeing with fresh eyes, of entering an old text from a new critical direction – is for women more than a chapter in cultural history: it is an act of survival. Until we can understand the assumptions in which we are drenched we cannot know ourselves.'[21]

Re-emphasizing the harm caused by the haphazard division of men and women into oppositional binaries, Rich observes again that women and men are both harmed by the rigid separation of roles, and she rejects the cultural constructions that 'masculinity made / unfit for women or men'.[22] Ultimately, Rich makes it abundantly clear that there is an urgent need for deep reconstruction of our culture:

The pact that we made was the ordinary pact
of men & women in those days

I don't know who we thought we were
that our personalities
could resist the failures of the race[23]

The exploitation and disregard of women in Western society produces an anger that Rich sees as potentially productive. In 'Song', the poet's indignation suffuses her survey of the wreck:

If I'm lonely
it's with the rowboat ice-fast on the shore
in the last red light of the year

that knows what it is, that knows it's neither
ice nor mud nor winter light
but wood, with a gift for burning[24]

This exploration of the origins of cultural inequality and injustices enables the poet to externalize her anger in contrast to the internalized, destructive anger in *Snapshots* – 'A thinking woman sleeps with monsters. / The beak that grips her, she becomes –'.[25] Rich asserts that a community of women can use this anger productively by challenging and disrupting the systems that trivialize and dehumanize them.

During the 1970s, Rich's life and writing demonstrate her dedication to radical feminist activism, with collections such as *Diving into the Wreck* and *Poems* (1975) signalling a shift in her poetic focus. Rich published *Of Woman Born: Motherhood as Experience and Institution* in 1976, the same year she came out as a lesbian. In this book, she uses material from history, psychology, and cultural anthropology to analyse the ways in which patriarchal institutions define and control what it is to be a woman and a mother. Rich's method dismantles traditional knowledge hierarchies by using specific details from her personal history as evidence, in addition to scientific and historical perspectives underscoring that the personal is political.

Although *Of Woman Born* received some scathing reviews from critics, this book made an indelible mark on feminist theory. Rich deconstructs and examines various aspects of motherhood to distinguish a woman's relationship with her children from the expectations imposed by male-dominated ideology, and she uses the mythology and history of the ancient past to create a portrait of motherhood and social life originating from women and their experiences.[26]

In *The Dream of a Common Language: Poems 1974–1977* (1978) Rich intensifies the connection of the personal and political. 'Twenty-One Love Poems', the central section of the collection, is an intimate portrait of a lesbian relationship that celebrates love based on mutuality instead of submission:

this we were, this is how we tried to love,
and these are the forces they had ranged against us,
and these are the forces we had ranged within us,
within us and against us, against us and within us.[27]

The repetition of these lines conveys the weight that the relationship must bear to survive outside of the boundaries of the patriarchal conception of love. For Rich, women must determine their own identities and stories, and women must be free from a system that requires validation from men.

In 1980, Rich published an essay, 'Compulsory Heterosexuality and Lesbian Existence', in which she radically challenges the perception of lesbianism. Questioning the presumption that 'species-survival, the means of impregnation, and emotional / erotic relationships should have become so rigidly identified with each other', she asks 'why such violent structures should be found necessary to enforce women's total emotional, erotic loyalty and subservience to men'.[28] By disclosing the basic assumptions of heterosexuality, Rich challenges the hegemony of sexuality defined by males and asserts that lesbianism is a continuum in which women should have the ability to determine their own relationships with each other.

The year before 'Compulsory Heterosexuality' was published, Rich explored the influence of the Women's Liberation movement on her poetry in a collection of essays *On Lies, Secrets, and Silence: Selected Prose, 1966–78* (1979). In 'Conditions for Work', Rich asserts that 'Feminism begins but cannot end with the discovery by an individual of her self-consciousness as a woman. It is not, finally, even the recognition of her reasons for anger, or the decision to change her life ... Feminism means finally that we renounce our obedience to the fathers and recognize the world they have described is not the whole world.'[29] This vision of feminism mirrors Rich's poetic mission – to live and write in language that is liberated from patriarchal ideology.

Rich's next collection of poetry *A Wild Patience Has Taken Me This Far: Poems, 1979–81* (1981) is grounded in her woman-centred and community-minded vision. These poems celebrate legendary as well as unknown women of the past to counter the popular representation of women as weak and subservient. 'For Memory' demonstrates Rich's belief in the power of the quotidian – of everyday life:

> The past is not a husk   yet change goes on
>
> Freedom. It isn't once, to walk out
>   under the Milky Way, feeling the rivers
> of light, the fields of dark—
>   freedom is daily, prose-bound, routine
>   remembering. Putting together, inch by inch
>   the starry worlds. From all the lost collections.[30]

Rich emphasizes daily life as a way to ground her vision of equality as a reality that can be created through the intentional choices of individual people in their day-to-day lives.

Beginning in the 1970s Rich scrutinizes the ways in which language is used to oppress women and marginalized groups. In *A Wild Patience*, she rejects metaphors and images that cause division and subjugation. Rich urges women to find new modes of expression that accurately describe their experience and draw on their power to reconnect society to the meaningful sources of life. The woman portrayed in 'Coast to Coast' embodies this vision of reintegration – she is seamlessly part of the landscape just as the landscape is part of her:

> Seeing through the prism Your face, fog-hollowed burning
> cold of eucalyptus hung with butterflies
> lavender of rockbloom
> O and your anger uttered in silence word and stammer
> shattering the fog lances of sun
> piercing the grey Pacific unanswerable tide
> carving itself in clefts and fissures of the rock
> Beauty of your breasts your hands
> turning a stone a shell a weed a prism in coastal light
> traveller and witness[31]

Conjoining contradictory images, such as 'burning cold', Rich asserts that experience can be more complex and inclusive with new uses of language. Similarly, she insists that the public and private spheres of existence cannot be divided or viewed in isolation; instead, these two areas of life need to enrich each other.

By the early 1980s, Adrienne Rich was established as a major American poet with numerous awards and professorial appointments attesting to her critical success. Charting the evolution of her poetic style and thematic focus, *The Fact of a Doorframe* (1984) presents selections from the poet's nine previous books of poetry and includes six previously unpublished poems.

Your Native Land, Your Life (1986) begins with 'Sources', a twenty-three-part poem in which Rich investigates her family origins and history; she is especially interested in her Jewish heritage and explores the extent to which this and other sources – however limiting, oppressive or paradoxical they may prove to be – influence her poetry and her life. In 'Sources', Rich sets out to excavate her past in order to create meaningful connections to her present life; as she explores her Jewish heritage that her father denied, she realizes even if she is not religious in the traditional sense, there is significance in 'wearing the star of David / on a thin chain at my breastbone'.[32] In order to change the present, Rich makes it clear that we must take responsibility for our origins – which we cannot choose – to extricate ourselves from helpless resignation.

'Sources', however, is only a starting point. In 'Contradictions: Tracking Poems', the third and final section of *Your Native Land*, Rich reminds us that 'our lives will always be / a stew of contradictions', yet she remains hopeful, viewing these paradoxes as a means of identifying with others:[33]

> remember: the body's pain and the pain on the streets
> are not the same   but you can learn
> from the edges that blur   O you who love clear edges
> more than anything   watch the edges that blur[34]

Identification does not conflate and level 'difference'. Rich wishes to retain and appreciate such difference, and in acknowledging the reality of the other begins to perceive her connectedness to separate, yet shared, experiences.

Rich continues to investigate the universal and particular aspects of personhood in her prose collection *Blood, Bread, and Poetry: Selected Prose 1979–1985* (1986), using her relocation from the East Coast to Santa Cruz, California, as an opportunity to reflect on her environment. Physical location is important to Rich, and in the foreword to this work, she asks how her environment informs her life and work: '*What happens to the heart of the artist, here in North America?*'[35] As Rich reconsiders the relationship between political activism and the personal exercise of creativity, she confirms the inevitable influence of her native land – its beauty and its flaws.

The specificity of location and landscape – dense forests, rivers, deserts – pervades Rich's next publication, *Time's Power: Poems 1985–1988* (1989). In 'The Desert as Garden of Paradise' Rich uses drought to discuss forfeited power and habituation:

> but where drought is the epic then there must be some
> who persist, not by species-betrayal
> but by changing themselves
>
> minutely, by a constant study
> of the price of continuity
> a steady bargain with the way things are[36]

Rich continues: 'You learn to live without prophets / without legends / to live just where you are.'[37] Learning to thrive in one's cultural moment requires knowledge of that moment and the conditions that created it.

In her next collection of poetry, Adrienne Rich moves from the local and personal to a world that includes and implicates the reader. In *An Atlas of the Difficult World: Poems 1988–1991* (1991), Rich reaches out to a broader audience in an effort to raise social consciousness in the aftermath of the Gulf War.[38] The title poem is divided into thirteen parts which directly address the reader in the second person – 'You': 'I promised to show you a map you say but this is a mural / then yes let it be these are small distinctions / where do we see it from is the question.'[39] Rich works through this complicated terrain providing glimpses of starving schoolchildren, abuse, and isolation. The poem ends: 'I know you are reading this poem listening for something, torn between bitterness and hope / turning back once again to the task you cannot refuse. / I know you are reading this poem because there is nothing else left to read / there where you have landed, stripped as you are.'[40] Rich wants to use her poetry as a tool that can alleviate real pain and misery, and feminist concerns are once again expanded to include all of humanity, as every person carries the burden of the patriarchal culture in some capacity.

Engaging a broader audience, *What is Found There: Notebooks on Poetry and Politics* (1993) contains twenty-eight entries that centre on the role of poetry in society. In 'Woman and Bird', Rich argues for the interplay between poetry, politics, and science:

> This impulse to enter, with other humans, through language, into the order and disorder of the world, is poetic at its root as surely as it is political at its root. Poetry and politics both have to do with description and with power. And so, of course, does science. We might hope to find the three activities – poetry, science, politics – triangulated, with extraordinary electrical exchanges moving from each to each and through our lives. Instead, over centuries, they have become separated – poetry from politics, poetic naming from scientific meaning, an ostensibly 'neutral' science from political questions, 'rational' science from lyrical poetry – nowhere more than in the United States over the past fifty years.[41]

Doris Earnshaw observes that *What Is Found There* is an exemplary continuation of Rich's desire to process 'the struggles to survive materially and spiritually in a world both violent and affluent' as well as the importance of knowing 'the art of the displaced, the homosexuals, the exiles, the nonwhites.'[42] Rich pursues these issues in prose as a complement to her poetic work.

Rich's next poetry collection, *Dark Fields of the Republic: Poems 1991–1995* (1995) intertwines figures from the past and present, erasing the boundary of historical time to communicate shared humanity. Chafing against the latent and pervasive oppression of women and minorities into the new millennium, Rich communicates her disbelief in 'Rachel': 'It's the end of a century. / If she gets to grow old, if there's anything / : anyone to speak, will they say of her, / *She grew up to see it, she was our mother, but / she was born one of them?*'[43] Rich speaks out against waning civil liberties, the continued suppression of non-white artists and citizens, and the military-industrial complex of the late twentieth century. While she does not want to succumb to the pessimism of her moment, she does want to understand it: 'don't think I was trying to state a case / or construct a scenery: / I tried to listen to / the public voice of our time.'[44] In the midst of the challenges, Rich insists on collective action and consciousness as the only means to transform the culture in the United States that has been dominated by patriarchy and violence.

In 1997, Rich won the National Medal for the Arts but declined the award. In an article in the *Los Angeles Times Book Review*, she explains that she cannot justify receiving a 'token' honour at a time when 'the radical disparities of wealth and power in America are widening at a devastating rate'.[45] Listing a range of issues from the decline of public education to the demonization of young black men, Rich laments, '[p]iece by piece the democratic process has been losing ground to the accumulation of private wealth.'[46] Though Rich decries the commodification and diminished position of the arts at the end of the twentieth century, she retains faith that art is still a 'regenerative process' that 'could help you save your life'.[47] The humanizing influence of the arts is a powerful political tool. Rich calls on artists 'to work out our connectedness, *as artists*, with other people who are beleaguered, suffering, disenfranchised'.[48] She made her refusal more than a personal statement of discontent, turning the nation's attention to the unacceptable inequalities throughout the United States.

In this political climate, Rich produced *Midnight Salvage: Poems 1995–1998* (1999). This collection is noted for its graphic images of violence, pain and sexuality. In her review of this collection, Sandra Cookson acknowledges that the poems' explicit rendering of human suffering is difficult to read but sees Rich's originality and courage as the foundation that enables the reader to engage in its dark content.[49] In *Midnight Salvage*, Rich adopts multiple perspectives – those of famous political activists, such as René Char or Tina Modotti, as well as the many voices speaking throughout 'The Night Has A Thousand Faces'.

Rich gathered several of her canonized, early essays alongside work spanning the 1990s in *Arts of the Possible: Essays and Conversations* (2001) to trace her trajectory as a woman, poet and activist. Her work has moved beyond feminism alone, and she challenges what she sees as the middle-class habit of self-absorption and apathy. Contending that second-wave feminism needs to open itself to larger concerns, she declares that 'Though some feminists (mostly women of color) insisted on intersections of race, class, and gender, emphasis was more often laid on women's individual class identifications and how they negotiated them, or on poverty and welfare, than on how class, poverty, and the need for welfare are produced and perpetuated in the first place.'[50] This critique notwithstanding, Rich remains emphatically committed to finding a common language and values that will promote collective action and broaden the individual's sense of responsibility from the self to others.

The final four collections published during Adrienne Rich's lifetime embody her dedication to human struggle in the midst of real and changeable history. In *Fox: Poems 1998–2000* (2001), Rich discloses her own feelings of helplessness in the face of the powerful political and social systems oppressing individuals: 'I as novice trembled / I should have been stronger   held us / together.'[51] The fear of powerlessness resurfaces in her later collection, *Telephone Ringing in the Labyrinth: Poems 2004–2006* (2007). Musing on her experience as a writer, Rich writes in 'Draft #2006':

> They asked me, is this time worse than another.
>
> I said, for whom?
>
> Wanted to show them something.   While I wrote on the
>
> chalkboard they drifted out. I turned back to an empty room.
>
> Maybe I couldn't write fast enough. Maybe it was too soon.[52]

Again, Rich reflects on meaningful social change, and the role of poetry in this process. The images of a woman with one arm tied behind her back,[53] and of the poet writing 'with a clawed hand',[54] appear in these later poems and point to Rich's own physical affliction – the arthritis that had plagued her for decades – as well as her fear of failure as a visionary poet. In spite of mounting anxiety she continues to push herself and her poetry to engage the difficult problems of existence, demanding: 'Don't stop asking me why.'[55]

In her essay *Poetry and Commitment* (2007), Rich underscores the revelatory power of poetry: 'Poetry has the capacity—in its own way and by its own means—to remind us of something we are forbidden to see. A forgotten future.'[56] As she considers her own past and the world around her, Rich remains confident in poetry as an essential reminder of what it means to be human. In her collection of essays, *A Human Eye: Essays on Art in Society 1997–2008* (2009), Rich reasserts that human sensibility has been dulled by the consumer demands of capitalism, and art is one way by which these economic impositions can be de-familiarized and challenged. Again, she insists on the intentionality of the individual in the face of tyranny, oppression, and unquestioned social mores. Sylvia Henneberg observes that this ethos of public responsibility also appears in Rich's writing on ageing and notes that Rich does not defer to old age as a justification of inactivity: 'Rich wastes no effort regretting or defying aging' and 'understands age not primarily as a personal drama with which she must come to terms but … as a public responsibility that requires certain kinds of action and certain kinds of art.'[57]

In *Tonight No Poetry Will Serve: Poems 2007–2010* (2011), published a year before her death, Adrienne Rich claims the title of 'endless beginner'.[58] Her poetic career demonstrates a lifelong dedication to the enlarging possibilities of self-exploration and careful questioning of cultural assumptions that are presented as givens. Her writing celebrates the quotidian as well as the extraordinary, explores the problematic dimensions of her own life as well as the political and cultural context in which she lives, and insists that the integration of local and global realities is essential for freedom and equality. Adrienne Rich's life and work were propelled by her determination to use her poetry to bring about transformative personal and social change.

Notes

1. Adrienne Rich, 'Legislators of the World', *The Guardian* (17 November 2006). Reprinted in *Poetry and Commitment* (New York: W. W. Norton, 2007), p. 26.
2. Adrienne Rich, *On Lies, Secrets, and Silence: Selected Prose 1966–1978* (New York: W. W. Norton, 1979), p. 39.
3. Adrienne Rich, Preface, *A Change of World* (New Haven, CT: Yale University Press, 1951), p. 11.
4. Adrienne Rich, *A Change of World*, p. 26.
5. Adrienne Rich, *A Change of World*, p. 54.
6. Adrienne Rich, *Collected Early Poems: 1950–1970* (New York: W. W. Norton, 1993), p. xix.
7. Adrienne Rich, 'Love in the Museum', *The Diamond Cutters, and Other Poems* (New York: Harper, 1955), pp. 89–90.
8. Adrienne Rich, *On Lies, Secrets, and Silence*, p. 42.
9. Adrienne Rich, *On Lies, Secrets, and Silence*, p. 42.
10. Adrienne Rich, *On Lies, Secrets, and Silence*, p. 44.
11. Adrienne Rich, 'Snapshots of a Daughter-in-Law', *Snapshots of a Daughter-in-Law* (New York: W. W. Norton, 1963), p. 25.

12. Adrienne Rich, 'The Knight', *Snapshots of a Daughter-in-Law*, p. 14.
13. Adrienne Rich, 'Spring Thunder', *Necessities of Life: Poems 1962–1965* (New York: W. W. Norton, 1966), p. 44.
14. Adrienne Rich, 'Implosions', *Leaflets: Poems 1965–1968* (New York: W. W. Norton, 1969), p. 42.
15. Adrienne Rich, *Leaflets*, p. 36.
16. Adrienne Rich, *Leaflets*, p. 59; emphasis in the original.
17. Adrienne Rich, *The Will to Change: Poems 1968–1970* (New York: W. W. Norton), p. 67.
18. Adrienne Rich, *Diving Into the Wreck: Poems 1971–1972* (New York: W. W. Norton, 1973), p. 22.
19. Adrienne Rich, *Diving Into the Wreck*, p. 23.
20. Adrienne Rich, 'Adrienne Rich, Winner of the 1974 National Book Award for *Diving into the Wreck*', *National Book Foundation*. Last accessed 27 August 2015. Available at: www.nationalbook.org/nbaacceptspeech_arich_74.html#.vd9jewk9kko.
21. Adrienne Rich, *On Lies, Secrets, and Silence*, p. 35.
22. Adrienne Rich, 'Merced', *Diving Into the Wreck*, p. 36.
23. Adrienne Rich, 'From a Survivor', *Diving Into the Wreck*, p. 50.
24. Adrienne Rich, *Diving Into the Wreck*, p. 20.
25. Adrienne Rich, *Snapshots of a Daughter-in-Law*, p. 22.
26. See Andrea O'Reilly (ed.), *From Motherhood to Mothering: The Legacy of Adrienne Rich's* Of Woman Born (Albany, NY: State University of New York Press, 2004).
27. Adrienne Rich, *The Dream of a Common Language: Poems 1974–1977* (New York: W. W. Norton, 1978), p. 34.
28. Adrienne Rich, 'Compulsory Heterosexuality and Lesbian Existence', *Signs*, 5(4) (1980): 637.
29. Adrienne Rich, *On Lies, Secrets, and Silence*, p. 207.
30. Adrienne Rich, *A Wild Patience Has Taken Me This Far: Poems 1978–1981* (New York: W. W. Norton, 1981), p. 22.
31. Adrienne Rich, *A Wild Patience Has Taken Me This Far*, pp. 6–7.
32. Adrienne Rich, 'Sources, xvi', *Your Native Land, Your Life* (New York: W. W. Norton, 1986), p. 18.
33. Adrienne Rich, *Your Native Land, Your Life*, p. 83.
34. Adrienne Rich, *Your Native Land, Your Life*, p. 111.
35. Adrienne Rich, Foreword, *Blood, Bread, and Poetry: Selected Prose 1979–1985* (New York: W. W. Norton, 1986), p. xiv.
36. Adrienne Rich, *Time's Power: Poems 1985–1988* (New York: W. W. Norton, 1989), p. 27.
37. Adrienne Rich, *Time's Power*, p. 30.
38. Examples include reviews by Gertrude Reif Hughes and Mary Hussman.
39. Adrienne Rich, 'An Atlas of the Difficult World', *An Atlas of the Difficult World: Poems 1988–1991* (New York: W. W. Norton, 1991), p. 6.
40. Adrienne Rich, *An Atlas of the Difficult World*, p. 26.
41. Adrienne Rich, *What is Found There: Notebooks on Poetry and Politics*, pp. 6–7.

42. Doris Earnshaw, Review of *What is Found There: Notebooks on Poetry and Politics*, by Adrienne Rich, *World Literature Today*, 68(4) (1994): 821.
43. Adrienne Rich, *Dark Fields of the Republic: Poems 1991–1995* (New York: W.W. Norton, 1995), p. 7.
44. Adrienne Rich, 'And Now', *Dark Fields of the Republic: Poems 1991–1995*, p. 31.
45. Adrienne Rich, *Arts of the Possible: Essays and Conversations* (New York: W.W. Norton, 2001), p. 99.
46. Adrienne Rich, *Arts of the Possible: Essays and Conversations*, p. 101.
47. Adrienne Rich, *Arts of the Possible: Essays and Conversations*, p. 102.
48. Adrienne Rich, *Arts of the Possible: Essays and Conversations*, p. 104.
49. See Sandra Cookson, Review of *Midnight Salvage: Poems 1995–1998*, by Adrienne Rich. *World Literature Today*, 74(4) (2000): 821.
50. Adrienne Rich, *Arts of the Possible: Essays and Conversations*, p. 5.
51. Adrienne Rich, 'Terza Rima', *Fox: Poems 1998–2000* (New York: W.W. Norton, 2001), p. 44.
52. Adrienne Rich, *Telephone Ringing in the Labyrinth: Poems 2004–2006* (New York: W.W. Norton, 2007), p. 94.
53. Adrienne Rich, 'I was there, Axel', *Tonight No Poetry Will Serve: Poems 2007–2010* (New York: W.W. Norton, 2011), p. 46.
54. Adrienne Rich, 'Circum/Stances', *Tonight No Poetry Will Serve: Poems 2007–2010*, p. 62.
55. Adrienne Rich, 'School Among the Ruins', *The School Among the Ruins: Poems 2000–2004* (New York: W.W. Norton, 2004), p. 25.
56. Adrienne Rich, *Poetry and Commitment*, p. 36.
57. Sylvia B. Henneberg, 'Of Creative Crones and Poetry: Developing Age Studies through Literature', *NWSA Journal*, 18(1) (2006): 120–1.
58. Adrienne Rich, 'Powers of Recuperation', *Tonight No Poetry Will Serve: Poems 2007–2010*, p. 76.

Selected Further Reading

Altieri, Charles, *Self and Sensibility in Contemporary American Poetry* (New York: Cambridge University Press, 1984).

Cookson, Sandra, Review of *Midnight Salvage: Poems 1995–1998*, by Adrienne Rich, *World Literature Today*, 74(4) (2000): 821.

Cooper, Jane Roberta (ed.), *Reading Adrienne Rich: Reviews and Re-visions 1951–1981* (Ann Arbor, MI: University of Michigan Press, 1984).

Dickie, Margaret, *Stein, Bishop, and Rich: Lyrics of Love, War, and Place* (Chapel Hill, NC: University of North Carolina Press, 1997).

Earnshaw, Doris, Review of *What is Found There: Notebooks on Poetry and Politics*, by Adrienne Rich, *World Literature Today*, 68(4) (1994): 821.

George, Diana Hume, 'A Poet's Work is Never Done', Review of *What is Found There: Notebooks on Poetry and Politics*, by Adrienne Rich, *The Women's Review of Books*, 11(3) (1993): 1, 3–4.

Henneberg, Sylvia B., 'Of Creative Crones and Poetry: Developing Age Studies through Literature', *NWSA Journal*, 18(1) (2006): 106–25.

Henneberg, Sylvia B., *The Creative Crone: Aging and the Poetry of May Sarton and Adrienne Rich* (Columbia, MO: University of Missouri Press, 2010).

Hudgins, Andrew, '"The Burn has Settled In": A Reading of Adrienne Rich's *Diving into the Wreck*', *The Texas Review*, 2.1 (1981): 49–65.

Hughes, Gertrude Reif, 'Eternal Vigilance'. Review of *An Atlas of the Difficult World: Poems 1988–91*, by Adrienne Rich, *The Women's Review of Books*, 9.3 (1991): 11.

Hussmann, Mary, 'On Adrienne Rich'. Review of *An Atlas of the Difficult World*, by Adrienne Rich, *The Iowa Review*, 22.1 (1992): 221–5.

Keyes, Claire, *The Aesthetics of Power: The Poetry of Adrienne Rich* (Athens, GA: University of Georgia Press, 1986).

Martin, Wendy, 'From Patriarchy to the Female Principle: A Chronological Reading of Adrienne Rich's Poems', in *Adrienne Rich's Poetry*, ed. Barbara Charlesworth Gelpi and Albert Gelpi (New York: W. W. Norton, 1975), pp. 175–89.

Martin, Wendy, *An American Triptych: Anne Bradstreet, Emily Dickinson, Adrienne Rich* (Chapel Hill, NC: University of North Carolina Press, 1984).

Martin, Wendy and Annalisa Zox-Weaver, 'Adrienne Rich: The Poetry of Witness', in *The Cambridge Companion to American Poetry* (New York: Cambridge University Press, 2016).

Milburn, Michael, Review of *An Atlas of the Difficult World: Poems 1988–1991*, by Adrienne Rich, *Harvard Review*, 1 (1992): 129–32.

O'Reilly, Andrea, *From Motherhood to Mothering: The Legacy of Adrienne Rich's* Of Woman Born (Albany, NY: State University of New York Press, 2004).

Ostriker, Alicia, 'Her Cargo: Adrienne Rich and the Common Language', *The American Poetry Review*, 8(4) (1979): 6–10.

Templeton, Alice, *The Dream and the Dialogue: Adrienne Rich's Feminist Poetics* (Knoxville, TS: University of Tennessee Press, 1994).

Werner, Craig, *Adrienne Rich: The Poet and Her Critics* (Chicago, IL: American Library Association, 1988).

Poetry by Adrienne Rich

A Change of World (New Haven, CT: Yale University Press, 1951).

The Diamond Cutters, and Other Poems (New York: Harper, 1955).

Snapshots of a Daughter-in-Law: Poems 1954–1962 (New York: W. W. Norton, 1963).

Necessities of Life: Poems 1962–1965 (New York: W. W. Norton, 1966).

Selected Poems (London: Hogarth Press, 1967).

Leaflets: Poems 1965–1968 (New York: W. W. Norton, 1969).

The Will to Change: Poems 1968–1970 (New York: W. W. Norton, 1971).

Diving Into the Wreck: Poems 1971–1972 (New York: W. W. Norton, 1973).

Poems: Selected and New 1950–1974 (New York: W. W. Norton, 1974).

Twenty-One Love Poems (Emeryville, CA: Effie's Press, 1976).

The Dream of a Common Language: Poems 1974–1977 (New York: W. W. Norton, 1978).
A Wild Patience Has Taken Me This Far: Poems 1978–1981 (New York: W. W. Norton, 1981).
Sources (Woodside, CA: Heyeck Press, 1983).
The Fact of a Doorframe: Poems Selected and New 1950–1984 (New York: W. W. Norton, 1984).
Your Native Land, Your Life (New York: W. W. Norton, 1986).
Time's Power: Poems 1985–1988 (New York: W. W. Norton, 1989).
An Atlas of the Difficult World: Poems 1988–1991 (New York: W. W. Norton, 1991).
Collected Early Poems: 1950–1970 (New York: W. W. Norton, 1993).
Dark Fields of the Republic: Poems 1991–1995 (New York: W. W. Norton, 1995).
Midnight Salvage: Poems 1995–1998 (New York: W. W. Norton, 1999).
Fox: Poems 1998–2000 (New York: W. W. Norton, 2001).
The School Among the Ruins: Poems 2000–2004 (New York: W. W. Norton, 2004).
Telephone Ringing in the Labyrinth: Poems 2004–2006 (New York: W. W. Norton, 2007).
Tonight No Poetry Will Serve: Poems 2007–2010 (New York: W. W. Norton, 2011).
Later Poems: Selected and New 1971–2012 (New York: W. W. Norton, 2013).

Prose/Essay Collections by Adrienne Rich

'Adrienne Rich, Winner of the 1974 National Book Award for *Diving into the Wreck*', *National Book Foundation*. Last accessed 27 August 2015. Available at: www.nationalbook.org/nbaacceptspeech_arich_74.html#.vd9jewk9kko.
Of Woman Born: Motherhood as Experience and Institution (New York: W. W. Norton, 1976).
Women and Honor: Some Notes on Lying (Pittsburgh, PA: Cleis Press, 1977).
On Lies, Secrets, and Silence: Selected Prose 1966–1978 (New York: W. W. Norton, 1979).
Blood, Bread, and Poetry: Selected Prose 1979–1985 (New York: W. W. Norton, 1986).
What is Found There: Notebooks on Poetry and Politics (New York: W. W. Norton, 1993).
Arts of the Possible: Essays and Conversations (New York: W. W. Norton, 2001).
Poetry and Commitment (New York: W. W. Norton, 2007).
A Human Eye: Essays on Art in Society 1997–2008 (New York: W. W. Norton, 2009).
'When We Dead Awaken: Writing as Re-Vision', *College English*, 34(1) (1972): 18–30.
'Compulsory Heterosexuality and Lesbian Existence', *Signs*, 5(4) (1980): 631–60.

5

'A work of art that the critic cannot even talk about': The Poetry of John Ashbery

Eleanor Spencer

In 2007, mtvU, the subsidiary of the MTV music television channel broadcast at US college campuses, announced that it had selected its first poet laureate. Many expected the inaugural laureate to be a rapper, a performance poet, or a fêted lyricist like Bob Dylan. The octogenarian poet John Ashbery was not an obvious choice, yet the general manager of mtvU Stephen Friedman explained that 'he resonates with college students that we've talked with'.[1] Free-floating fragments of Ashbery's verse chosen by college students appeared in eighteen promotional 'shorts' on the channel – 'like commercials for verse', writes Melena Ryzik – and the full texts of the poems were made available on the website mtvu.com.[2] Ashbery, who was the poet laureate of New York State from 2001 to 2003, later said of his unlikely appointment to the role, 'it seemed like it would be a chance to broaden the audience for poetry'.[3]

How do we reconcile this desire to 'broaden the audience for poetry' amongst the MTV generation with Ashbery's reputation as a 'difficult' or even 'incomprehensible' poet? Or with his declaration that 'To create a work of art that the critic cannot even talk about ought to be the artist's chief concern'?[4] It would seem that college students have little hope of understanding Ashbery's verse when even the doyenne of American academicians Helen Vendler (no stranger to recondite 'poets' poets', having written extensively on Wallace Stevens) confesses to being frequently flummoxed by the 'resistant incoherence' of Ashbery's verse, and by the often 'too private ... too abstruse ... too silly' associative 'games' that he plays.[5] Ashbery himself has bemusedly noted 'I live with this paradox; on one hand I am an important poet, read by younger writers, and on the other hand, nobody understands me. I am often asked to account for this state of affairs, but I can't.'[6]

It is the difficulty of forming any comfortable 'understanding' of such texts that in the earlier stages of his career led several notable critics to attack with startling vitriol not only the poetry, but also the poet himself. In 1962 John Simon summarily dismissed the so-called 'New York School' – amongst them Ashbery, Barbara Guest, and Kenneth Koch – as 'abstract expressionists in words ... every bit as undistinguished and indistinguishable as their confreres of the drip, dribble, and squirt', yet singled the supposedly 'indistinguishable' Ashbery out for particular reproach.[7] *The Tennis Court Oath* was, Simon pronounced, 'garbage', largely because 'Mr. Ashbery has perfected his verse to the point where it almost never deviates into – nothing so square as sense! – sensibility, sensuality, or sentences.'[8] In 1970, J. W. Hughes, moved to apoplexy by the publication of *The Double Dream of Spring*, bizarrely called Ashbery 'The Doris Day of modernist poetry', and accused him of playing 'nasty Symbolist–Imagist tricks on his audience while maintaining a façade of earnest innocuousness'.[9] Clearly, when faced with a body of verse that seems not only to resist but also to mock their analytical endeavours, some critics begin to feel hoaxed or hoodwinked. However, T. S. Eliot famously declared that 'Genuine poetry can communicate before it is understood,' and it may be that it is only in the act of relinquishing our desire (or even our *need*) to 'understand' that we can begin to truly appreciate Ashbery's verse.[10] Indeed, Adam Phillips, in his review of *Notes from the Air: Later Selected Poems*, suggested that 'Ashbery's poetry makes you wonder what the wish to understand may protect you from; what the pleasures are of not understanding.'[11]

Lines like these from the sestina 'Farm Implements and Rutabagas in a Landscape' (1970) seem designedly opaque, gleefully impervious to the attempts of critics and readers alike to understand or to evaluate them:

> The first of the undecoded messages read: "Popeye sits in thunder,
> Unthought of. From that shoebox of an apartment,
> From livid curtain's hue, a tangram emerges: a country."
> Meanwhile the Sea Hag was relaxing on a green couch: "How pleasant
> To spend one's vacation *en la casa de Popeye*," she scratched
> Her cleft chin's solitary hair[.][12]

The painterly title, promising an agreeable agrarian scene, bears no obvious relation to the poem, which casts the characters of the popular 1930s 'Popeye the Sailor' newspaper comic strips in a melodramatic, mythopoeic soap opera. Ashbery admits that he often begins with a title – a phrase overheard, a scrap of newsprint – without any conception of how the resultant poem may look or sound; 'A possible title occurs to me and it defines an area ... to move around in and uncover.'[13] Both the seemingly arbitrary title and the 'highly artificial' sestina form, then, are the terms of a challenge that the poet sets himself:

> [T]hese forms such as the sestina were really devices at getting into remoter areas of consciousness. The really bizarre requirements of a sestina I use as a probing tool rather than as a form in the traditional sense. I once told somebody that writing a sestina was rather like riding downhill on a bicycle and having the pedals push your feet. I wanted my feet to be pushed into places they normally wouldn't have taken.[14]

Ashbery's use of form as an experimental 'probing tool', preceding any conscious subject or content, stands in opposition to the Romantic notion of form as an organic accretion or process. The 'bizarre requirements' of this contorted form prove generative rather than constrictive, though. The poet casts a seine net through the 'remoter areas of consciousness' (both his individual consciousness and the collective or cultural consciousness), and brings into conjunction an unlike and unlikely catch of images, vocabularies, and references; Greek mythology, newspaper comic strips, secret agent novels, bourgeois platitudes ('How pleasant!'), and a Song Dynasty Chinese puzzle.

This is not so much an 'undecoded message' as an 'undecodable message', then; or, more radically, perhaps not even a 'message' at all, but a literary puzzle or a game. Joseph M. Conte suggests that the sestina 'views itself as a game, puzzle, or assemblage; the form has an accomplice in this endeavor, namely the multiple contexts and voices which function as the shifting signs or counters of the game'.[15] Many of Ashbery's poems present themselves as games to be played or puzzles to be solved. Poems such as 'Riddle Me' (1987) and 'Chinese Whispers' (2002) explicitly associate themselves with verbal games, whereas incomplete titles like '... by an Earthquake' and 'Outside My Window the Japanese ...' invite the readers to 'fill in the blanks' as though on the TV game show *Blankety Blanks*.

Ashbery's poetry is radically egalitarian, in that it is a poetry that renders the standard 'critical toolkit' obsolete, and therefore puts everyone – scholar and student, critic and casual reader alike – on a level (equally bewildered) playing field. It is a poetry that, in its frequent opacity, allows (or even invites) the reader to project upon it all manner of motivations and meanings, as M. Wynn Thomas points out; 'Is his work a libertarian, democratic, catholic approach to the world [as] its champions claim? Or is it, as others say, the corrupt aesthetic of capitalist consumerism? You could argue that it is both.'[16] As such, much of the existing criticism on Ashbery's poetry reveals rather more about the critic than it does about the poetry.

Similarly democratic is Ashbery's madcap mixing and merging of the lexis, images, and reference points of 'high' and 'low' culture. Conte suggests that whereas 'a modernist such as Ezra Pound packs his bag with allusions to the high art of distant epochs ... the postmodernist is more comfortable with references to more popular modes'.[17] Like the conductor in 'The Explanation', Ashbery brings all things to bear in and on his art:

> The conductor, a glass of water, permits all kinds
> Of wacky analogies to glance off him, and, circling outward,
> To bring in the night. Nothing is too 'unimportant'
> Or too important, for that matter. The newspaper and the garbage
> Wrapped in it, the over, the under.[18]

Whilst Ashbery notes 'there's a lot of pop in my poetry ... A lot of my poetry comes out of popular American culture like comic strips and B movies and song titles and stuff like that,' he suggests that this ostensible 'at homeness' with and within popular culture in fact masks a fundamental sense of estrangement:

> I've always felt that way, even as a child, I guess because my interests, in poetry in particular, are not those of most Americans, and yet I continue to have them and to also be interested in things that other Americans are interested in. But I've always felt somewhat at a remove from the world around me in America ... When I was very young I read Thomas Mann's novella *Tonio Kruger* and identified very much with the hero of that, who looks into the houses of bourgeois families at night and realizes how estranged he feels and how much he would like to join that world, but can't.[19]

We might think here of Wallace Stevens' figure of the 'contemporary Romantic' who

> happens to be one who still dwells in an ivory tower, but who insists that life would be intolerable except for the fact that one has, from the top,

> such an exceptional view of the public dump and the advertising signs of Snider's Catsup, Ivory Soap and Chevrolet Cars. He is the hermit who dwells alone with the sun and the moon, but insists on taking a rotten newspaper.[20]

Unlike Stevens' 'contemporary Romantic', Ashbery is not content with merely an 'exceptional view of the public dump'; he escapes his ivory tower and, like a poetic skip rat, picks his way through 'the wrapper on a can of pears, / The cat in the paper bag, the corset, the box / From Esthonia: the tiger chest, for tea'.[21] Whereas Stevens' 'Man on the Dump' rejects the 'trash' of slack prosaicisms and newspaperese, it is precisely this 'low' language which Ashbery seeks as treasure.

Ashbery's collocation and juxtaposition of the disparate and disposable 'material' of twentieth-century American experience is a kind of linguistic or literary collaging. He was introduced (or rather, introduced himself) to the work of the Surrealist artists at the age of nine, reading an article in *Life* magazine on the 'Fantastic Art, Dada, and Surrealism' exhibition at the Museum of Modern Art in 1936. Ashbery recalls, 'It was tremendously exciting and although I probably didn't say I wanted to be a surrealist when I grew up, it did take me in that direction. I started taking painting classes and looked at books about surrealism.'[22] Ashbery idolized Max Ernst, the prolific collage artist and pioneer of the Dada movement, and during his teenage years an obsession with film, and with low budget B movies in particular, informed the eclectic, outlandish visual vocabulary requisite for the Surrealist artist. Ashbery's first visual collages date from his undergraduate years at Harvard in the mid-1940s and his sporadic work in the medium over the past sixty years has tended to juxtapose the 'old world' European art historical tradition with the 'new world' brash Technicolor of mid-twentieth-century America. In 2008, Ashbery exhibited two dozen small collages at the Tibor de Nagy Gallery in New York, the majority of which date from the 1970s. There was a pleasing circularity in this as, when the gallery first opened its doors in 1950, Ashbery was a guest at the opening night party, and his first chapbook *Turandot and Other Poems* was published under the gallery's imprint in 1953.

In this small body of work, we can see what M. Wynn Thomas calls Ashbery's 'omnivorous aesthetic' in action.[23] Most of the collages consist of three elements: a postcard (most often a landscape); several cut-and-paste images (Marvel superheroes, reclining glamour girls, Renaissance portraits, rosy-cheeked children, all obliviously incongruous in their new surroundings); and a puzzling title, often in

French ('Poisson d'Avril', 'L'Heure Exquise', 'Mannerist Concern'). The playfulness of all these works is made explicit in 'Chutes and Ladders I (for Joe Brainard)' (2008) and 'Chutes and Ladders III (for David Kermani)' (2008). Using photocopies of antique game boards as backgrounds, these larger works invite onlookers to 'play' a game. Significantly, there is little discernible difference between 'up' and 'down' on these game boards. Many of the superimposed images are turned on their heads, and the 'player' is dispossessed of any real sense of high (culture) or low (culture), progress or recession, winning or losing. This disorientation, we sense, is the aim of the game.

What Ashbery's collages do with images, his poems do with language. *The Tennis Court Oath* (1962), widely regarded as Ashbery's most challenging volume, is the most notable product of Ashbery's *collagiste* period. Its eponymous poem takes its title from the French Neoclassicist Jacques-Louis David's 1791 painting of that pivotal pledge taken by the Third Estate during the first days of the French Revolution. Ashbery is not as interested in the polished finished painting, though, as in the unfinished preparatory drawings in which David's dynamic figures remain entirely unclothed, the artist having first taken pains to render minutely their musculature. Only their faces have been painted in, creating a collage-like 'cut and paste' effect. The image is unintentionally comic; the figures' animated facial expressions and aggressive stances contrast utterly with the vulnerability of their naked bodies. David Shapiro suggests that 'the whole effect is thus a typical dreamlike embarrassment: To be caught with one's pants down, while initiating a great revolution with one's peers.'[24] It is precisely the incompleteness of the image – the provisional quality of David's drawing, and the contingency that led to it being left unfinished – which appeals to Ashbery. As with 'Farm Implements', though, the painterly title has nothing to do with the poem that follows; Ashbery makes no further reference either to David or to the events of the Revolution. Even the title of this poem is a flimsy scrap of paper, frustrating the readers' expectation that a title should be instructive, informative, and indicative.

What the poem shares with David's drawing is a pervasive sense of incompleteness and interrupted-ness, and it is only in this constant inconstancy, this consistent inconsistency, that the poem coheres:

What had you been thinking about
the face studiously bloodied
heaven blotted region
I go on loving you like water but

there is a terrible breath in the way all of this
You were not elected president, yet won the race
All the way through fog and drizzle
When you read it was sincere the coasts
stammered with unintentional villages the
horse strains fatigued I guess … the calls …
I worry[.][25]

David Herd notes that 'One of the ways Ashbery made a number of the poems in *The Tennis Court Oath* as disjointed and unaccommodating as they are was by the practice of cut-ups.'[26] The cut-up is an aleatory poetic technique in which a text is first dissected into words or phrases and then rearranged to create a new text. The technique was conceived by Tristan Tzara in his short piece, *TO MAKE A DADAIST POEM* (1920), and he demonstrated the process during a Dadaist rally in the 1920s, 'assembling' a poem by pulling words at random from a hat. Ashbery used not one text but many, amongst them 'American magazines he bought in Paris, "things like *Esquire* and *Life*", … pulp fiction like William Le Queux's *Beryl of the Biplane*',[27] and '*Soundings* … a popular novel by A. Hamilton Gibbs, which Ashbery found in his parents' home in Sodus'.[28] These mass-market American publications contrast strikingly with the rarefied European art historical inspiration for the poem's title. Ripped (quite literally) from their contexts, these 'found' words and phrases have what Shapiro calls 'the tone and look of shattered newsprint' and 'a flat prose quality'.[29] The poems in *The Tennis Court Oath* differ from those in his earlier volume *Some Trees* (1956) in the dizzying rapidity of the disintegration or discarding of images and lexical fields. An image no sooner flashes up in front of us than it is unceremoniously papered over by a new image, as though on a billboard or advertising hoarding.

Does Ashbery's use of the cut-up technique stem from what we might call an aesthete's 'magpie instinct' for collecting and collating linguistic curios? Or is it a political, rather than an aesthetic, strategy, whereby Ashbery (mis)appropriates this language in order to attack and undermine the dominant discourse of mid-century America? Ashbery has stated that 'American vernacular is an important stimulus for me,' but does not elaborate as to whether it is grist to his mill or the grit in the oyster shell.[30] When Ashbery takes his scissors to a populist magazine or a piece of genre fiction, is it an act of homage, or is it, as David Herd argues, a 'particularly hostile' act of symbolic violence (and, of course, physical violence) against the linguistic order?[31] One way of interpreting Ashbery's use of the cut-up technique is as a response to the question posed by one of his earliest collected poems, 'The Painter' (1956). In this narrative sestina, the eponymous artist envisages a masterpiece of self-abnegation: 'painting the sea's portrait … / … he expected his subject / To rush up the sand, and, seizing a brush, / Plaster its own portrait on the canvas.'[32] The artist struggles with the realization that every painting, no matter the subject or sitter, is to some extent a self-portrait, as the creating self cannot be fully expunged from the creative process. The radical collage and cut-up techniques that we see both in Ashbery's visual collages and in *The Tennis Court Oath* are experiments in expunging – or at least, decentring the artist – from the art. In those cut-up poems, the poet becomes the organizer rather than originator. The cut-up technique introduces a degree of chance and arbitrariness into the poetic process, thus challenging the Romantic (and persistent) notion of the poem as an organic mode of self-expression.

Whilst the lyric 'I' and the second person 'you' occur frequently in 'The Tennis Court Oath', any sense of this 'I' issuing from a singular, consistent speaker and any sense of this 'you' indicating a singular consistent addressee, is undermined by the rapid shifts in register, lexis, and subject. Shapiro suggests that 'The "I" may now merely be the "I" not of a persona but of a piece of newspaperese or newspaper, or part of a story pasted, as it were, upon the poem.'[33]

One reading of this disbanding of the traditional lyric 'I' is that Ashbery conceives of a contemporary version of Ralph Waldo Emerson's self-dissolution in nature. In the 1836 essay 'Nature' Emerson advocates a state of self-forgetfulness in which a unity with the 'infinite' and the 'Universal' may occur:

> Standing on the bare ground, — my head bathed by the blithe air, and uplifted into infinite spaces, — all mean egotism vanishes. I become a transparent eye-ball; I am nothing; I see all; the currents of the Universal Being circulate through me; I am part or particle of God.[34]

Ashbery's 'I' also exists within this state of self-forgetfulness but 'all mean egotism' has been lost not in *nature*, but in *culture*; specifically, the mass-produced, material and textual culture of mid-twentieth-century America. Ashbery's 'I' has become 'a transparent eye-ball' who (or which) sees all, and through whom (or which) the roiling currents of collective American consciousness rush. Ashbery has said in interviews that he often writes his poetry while watching television, as though to tune out of his own singular consciousness or to tune in to a collective broadcast consciousness.[35] That Ashbery's 'I' is a kind of 'hive mind' – a decentralized, communal (un)consciousness – is suggested in the first stanzas of the title poem of *Hotel Lautréamont* (1992):

> Research has shown that ballads were produced by all of society
> working as a team. They didn't just happen. There was no guesswork.

> The people, then, knew what they wanted and how to get it.
> We see the results in works as diverse as 'Windsor Forest' and 'The Wife of Usher's Well,'
>
> ...
>
> Working as a team, they didn't just happen. There was no guesswork.
> The horns of elfland swing past, and in a few seconds
> we see the results in works as diverse as 'Windsor Forest' and 'The Wife of Usher's Well,'
> or, on a more modern note, in the finale of the Sibelius violin concerto.[36]

The poem is a pantoum: an elaborate verse form in which the second and fourth lines of one quatrain become the first and third lines of the next. This highly patterned repetition creates a sense of the ceaseless cycling and recycling of thoughts and phrases in our collective consciousness. The title of Ashbery's 2002 volume, *Chinese Whispers*, also points towards the possibility of creative collectivism; each 'player' may have a hand in creating the final product of the game.

Are we to read this 'radical flattening out' of the lyric 'I' as an uplifting surrender of 'all mean egotism', as in Emerson's 'Nature'? Or is it Ashbery's clear-sighted critique of the ways in which mass-produced material culture may perniciously erode our autonomy and distinctiveness?[37] Certainly, we find in some poems an almost apocalyptic vision of America. In 'America' (1962), we find what Herd calls the 'recurring motif ... of accumulation' – an accumulation of 'images of self-defeating accumulation', even.[38] The opening lines direct the reader's gaze upwards to a cluttered heaven ('Piling upward / the fact the stars'), and a few lines later an endless traffic jam stretches as far as the eye can see ('We were parked / Millions of us / The accident was terrible.')[39] This accretion of 'things' is seemingly unstoppable, automatic:

> The stones piled up—
> The ribbon—books. miracle. with moon and the stars
>
> The pear tree
> moving me
> I am around and in my sigh
> The gift of a the stars.

In this landscape (or dreamscape?) of 'things', it is the 'I' – whoever that is – that becomes inanimate, insensible, and moveable, and the industrial or mechanical that becomes sinisterly sentient and purposeful, as in the lines 'of course the lathes around / the stars with privilege jerks', and 'Cars / blockade the streets wish'. Whilst the visual iconography and bombastic rhetoric of a Fourth of July parade flares and blares in this poem ('these stars in our flag', 'Some tassels', 'pageant of history', 'liberty') we are left with the sense that America – or *this* 'America', at least – is not 'the Land of the Free'.

The contemporaneous poem 'They Dream Only of America' (1962) is described by Shapiro as 'one of the most horrifying of Ashbery's middle period poems'.[40] We find 'The American Dream' turned, or turning, into a nightmare: 'They dream only of America / To be lost among the thirteen million pillars of grass.'[41] The image of the 'pillars of grass' evokes Walt Whitman's *Leaves of Grass*, but the shift from 'leaves' to 'pillars' is a shift from nature to architecture, from the pastoral to the urban; they paved paradise and put up a parking lot. That this aspirational 'dream' of becoming assimilated or 'lost' within the 'thirteen million' is a misguided or even dangerous one is suggested in the sudden interjection '"This honey is delicious / Though it burns the throat."' America is not, it warns, the promised land of milk and honey. Vague images of threat and debility pervade the poem; an unknown 'they' hide out in a barn either tracking or being tracked by a murderer, and that all-American rite of passage, the road trip, is curtailed by a headache. In the fifth stanza there is an apparently paranoid search for 'signs' within this shifting dreamscape, though for signs of *what* we are not told. In the final stanza, a quoted speaker (though not necessarily the same speaker as before) bleakly concludes that 'There is nothing to do / For our liberation, except wait in the horror of it.' Is this 'liberation' the sudden waking from a bad dream? To what reality will the dreamer awake, though? The final line reads as a desolate admission that without America – without the 'thirteen million' – the speaker is 'lost' and is 'nothing'; his selfhood, though eroded, is dependent on his buying in to that 'dream', however nightmarish it may have become. Ashbery recalls that he 'wrote ['They Dream Only of America'] in the spring of 1957' whilst living as an American émigré in Paris. 'At the time,' he explains, 'I was beginning to get all anxious about going back to New York.'[42] Absence from America did not make Ashbery's heart grow fonder; on the contrary, it seemed to throw into sharper relief the poet's anxieties about his homeland.

In 1975, something of an *annus mirabilis* for Ashbery, *Self-Portrait in a Convex Mirror* won an unprecedented triple crown: the National Book Critics Circle Award, the National Book Award, and the Pulitzer Prize. In 'The One Thing That Can Save America' (1975) from that volume, Ashbery seems to reprise his earlier concerns. Despite its didactic title, the poem does not hector or moralize; rather, it asks a series of bewildered and bewildering questions of the reader: 'Is anything central? / Orchards flung out on the land, / Urban forests, rustic plantations, knee-high hills?'[43] This America seems somehow unreal; an ersatz America laid on for the benefit of tourists. 'Urban forests' and 'knee-high hills' are surely self-contradictory or self-cancelling terms, and 'rustic plantation' seems clearly tautological. The reference to 'scenery mingled with darkness' in this first verse paragraph brings to mind not real landscape but the scenery waiting in the wings of a theatre. The speaker's concern with the 'centrality' of these topological features and their names seems to be a concern about the possibility of experiencing authentic or objective 'reality'; whilst these are 'connected' to his 'version of America', the speaker explains, 'the juice is elsewhere'. What initially advertises itself as an oration on the sorry state of the nation, though, suddenly becomes a musing on the poet-speaker's *ars poetica*:

> I know that I braid too much my own
> Snapped-off perceptions of things as they come to me.
> They are private and always will be.
> Where then are the private turns of event
> Destined to boom later like golden chimes
> Released over a city from a highest tower?
> The quirky things that happen to me, and I tell you,
> And you instantly know what I mean?

It is perhaps ironic that it is in this relatively 'conventional' and coherent text (we are, after all, able to refer with reasonable confidence to a single 'speaker' here) that Ashbery seems most concerned with the lucidity and intelligibility of his verse. In the fragmentary cut-up poems of *The Tennis Court Oath*, Ashbery seemed to have altogether rejected the classical principle of mimesis. As William Burroughs, that other great mid-century exponent of the cut-up technique, suggests, what those poems represent is not a visible external reality but the process or experience of perception and consciousness itself:

> [Cut-ups] make explicit a psychosensory process that is going on all the time anyway. Somebody is reading a newspaper, and his eye follows

> the column in proper Aristotelian manner, one idea and one sentence at a time. But subliminally he is reading the columns on either side and is aware of the person sitting next to him … That's a cut-up – a juxtaposition of what's happening outside and what you're thinking of[.][44]

In *Self-Portrait in a Convex Mirror* we find some of Ashbery's most sustained poetic examinations of the (im)possibilities of mimesis. The collection's title poem begins as an ekphrastic study of Parmigianino's self-portrait of the same name (c. 1524), which depicts the artist's distorted reflection as seen in a convex mirror. The artist's hand, foregrounded, is disproportionately large, elongated by its proximity to the mirror, whereas the shadowy room in which the artist sits seems to stretch elastically into the distance:

> As Parmigianino did it, the right hand
> Bigger than the head, thrust at the viewer
> And swerving easily away, as though to protect
> What it advertises.[45]

Parmigianino's portrait offers a distorted and twice mediated re-presentation of the sitter and the scene: 'the portrait / Is the reflection once removed', the speaker acknowledges, the line break indicating the distance and difference between them. Whereas most self-portraits are indistinguishable from portraits, Parmigianino plainly 'advertises' that he is sitter and artist both. Similarly, Ashbery's poem foregrounds a scepticism as to the possibility and the desirability of mimesis: 'words are only speculation' / (From the Latin *speculum*, mirror)'. If 'Self-Portrait' is indeed Ashbery's self-portrait, then it is an image of a poet who is acutely aware that language is only 'a weak instrument though / Necessary'. Throughout the poem, we are offered images of the vertiginous variousness of experience. Like the room behind Parmigianino, spatial and chronological horizons stretch off into indistinctness where the eye and the imagination cannot follow: 'The city falling with its beautiful suburbs / Into space always less clear, less defined', or the 'further tributaries / … that … empty themselves into a vague / Sense of something that can never be known'. Any attempt to fix 'this flow', whether in words or in brushstrokes, is bound to fail or fall short, as Ashbery explains in an interview with David Lehman; 'Art with any serious aspirations toward realism still has to take into account that fact that reality escapes laws of perspective and logic, and does not naturally take the form of a sonnet or a sonata.'[46]

'Ode to Bill' (1975) is pervaded by a similar second-guessing concern with the possibility of mimesis, as the speaker asks:

What is writing?
Well, in my case, it's getting down on paper
Not thoughts, exactly, but ideas, maybe:
Ideas about thoughts. Thoughts is too grand a word.
Ideas is better, though not precisely what I mean.[47]

Even when (or perhaps, *especially* when) trying to elucidate the nature of writing, words are no more than blunt instruments, crude approximations of experience – 'not … exactly', 'maybe', 'too grand', or 'not precisely what I mean'. Here, we might again think back to Stevens' 'The Man on the Dump' in which the nameless 'Man' sits on this 'dump' of tired and tainted words, and 'beats an old tin can, lard pail' in hope of 'get[ting] near' the reality – 'The the' – which language can no longer adequately represent.[48] Stevens' 'Man on the Dump' retains a belief in the possibility of mimesis, the idea that an external reality can be accurately reproduced or represented in language – but only in the 'right' language. Ashbery, however, seems less invested in upholding the traditional hierarchical relationship between signified (that which is material) and signifier (that which is linguistic). David Spurr suggests that in 'Grand Galop' (1975), 'Ashbery introduces a universe in which word and object have merged'.[49] In this universe 'All things seem mention of themselves. / And the names which stem from them branch out to other referents.'[50] Language is not merely reflective of reality, but constitutive of its own parallel, simultaneous 'reality'. However, this is not the first time that 'word' and 'object' have appeared interchangeable; in the title poem of the earlier volume *Rivers and Mountains* (1666), the physical landscape and the inscribed page seem overlaid, transposable.

On a secret map the assassins
Cloistered, the Moon River was marked
Near the eighteen peaks and the city
Of humiliation and defeat – wan ending
Of the trail among dry papery leaves
Gray-brown quills like thoughts
In the melodious but vast mass of today's
Writing through fields and swamps
Marked, on the map, with little bunches of weeds.[51]

Words like 'leaves', 'quills', and 'print' simultaneously belong to two different lexical fields – that of nature and that of writing – creating what Spurr describes as 'a deliberate confusion of metaphorical tenor and vehicle in this passage … It is not that the act of writing is compared to a journey across a landscape, or vice-versa; rather, they constitute the same activity: to write is to move, to act.'[52]

The possibility of communicating 'truthfully' in language remains a concern in Ashbery's later work, too. In 'Paradoxes and Oxymorons' (1981) the poet-speaker ostensibly announces his intention to eschew allusiveness and wordplay in favour of 'plain' speaking. John Shoptaw suggests that 'the poem … voices Ashbery's populist impulse to reach the common reader'; however, the addressed reader seems reluctant to be 'reached', 'look[ing] out a window', deliberately not meeting the poet-speaker's gaze.[53] In the second stanza, the poem begins its inevitable slide into linguistic cross-questioning and second-guessing: 'What's a plain level? It is that and other things, / Bringing a system of them into play. Play?'[54] The poet-speaker then levels at this unresponsive reader a charge that countless readers and critics have levelled at Ashbery, accusing him of playing a kind of poetic knock-and-run game:

> I think you exist only
> To tease me into doing it, on your level, and then you aren't there[.]

As Shoptaw concludes, Ashbery 'yields himself to the reader, who nevertheless continues to "miss" him', thus demonstrating the difficulty of 'truthful' communication, even on 'a very plain level'.[55]

Ashbery's 1979 volume *As We Know* contained the long poem 'Litany', often regarded by critics and readers as one of Ashbery's most demanding texts. Harold Bloom describes it as 'a highly problematic and at moments magnificent long poem of some sixty-five pages, in two quite separate columns'.[56] On the one hand, the poem's daunting double-columned structure is a new formal departure for the poet; on the other, it is merely a making visible of the familiar polylogic or polyvocal strategies of his earlier verse. The interrogative interplay of voices and perspectives that was largely implicit in a poem like 'Syringa' (1977) is now explicitly indicated on the page, in what we might interpret as an obliging concession to the reader:

For someone like me	*So this must be a hole*
The simple things	*Of cloud*
Like having toast or	*Mandate or trap*
Going to church are	*But haze that casts*
Kept in one place.	*The milk of enchantment*
Like having wine and cheese.	*Over the whole town,*
The parents of the town	*Its scenery, whatever*
Pissing elegantly escape	*Could be happening*

knowledge
Once and for all. The
Snapdragons consumed in a
wind
Of fire and rage far over
The streets as they end.

Behind tall hedges
Of dark, lissome knowledge[.]

Though the left-hand column refers in the singular first person to 'someone like me', neither of the columns can be certainly associated with the poet, or with any identifiable speaker, figure, or viewpoint.[57] There is no obvious hierarchical relationship between the two columns, and no obvious 'right' way in which to read this poem. Ashbery says of the poem, 'I thought it would be interesting to have to pay attention to two separate poems at the same time; it would be like eavesdropping on two different conversations at a cocktail party.'[58] The extent to which the two columns are 'two separate poems' is debatable. Certainly, the columns seem frequently to echo or mimic, and to comment on or contradict one another, though the reader may well be led to question whether they are projecting onto this poem (or these poems) sense and synchronicity where there are none.

Since the early 1990s Ashbery has been startlingly prolific, publishing fourteen new volumes of verse between 1991 and 2015. There has been relatively little sustained treatment of the later Ashbery, and, as John Emil Vincent notes, 'critics have suggested that Ashbery is producing books too quickly for criticism to keep up.'[59] The criticism that has 'kept up' proves that Ashbery's later work is just as provocative as his earlier volumes. On one hand, Langdon Hammer enthuses that 'Ashbery's phrases always feel newly minted; his poems emphasize verbal surprise and delight, not the ways that linguistic patterns restrict us,'[60] and on the other, Michael Robbins mockingly describes Ashbery as 'the Duracell bunny of American poetry' who 'has been writing the same book for more than fifteen years'.[61] However, such insinuations that later Ashbery is a poetic pile-up of the sort decried in 'America', are surely refuted by the sheer variety of his poetic projects since 1987, as catalogued by Vincent:

> *April Galleons* is a fairly slim volume of mostly one-page lyrics[;] *Flow Chart* is a 216-page poem[;] *Hotel Lautréamont* is a large collection of long-lined, often several-page lyrics[;] *And the Stars Were Shining* is a slim collection of slender lyrics crowned by a thirteen-part long poem[;] *Can You Hear, Bird* is a very long alphabetized collection of lyrics[;] *Girls on the Run* is a fifty-six-page poem[;] *Wakefulness* an entirely lineated collection of single lyrics[;] while the volumes that follow it are riddled with prose poems.[62]

What these otherwise unlike volumes have in common is a certain restiveness and need to experiment; as Hammer writes, 'Again and again he sets out to determine freshly what matters, knowing that there can be no rules for finding it, including those he has invented.'[63] This is not novelty for novelty's sake, but novelty as necessity.

Whereas the earlier poems evidence what we might call Ashbery's 'magpie' instinct for borrowing incongruent scraps of language, what we see in his later work is what Ashbery himself has called a 'cuckoo instinct that makes me enjoy making my home in somebody else's nest'.[64] In the poems of *The Tennis Court Oath*, lexis or a particular voice are no sooner picked up than they are summarily dropped or overwritten, but in this later work we see instances of more sustained engagement with other texts. 'Sir Gammer Vans', the final poem of *Chinese Whispers* (2002), borrows its title, governing premise, and several verbatim lines from the English fairy tale published by Joseph Jacobs in *More English Fairy Tales* (1894). The original 'Sir Gammer Vans' is a lying tale, a kind of nonsense form in which every statement made is either immediately or subsequently shown to be a falsehood, or a logical impossibility. Ashbery's version intersperses contemporary American discourse ('wouldn't commit himself to a used Chevy') with the borrowed lines and lexis ('*sir*', 's'blood I said') of the archaic English folk text:

> Last Sunday morning at six o'clock in the evening as I was sailing
> over the tops of the mountains in my little boat a crew-cut stranger
> saluted me, so I asked him, could he tell me whether the little old
> woman was dead yet who
>
> was hanged last Saturday week for drowning herself in a shower of feathers?
> 'Ask Monk Lewis what he thinks "been there done that" means in the
> so-called
> evening of life. Chances are he'll regale you with chess moves. All I
> want is my damn prescription.' 'And you shall have it, *sir*,' he answered
> in a level voice.[65]

If Ashbery is, as some mystified readers have concluded, a nonsense poet, then this is a different, more demotic brand of nonsense. As Vincent notes, 'Such a fairy tale elicits delight from the obviousness of its nonsense, the fact that the listener knows and can expect that all the assertions in the story are either frank nonsense or are forthrightly contradicted.'[66] In this poem, all the readers are in on the joke; everyone knows the rules of this particular game.

Ashbery's twenty-sixth volume, *Breezeway*, was published in 2015, and it is clear that the poet is not quite finished with 'games'. These short lyrics continue the play of Chinese whispers with a plethora of substitutions and aural slips; in the title poem we find 'to bark down' where we would expect 'to back down', and 'winch' where 'wench' might make more sense in the context (though not much more).[67] As ever, Ashbery delights in the irreverent mix and mash-up of high and low culture:

> Will research tell us tomorrow
> of normal morals? Take a Brooklyn family
> in fracture mode, vivid,
> energizing, throbs to the earlobes. Thanks
> to a snakeskin toupee, my grayish push boots
> exhale new patina / prestige. Exeunt the Kardashians.[68]

We know by now not to be too trusting of Ashbery's titles, but the title of this poem, 'Seven-Year-Old Auroch Likes This', is suggestive in several ways. The Auroch was a species of wild ox hunted to extinction in the seventeenth century, and to the millennial generation, the phrase 'Likes This' is part of the familiar phraseology of Facebook. The Shakespearean stage direction, 'Exeunt the Kardashians', then, may well be a warning to those ubiquitous social media superstars from a poet who, at eighty-seven years of age, has seen the rise and fall of the *Rota Fortunae* of celebrity over and over again.

This is not the predictable griping of an ageing poet against the rise of social media, though. In a 2015 interview, Ashbery said 'I'm not [on social media], but I wish I was ... Because it might offer new possibilities on the horizon.'[69] If social media does indeed offer 'new possibilities' then they are possibilities presaged even in Ashbery's earliest poetry. His decentred, digressive, polyphonic, and multifarious verse anticipates so clearly this early twenty-first-century (un)reality of 24/7 connectivity and attention spans of 140 characters. We have finally arrived in the world in which the prophetic Ashbery has lived all along; 'it is no longer the imaginary world but the real one, and it is exploding all around us like a fireworks factory in one last dazzling orgy of light and sound.'[70]

Notes

1. Melena Ryzik, 'John Ashbery: An 80-year-old Poet for the MTV Generation', *The New York Times* (Arts) (27 August 2007). Last accessed on 17 August 2015. Available at: http://www.nytimes.com/2007/08/27/arts/27iht-27laur. 7268746.html?_r=0
2. Melena Ryzik, 'John Ashbery: An 80-year-old Poet for the MTV Generation'.

3. Melena Ryzik, 'John Ashbery: An 80-year-old Poet for the MTV Generation'.
4. 'Brice Marden', first published in *ARTnews* (March 1972). Reprinted in John Ashbery, *Reported Sightings: Art Chronicles 1957–1987* (New York: Alfred A. Knopf, 1989), p. 214. These lines are often misquoted, for example in the online magazine *Slate*, as 'to produce a poem that the critic cannot even talk about'.
5. Helen Vendler, 'John Ashbery, Toying With Words', *The New York Times*, Sunday Book Review (8 December 2009). Last accessed 15 July 2016. Available at: http://www.nytimes.com/2009/12/13/books/review/Vendler-t.html?pagewanted=all&_r&_r=1&
6. Peter Stitt, 'John Ashbery, The Art of Poetry, No. 33', *Paris Review*, 90 (Winter 1983). Last accessed on 17 August 2015. Available at: http://www.theparisreview.org/interviews/3014/the-art-of-poetry-no-33-john-ashbery
7. John Simon, 'More Brass Than Enduring', *Hudson Review*, 15(3) (Autumn 1962): 458.
8. John Simon, 'More Brass Than Enduring': 458.
9. J. W. Hughes, *The Saturday Review* (8 August 1970): 34.
10. T. S. Eliot, 'Dante' (1929), in *Selected Essays: 1917–1932* (New York: Harcourt, Brace and Company, 1932), p. 200.
11. Adam Phillips, Review of *Notes From the Air: Selected Later Poems* by John Ashbery, *The Observer*, Poetry (30 December 2007). Last accessed on 17 August 2015. Available at: http://www.theguardian.com/books/2007/dec/30/poetry.features
12. John Ashbery, 'Farm Implements and Rutabagas in a Landscape' (1970), *Selected Poems* (Manchester: Carcanet, 2002), p. 105. Where poems have been included in the *Selected Poems* or *Notes from the Air: Selected Later Poems* volumes, I will cite these volumes; those poems which have not been included will be cited in their original collections.
13. Janet Bloom and Robert Losada, 'Craft Interview with John Ashbery', *New York Quarterly*, 9 (1972): 24. Reprinted in William Packard (ed.), *The Craft of Poetry: Interviews from The New York Quarterly* (Garden City, NY: Doubleday, 1974), p. 124. It is this reprinting that I will cite hereafter.
14. William Packard, *The Craft of Poetry: Interviews from The New York Quarterly*, p. 124.
15. Joseph M. Conte, *Unending Design: The Forms of Postmodern Poetry* (Ithaca, NY: Cornell University Press, 1991), p. 175.
16. Nicholas Wroe, 'Parallel Lines', *The Guardian*, Books (23 April 2005). Last accessed 17 August 2015. Available at: http://www.theguardian.com/books/2005/apr/23/featuresreviews.guardianreview13
17. Joseph M. Conte, *Unending Design: The Forms of Postmodern Poetry*, p. 175.
18. John Ashbery, 'The Explanation' (1977), *Houseboat Days* (New York: Viking Press, 1977), p. 14.

19. Erica Wright, 'Houses at Night: Erica Wright interviews John Ashbery', *Guernica* (8 February 2008). Last accessed 17 August 2015. Available at: https://www.guernicamag.com/interviews/houses_at_night_1/
20. Wallace Stevens, *Opus Posthumous: Poems, Plays, Prose*, rev. edn (New York: Vintage Books: 1990), p. 212.
21. Wallace Stevens, 'The Man on the Dump' (1942), *The Collected Poems* (New York: Vintage Books, 1990), p. 201.
22. Nicholas Wroe, 'Parallel Lines'.
23. Nicholas Wroe, 'Parallel Lines'.
24. David Shapiro, *John Ashbery: An Introduction to the Poetry* (New York: Columbia University Press, 1979), p. 54.
25. John Ashbery, 'The Tennis Court Oath' (1962), *The Tennis Court Oath*. Wesleyan Poetry Program (Middletown, CT: Wesleyan University Press, 1977), p. 11.
26. David Herd, *John Ashbery and American Poetry* (Manchester: Manchester University Press, 2000), p. 82.
27. David Herd, 'John Ashbery in conversation with David Herd', *PN Review*, 21(1) (September–October 1994): 34.
28. John Shoptaw, *On the Outside Looking Out: John Ashbery's Poetry* (Cambridge, MA, and London: Harvard University Press, 1994), p. 53.
29. David Shapiro, *John Ashbery: An Introduction to the Poetry*, p. 55.
30. Rich Kelley, 'The Library of America Interviews John Ashbery', *Library of America e-newsletter* (October 2008). Last accessed 17 August 2015. Available at: http://www.loa.org/images/pdf/LOA_Ashbery_interview_on_Collected_Poems.pdf
31. David Herd, *John Ashbery and American Poetry*, p. 82.
32. John Ashbery, 'The Painter' (1956), *Selected Poems*, p. 20.
33. David Shapiro, *John Ashbery: An Introduction to the Poetry*, p. 56.
34. Ralph Waldo Emerson, 'Nature', *The Complete Prose Works* (London: Ward, Lock, 1890), p. 311.
35. Adam Phillips, Review of *Notes From the Air: Selected Later Poems* by John Ashbery.
36. John Ashbery, 'Hotel Lautréamont', *Notes from the Air: Selected Later Poems* (Manchester: Carcanet, 2007), p. 70.
37. David Shapiro, *John Ashbery: An Introduction to the Poetry*, p. 56.
38. David Herd, *John Ashbery and American Poetry*, p. 79.
39. John Ashbery, 'America' (1962), *The Tennis Court Oath*, p. 15.
40. David Shapiro, *John Ashbery: An Introduction to the Poetry*, p. 57.
41. John Ashbery, 'They Dream Only of America' (1962), *The Tennis Court Oath*, p. 13.
42. Mark Ford, *John Ashbery in Conversation with Mark Ford* (London: Between the Lines, 2003), p. 44.
43. John Ashbery, 'The One Thing That Can Save America' (1975), *Self-Portrait in a Convex Mirror* (Manchester: Carcanet, 1977), p. 44.

44. Conrad Knickerbocker, 'William S. Burroughs, The Art of Fiction No. 36' (Interview), *The Paris Review*, 35 (Fall 1965). Last accessed 17 August 2015. Available at: http://www.theparisreview.org/interviews/4424/the-art-of-fiction-no-36-william-s-burroughs
45. John Ashbery, 'Self-Portrait in a Convex Mirror', *Selected Poems* (Manchester: Carcanet, 2002), p. 188.
46. John Ashbery, 'Hunger and Love in Their Variations', in John Ashbery, Joe Shannon, Jane Livingston and Timothy Hyman (contrs.), *Kitaj: Paintings, Drawings, Pastels* (London: Thames and Hudson, 1983), p. 10.
47. John Ashbery, 'Ode to Bill' (1975), *Self Portrait in a Convex Mirror*, p. 50.
48. Wallace Stevens, 'The Man on the Dump' (1942), *The Collected Poems*, p. 201.
49. David Spurr, 'John Ashbery's Poetry of Language', *The Centennial Review*, 25 (Spring 1981): 152.
50. John Ashbery, 'Grand Galop' (1975), *Self Portrait in a Convex Mirror*, p. 14.
51. John Ashbery, 'Rivers and Mountains' (1966), *Selected Poems*, p. 49.
52. David Spurr, 'John Ashbery's Poetry of Language': 155.
53. John Shoptaw, *On the Outside Looking Out: John Ashbery's Poetry*, p. 255.
54. John Ashbery, 'Paradoxes and Oxymorons' (1981), *Selected Poems*, p. 283.
55. John Shoptaw, *On the Outside Looking Out: John Ashbery's Poetry*, p. 255.
56. Harold Bloom, quoted in 'The Poetry Symposium', *The New York Times*, Sunday Book Review (21 November 2004). Last accessed 17 August 2015. Available at: http://www.nytimes.com/2004/11/21/books/review/the-poetry-symposium.html?_r=0
57. John Ashbery, 'Litany' (1979), *As We Know* (New York: Viking Press, 1979), pp. 3–68.
58. Mark Ford, *John Ashbery in Conversation with Mark Ford*, p. 60.
59. John Emil Vincent, *John Ashbery and You: His Later Books* (Athens, GA, and London: University of Georgia Press, 2007), p. 3.
60. Langdon Hammer, 'But I digress' (Review of *Notes from the Air: Selected Later Poems*), *The New York Times*, Sunday Book Review (20 April 2008). Last accessed 17 August 2015. Available at: http://www.nytimes.com/2008/04/20/books/review/Hammer-t.html?_r=0
61. Michael Robbins, 'Remember the Yak' (Review of *Planisphere*), *London Review of Books*, 32(17) (September 2010): 25–6.
62. John Emil Vincent, *John Ashbery and You: His Later Books*, p. 4.
63. Langdon Hammer, 'But I digress' (Review of *Notes from the Air: Selected Later Poems*).
64. David Lehman, 'The Shield of a Greeting: The Function of Irony in John Ashbery's Poetry', in David Lehman (ed.), *Beyond Amazement: New Essays on John Ashbery* (Ithaca, NY: Cornell University Press, 1980), p. 111.
65. John Ashbery, 'Sir Gammer Vans', *Notes from the Air: Selected Later Poems*, p. 324.
66. John Emil Vincent, *John Ashbery and You: His Later Books*, p. 170.

67. John Ashbery, 'Breezeway' (2015), *Breezeway* (New York: HarperCollins, 2015). p. 14.
68. John Ashbery, 'Seven-Year-Old Auroch Likes This' (2015), *Breezeway*, p. 4.
69. Adam Fitzgerald, 'John Ashbery' (Interview), *Interview* (April 2015). Last accessed 17 August 2015. Available at: http://www.interviewmagazine.com/culture/john-ashbery/
70. John Ashbery, 'Re-establishing Raymond Roussel', *Portfolio & Art News Annual*, 6 (Autumn 1962), reprinted in Raymond Roussel, ed. Trevor Winkfield, *How I Wrote Certain of My Books* (Boston: Exact Change, 1995), p. xvii.

Further Reading

Conte, Joseph M., *Unending Design: The Forms of Postmodern Poetry* (Ithaca, NY: Cornell University Press, 1991).

Ford, Mark, *John Ashbery in Conversation with Mark Ford* (London: Between the Lines, 2003).

Herd, David, *John Ashbery and American Poetry* (Manchester: Manchester University Press, 2000).

Lehman, David, *Beyond Amazement: New Essays on John Ashbery* (Ithaca, NY: Cornell University Press, 1980).

Packard, William, *The Craft of Poetry: Interviews from The New York Quarterly* (Garden City, NY: Doubleday, 1974).

Shapiro, David, *John Ashbery: An Introduction to the Poetry* (New York: Columbia University Press, 1979).

Shoptaw, John, *On the Outside Looking Out: John Ashbery's Poetry* (Cambridge, MA, and London: Harvard University Press, 1994).

Vincent, John Emil, *John Ashbery and You: His Later Books* (Athens, GA, and London: The University of Georgia Press, 2007).

6

Sylvia Plath in the Early Twenty-First Century

Tracy Brain

The Fifty-Year Anniversaries

Sylvia Plath's work is absolutely of its time, yet continues to speak to readers. Over the last half-century, her writing has demonstrated a powerful ability to increase in currency. It resonates with readers from diverse cultures, in numerous languages. This essay evaluates responses to four significant Plath anniversaries that occurred in late 2012 and early 2013. There is the anniversary of the writing of the October poems of 1962, in what has been called Plath's 'miracle month'.[1] There is the anniversary of *The Bell Jar*'s original publication in January of 1963. There is the anniversary of Plath's death, on the eleventh day of the following month. And there is the anniversary of the discovery of the *Ariel* manuscript she left on her desk at that time. The multitude of reactions to this concurrence of fifty-year anniversaries presents a perfect opportunity for teasing out the ways that Plath is being read in the second decade of the twenty-first century, and for assessing the degree to which debates about her writing have developed since these important events.

For Clea Gibson, these anniversaries present us with 'a chance to view [Plath's] work anew'.[2] Tess Taylor makes a similar point: 'It's as if the tragedy of her death is beginning to burn away to allow us to read her in new ways.'[3] Amongst these 'new ways', scholars have been looking closely at the ever-developing archive of Plath's manuscripts; putting her work in the context of writers she hasn't formerly been read alongside; looking attentively at her visual art; evaluating the ways she has been taken up by different cultures and causes; measuring her far-reaching influence; seeing her poems in dialogue with Ted Hughes' rather than in opposition to him; considering how politics, history and other contemporary concerns informed her literary production; and reappraising the generic boundaries under which her work has formerly been classified. These scholarly enterprises have been filtering into the larger world of Plath's readers, as the avalanche of responses to these landmark moments show.

Plath has long been the subject of articles, essays and books, not to mention films, television documentaries and radio programmes – what can be fairly described as an 'ever-profitable Plath industry'.[4] This quartet of anniversaries generated a considerable increase in the number of words about her during the period from October 2012 through to October 2013, with the preponderance of material appearing in the early months of 2013. It is this one-year time frame on which I want to focus here. As Emma Garman announces in her opening sentence, as if sending out an invitation to a huge birthday party, 'The gossipiest, most divisive and arguably most compelling literary legend of them all … is turning 50.'[5]

We can take a cue from Plath herself in marking these anniversaries; and, moreover, in examining them. Belinda McKeon makes the fitting observation that '"Daddy" is itself a poem built on a bedrock of anniversaries.'[6] We might add that 'The Applicant' is, too: 'But in twenty-five years she'll be silver, / In fifty, gold.'[7] So is 'Lady Lazarus': 'I have done it again. / One year in every ten / I manage it – '.[8] The very titles of 'A Birthday Present' and 'Poem for a Birthday' foreground the magnitude of the most routine and common of human anniversaries. Ted Hughes' own collection, *Birthday Letters* (1998), pays homage to the importance such occasions had for Plath, and to her life-long tradition of commemorating them with letters and poems.

The titles of many of these half-century pieces are revealing: 'Fifty Years Gone, Yet Plath Lives On';[9] 'Why Sylvia Plath Still Haunts Us';[10] 'Out of the Ash, Sylvia Plath's Legend Rises Anew';[11] 'Debate Continues to Rage Over Lady Lazarus, Sylvia Plath';[12] 'Why Sylvia Plath Remains an Icon'.[13] Many are self-conscious about the circumstances that occasioned them, and about the need to take stock of Plath's meaning fifty years on.

These titles seem to promise so much – they are so dramatic, so emphatic, in their pronouncements. They appear to move seamlessly between attention to Plath herself and to her work; though this is perhaps the effect of accumulation, the unintentional consequence – as has so often been the case – is to imply that the woman and her writing are the same thing.

For the most part, the pieces themselves are far more nuanced than the proliferation of titles would indicate. Yet the question of why Plath continues to haunt us is a difficult one to answer. Perhaps this is because the reasons are too multiple, contingent, and contradictory to classify in any simple way. Many of these writers, nonetheless, make some suggestive observations in feeling their way towards addressing it. What is apparent – though with a few notable exceptions – is that Plath criticism has moved on in the last decade, influencing journalism and general readers towards a more sophisticated engagement with her writing and a knowingness about the concatenation of factors that influence our ways of making sense of it.

A New *Bell Jar* and a New *Ariel*

We cannot make sense of *Ariel* without considering it alongside *The Bell Jar*. This is not simply because Plath literally wrote some of these poems on the back of manuscript pages from her novel, very probably reading the prose on one side of the sheet before going on to compose a poem on the other.[14] The connections between *The Bell Jar* and *Ariel* – though extremely specific in terms of the links between particular sentences and lines – also touch on Plath's larger concerns and methodology. Moreover, the simultaneity of anniversaries – the writing of the October poems, the publication of *The Bell Jar*, Plath's death, the discovery of the *Ariel* manuscript – emerges out of the enmeshed relationship between Plath's prose and poetry.

For Lavinia Greenlaw, Esther Greenwood's thoughts 'heighten and fix in images as brilliant and exact as any poems'.[15] One example of this occurs in *The Bell Jar*'s first paragraph. With only eight words – 'the fusty, peanut-smelling mouth of every subway' – Plath captures the historical and cultural mood, the novel's setting, the sensory experiences of sight and scent, and the heroine's sardonic and utterly clear and original view of her world.[16] Again and again in *The Bell Jar*, Plath demonstrates a rare combination of a poet's economy and a novelist's ability never to lose sight of the story she is telling. Plath could not have written a novel with *The Bell Jar*'s visual and linguistic precision, freshness and power if she were not a poet.

Nor could she have achieved the compelling narrative voices and enthralling stories that underpin the poems if she were not a novelist. One example of this can be found in the drama of the trapped speaker in 'Gulliver'. She talks to herself in the second person, chiding and inciting herself to escape her predicament: 'You, there on your back'.[17] The second person always strikes me as a point of view that can manage a particularly intense rhetorical blend of intimate involvement and illusory detachment (as if to pretend, *this isn't really me, it's you*). The speaker of 'Gulliver', like so many of *Ariel*'s narrators, possesses the idiomatic chattiness and energy that we find in Esther Greenwood's voice. The latter, on rare occasions – and especially when in deepest crisis – can also slip into the second person: 'The more hopeless you were, the further away they hid you.'[18] Kate Moses reminds us that Esther tells her story retrospectively, from the vantage point of a mother. Moses then goes on to make the connection between the novel and the poems: 'Plath's *Ariel* was no less a story of redemption than *The Bell Jar*: the story of a woman, a mother, a daughter, a wife, an artist who still believed not just in the possibility of happiness, but in herself.'[19] Add to this Plath's deliberate care over the novelistic narrative arc in *Ariel*; her determination that the individual poems should accumulate meaning through their connections to one another and be sequenced as if they were chapters; her wish to tell a story beginning with the word 'Love' and ending with the word 'spring'.

Marsha Bryant reminds us of another key textual relationship between Plath's fiction and poetry: that of advertising, which creates 'drama through inflated rhetoric and outrageous claims. And like Plath's poems, fifties ads transformed domestic space into a dreamscape of daily miracles.'[20] This commercial rhetoric – and the impossible promises of the products it promotes – is mocked in the clothing offered to the speaker of 'The Applicant'. The suit 'is waterproof, shatterproof, proof / Against fire and bombs through the roof'.[21] There are many comparable instances in *The Bell Jar*. One occurs when Esther alludes sardonically to the 'size seven patent leather shoes I'd bought in Bloomingdale's one lunch hour with a black patent leather belt and black patent leather pocket-book to match' as well as the 'skimpy, imitation silver-lamé bodice stuck on to a big, fat cloud of white tulle' which she wears 'on some Starlight Roof, in the company of several anonymous young men with all-American bone structures hired or loaned for the occasion'.[22] In the poem and in the novel, it is all empty, fake, and ludicrously dissatisfying.

Emily Temple sums up *The Bell Jar*'s historical relevance: 'in the last 50 years, Sylvia Plath's one and only novel has become a cult favorite, a classroom staple, and a source of inspiration and solace for thousands of young people'.[23] Edel Coffey reflects directly on why *The Bell Jar* continues to be pertinent: 'it is a coming-of-age-tale that focuses on the difficulty of moving … into the uncertain world of adulthood'; moreover, 'Esther's voice still feels contemporary, despite the period detail that pervades the novel.'[24] One of my favourite such 'period details' is the reference to 'those "P.Q.'s wife wears B.H. Wragge" ads'.[25] It is yet another of the novel's numerous allusions to advertising and commodification. With the word 'those' Plath captures their pervasiveness and familiarity as a cultural code, as well as the specific recognizability of this particular ad.

The ad – just one short sentence – promises not merely an item of clothing, but also the kind of person its wearer can become by purchasing it: like Betsy, elegant and happy and beautiful but non-threatening. She is a sexually well-adjusted and normative woman who is so desirable she belongs to a man; she is before all else 'P.Q.'s wife'. The ad also promises the socio-economic position a woman can occupy by being seen in B. H. Wragge clothes: 'As the 1950s came along' and B. H. Wragge's 'college age customers were married and became young matrons, he added dresses and evening wear'.[26] These 'young matrons', then, were dutifully domestic but nonetheless glamorous and well-heeled and carefully groomed, with husbands who could afford to package them accordingly.

A recurring emphasis in the anniversary articles is the very personal impact that *The Bell Jar* has had on readers with aspirations to be much more than 'P.Q.'s' beautifully dressed 'wife'. Andrew Wilson believes 'that many, many women and many people connected with Plath's poetry and her work to such an extent because they saw her as a person, as a real woman dealing with very real concerns'.[27] For Jessica Ferri, Plath 'remains an icon because we can assign whatever story we'd like to her life', and there are 'a whole slew of reasons to read' her: '*The Bell Jar*'s surprising humor, the violent and beautiful poetry of *Ariel*, the vivacious journals that are both completely relatable and horribly neurotic'.[28] For Megan Behrent, 'Fifty years later, Plath's voice still has profound resonance. In a world where the gains of the women's movement have been severely eroded, her tale is all too relevant.'[29] For Sarah Churchwell, Plath is reborn like Lady Lazarus 'for a fresh generation of readers'. This is because Plath is 'a lightning rod for our culture's attitudes towards women' and because 'her virtuosity is on display throughout' *Ariel*; 'women poets had never written like this before'.[30] For Andrew Wilson, 'We sort of project all of our fantasies onto her.'[31]

Ali Smith and Mariella Frostrup are far from alone in recent counters to previous doom-readings of *The Bell Jar*. Smith remarks that it is 'so witty, so unexpectedly funny, so sharp, so artless seeming, so beautifully made'. Frostrup notes that it is 'full of all the vitality and excitement and expectation'[32] of a young woman. Jennifer Egan echoes this point: 'what I retained from *The Bell Jar* was mostly a sense of the narrator's irrepressible effervescence'.[33] Margaret Drabble captures *The Bell Jar*'s uniqueness, and legacy, perfectly: 'This is a novel about ambition and desire, about a woman's refusal even to contemplate life as a doormat. Esther wants everything. She's funny, vivid, extreme. There had been few heroines like her in fiction, but many more were to follow in her wake.'[34] Drabble's point is made literally in the novel, when Esther tells us: 'And I knew that in spite of all the roses and kisses and restaurant dinners a man showered on a woman before he married her, what he secretly wanted when the wedding service ended was for her to flatten out underneath his feet like Mrs Willard's kitchen mat.'[35]

Mariella Frostrup sees evidence in the novel for Plath's 'awareness of how different her writing is to what went before'. Ali Smith develops this point, arguing that *The Bell Jar* is self-consciously about 'reading materials', showing that 'there are other ways to understand how fictions work'.[36] We see this again and again in the novel, for instance when Esther comments that 'I didn't know magazines bought stories in lots of six,'[37] once more alluding to commerce and commodification, in this case of literature itself. Everything is for sale – poet and poem, body and word, artefact and myth. It is an idea that is also at the root of Lady Lazarus's pronouncement that 'there is a charge, a very large charge / For a word or a touch / Or a bit of blood / Or a piece of my hair or my clothes'. The 'charge' here is not only a literal electric shock and dramatic thrill. It is also the price that spectators must pay for watching the spectacle, and for material contact with it – as well as the toll it takes on the performer.

But there is more to writing than its mere sale, of course, and in *The Bell Jar* Esther has a silent fantasy of telling Buddy that 'a good poem lasts a whole lot longer than' the 'dust' of the human bodies he cuts up.[38] Later in the novel, she declares, 'I hated the very idea of the eighteenth century, with all those smug men writing tight little couplets and being so dead keen on reason.'[39] Esther's position here is that of a young, aspiring woman writer facing the heavy weight of male literary and intellectual tradition. She is specific about the technical and conceptual aspects of this tradition from which she wants to free herself. We might see Esther's statement as a kind of justification for the lyric and the prominence it gives to subjectivity. Yet given the complexity of Plath's own writing, both in form and in content, it would be misguided to read Esther's statement as Plath's own manifesto.

Plath herself does not advocate for a poetics that is purely personal and technically uncontrolled. As she put it in her famous interview with Peter Orr in October 1962:

> I cannot sympathise with these cries from the heart that are informed by nothing except a needle or a knife ... I believe that one should be able to control and manipulate experiences ... with an informed and an intelligent mind. I think that personal experience is very important, but ... it should be *relevant*, and relevant to the larger things, the bigger things such as Hiroshima and Dachau and so on.[40]

Jacqueline Rose reminds us that if *The Bell Jar* 'is important, it is because it weaves its brilliant depiction of the tortuous professional and personal life of a young would-be female writer into the landmark events of 1950s America'.[41] The same point could be made of *Ariel*, full as it is of individual stories and voices that are underpinned by a wide frame of references reaching beyond any single self. Though the following categories are incomplete and rudimentary, and bleed into one another, *Ariel* encompasses the consequences of contemporary medicine and science ('Thalidomide', 'Lesbos'); the imagery of war wounds ('The Applicant', 'Lady Lazarus'); world history ('Cut', 'The Courage of Shutting-Up', 'Berck-Plage', 'Getting There', 'Daddy'); and environmental toxins ('Elm', 'The Detective', 'Fever 103').

Sharon Olds tells us, 'my debt to Plath is incalculable: her fierceness and originality and embodiment of family passions had been long and powerfully present when I began to write the poems of my adult life'.[42] For Liesl Schillinger, 'the question that today has fresh urgency is how she *wrote*'. A 'new generation of women' are attuned to what the poet Sandra Beasley describes as Plath's 'struggle to make her way in the professional world' and what Mark Wunderlich accounts for as the 'permission' Plath gives them 'to express a particular kind of rage that is not self-annihilating and is not simply bitchy'. The poet Tracy K. Smith is drawn to 'extreme urgency of emotion with lyric precision and forms',[43] while the writer Sarah Manguso argues that 'Though the facts of her life won't soon fade from historical memory, Plath is now, at least, more poet than suicide.'[44]

It is important when evaluating Plath's legacy that we do not see it as beginning and ending with *Ariel*. The poet Craig Morgan Teicher considers Plath's first published book of poetry, *The Colossus*. Here, he finds 'the way toward the poet Plath would become', so that 'the excruciatingly intense gaze that Plath has been honing begins to become not just the poems' tool, but their subject'.[45] The poet Dan Chiasson's remarkably attentive meditation on *Ariel* is called 'Sylvia Plath's Joy'. His title – in particular, the last word of it, 'Joy' – is symptomatic of the depth of the change in how she is regarded. He writes:

> A time of day, dawn, made sharp by anticipated interruption; a house animated by children, their happiness, their demands, their balloons and playthings; the potential for violence innate in all beauty, as well as the awful beauty of violence; the feeling of elation at filling a house with the clacking of a typewriter, and the fear of the silence when the typing ends: these elements are my personal *Ariel*.

Chiasson's penultimate sentence is this: 'Add to the available accounts of Plath (there are so many) this, please: nobody brought a house to life the way she did.'[46] It is a revisionist plea.

Other writers express similarly transformative views in the anniversary pieces. Austin Allen describes 'Poppies in October' as '*both* an ecstatic celebration of her creative / destructive powers and a quiet pre-elegy for herself'.[47] Felicity Plunkett addresses the same theme in different terms, stating that 'From a young age, Plath was aware of the posthumous lives of artists and set about curating her own.'[48] Plath alludes to this 'curating' in a letter to her mother on 20 November 1961. She writes, 'Did I tell you I got 100 pounds ($280) for about 130 pages of poetry manuscript of mine from a bookseller in London who is buying stuff for the University of Indiana?'[49] This '130 pages' was the start of the Lilly Library's Plath archive. James Parker makes the point that '*Ariel* has more than one voice,' something that was celebrated on 26 May 2013, when '40 leading female poets and performers read one poem each from the restored edition'[50] of *Ariel* at the Royal Festival Hall. Parker goes on to describe Plath's world as 'exerting its tractor-beam fascination on American culture'.[51]

One of countless perfect examples of this 'tractor-beam fascination' occurs when Esther Greenwood glimpses the myth-making that surrounds what might be regarded as one of the most consummately American foods ever created:

> we had been shown around the endless glossy kitchens and seen how difficult it is to photograph apple pie à la mode under bright lights because the ice-cream keeps melting and has to be propped up from behind with toothpicks and changed every time it starts looking too soppy.[52]

What we have here is again poetic as much as fictional: it is acutely visual, and possesses the wry tone that runs beneath the *Ariel* poems. In the opening lines of 'Lesbos',[53] Plath turns her lens on another peculiarly American version of staged consumer fakeness, and the part that photographic production plays in it: 'Viciousness in the kitchen! / The potatoes hiss. / It is all Hollywood, windowless, / The fluorescent lights wincing on and off like a terrible migraine.'[54] Jacinta's Le Plastrier describes the *Ariel* poems as a 'fusing' of 'almost-perfected, virtuosic technical skills, groomed and grittily disciplined over her lifetime's writing, with a new plumbing of free-verse innovation', and an attention to a 'physicalised, internal reverberation'.[55] Le Plastrier experiences this fusing especially in 'Daddy', but we have seen that this is something we encounter in other poems too, as well as in *The Bell Jar.*

New Controversies

It is in this context that we can place one of the most notable controversies that emerged at the time of these half-century milestones: that is, the passionate responses elicited in readers by Faber & Faber's release of a new cover for *The Bell Jar*'s fiftieth anniversary edition.[56] It 'shows a bright picture of a woman looking into a powder compact'.[57] Again, the titles of the articles tell the story: '*The Bell Jar*'s New Cover Derided for Branding Sylvia Plath Novel as Chick Lit';[58] '*The Bell Jar* Gets a Hideous Makeover';[59] 'Silly Covers for Lady Novelists';[60] '*The Bell Jar* Cover Inspires Online Parodies'.[61] Condemnation of the new cover, however, is not unanimous. Kirsty Grocott gives her own article a kind of counter-title: '*The Bell Jar*'s New Cover is Just Perfect: No Chick-Lit in Sight',[62] while Janet Badia concludes her own title with a circumspect question mark: '*The Bell Jar* as Chick Lit?' Badia writes, 'one has to imagine that Plath, who strove to get as much of her writing into print as she could, would have welcomed' the new cover.[63] Badia's is a convincing view, particularly for readers who will regard the new cover as a much-needed departure from the many editions of *The Bell Jar* that are decorated with Plath's own image.[64]

The debate about the cover results in an interesting discussion about the nature of Plath's work and audience. Cathy Rentzenbrink is concerned that those who deride the cover's supposed association with 'chick lit' do so out of an assumption 'that reading is for the elite'.[65] Jacqueline Rose reminds us of how seriously Plath took 'popular fiction', and has a 'hunch that [Plath] would have loved' the new cover.[66] Elizabeth Winder makes the important point that 'Sylvia Plath was fully immersed in the material culture of her time. She took real pleasure in clothes, makeup, magazines, and food – a fact that runs counter to crude reductions of Plath as a tortured artist;'[67]

Rentzenbrink admires the new cover's attention to 'the uneasy relationship between art and commerce' and to women's often 'complicated relationship with their appearance'.[68] This subject matter threads its way not just through Plath's novel, but through her stories and poems too.

The cover could be regarded, as Maeve O'Brien suggests, as 'deeper than people may first imagine', providing 'a new way of reading a writer – fifty years after her death'.[69] As Grocott, Badia, and others argue, the design is attentive to *The Bell Jar*'s deliberate and sustained critique of women's preoccupation with their bodies as commodities, and with social expectations of female beauty and presentation. Plath examines the destructive effects of these expectations. Many of her narrators express dismay in the face of the pressure to be beautiful, and do so in tones that blend knowing irony with complicity. We see this in the speaker of 'Death & Co.' ('He tells me how badly I photograph'[70]); in Esther Greenwood ('I didn't want my picture to be taken because I was going to cry'[71]); and in the speaker of 'The Applicant' ('A living doll, everywhere you look'[72]). In 'Tulips', the female speaker is relieved when her admission to hospital allows her to relinquish responsibility both for her material goods and for her body: 'My body is a pebble to them, they tend it as water / Tends to the pebbles it must run over … / Now I have lost myself I am sick of baggage.'[73]

The dispute about *The Bell Jar*'s new packaging obscures a significant point. Peter K. Steinberg has undertaken a scrupulous study of textual variants in the editions of *The Bell Jar* that have appeared since its first publication in January of 1963. He demonstrates that 'dozens – if not hundreds – of minor changes and a few major ones to the text … have distorted the way that Plath intended her novel to be read'. Steinberg argues with conviction when he ends his essay with the plea, 'As we approach the fiftieth anniversary of the first publication of *The Bell Jar*, those in control of Plath's estate need to consider reinstating the … version sanctioned by Plath.'[74] While I would not wish to underplay the significance of what a book's cover says about it, and the effect it has on readers, it seems that a vital conversation about the text itself has been sidelined.

Emily Temple reproduces thirty of the novel's many different covers, from multiple countries, and goes on to write, 'we've taken a look at the many changes the cover has gone through over the years – some beautiful, some strange, and some that make us think about it the story [*sic*] in a whole new way'.[75] What is striking here is Temple's recognition of a new order of reader sophistication and knowingness. Temple presumes that the novel's production has an impact on interpretation, and that its packaging manipulates audience response. She is far from alone in recognizing that *The Bell Jar* is constructed by factors external to Plath's own words. Kirsty Grocott reveals how her reading of the book is informed by her own stage of life and experiences, seeing personal context as another crucial factor in reader response. As a young woman, she regarded 'Mrs Greenwood as a mere symbol of the old order, the very thing that Esther was fighting against'. Revisiting the book twenty years later, she 'identified with Esther's mother, imagining if one of my children became ill like Esther does'.[76]

What is remarkable is the novel's mutability; the way it speaks to readers of different ages, and changes with each reading. *The Bell Jar* made Lena Dunham 'feel less alone', which in her view is what 'art is for'.[77] Lesley McDowell describes *The Bell Jar* as 'timeless in its bravery and need for the truth'.[78] Sarah Galo is one of an increasing number of recent readers who want to see Plath's work in ways that reach beyond her death and mental illness. For Galo, *The Bell Jar* helped her to feel 'that someone understood the anxiety of being a young woman in a crazed-and-difficult world'. She remarks on the novel's contemporary relevance: 'in light of the leaks about the NSA surveillance, we find ourselves in an environment too familiar to our protagonist'.[79] *The Bell Jar*'s new cover seems to allude directly to the 'make-up kit'[80] or 'gilt compact' in whose mirror Esther scrutinizes a 'face that … looked bruised and puffy and all the wrong colours'.[81] It captures exactly the anxieties and forms of surveillance to which Galo alludes.

But *The Bell Jar*'s new design is not the only controversy to emerge out of these Plath half-centuries. Of the deluge of essays occasioned by these Plath anniversaries, one has drawn vociferous protests from readers. The level of disquiet calls to mind the virulent critical objections to Anne Stevenson's 1989 book, *Bitter Fame*, made for similar reasons.[82] Terry Castle's 'The Unbearable' is described by Beth Towle as a 'quasi-review'.[83] Stevenson herself, somewhat ironically given the argument of her own book, objects to the fact that 'The Unbearable' does 'little to shift the popular emphasis from [Plath's] sensational story to her remarkable poetry'.[84] No matter who voices this objection, it is nonetheless a legitimate one. Castle refers scornfully to Plath's 'short and appalling life' in the first sentence. She recycles long-familiar caricatures of the writing and 'Plath's story – Otto the bogeyman of "Daddy" and smother-mother Aurelia'.[85]

Towle does a convincing job of enumerating Castle's 'own personal grudge against Sylvia Plath'. Castle's 'Bad Mom' reading of Plath is couched in reductive biographical terms that many Plath readers and critics have left behind.[86] It is difficult to remain impartial when Castle ends her essay by blaming Plath for the tragic suicide of Nicholas Hughes in 2009. It is challenging to maintain any effort to see the best in what a given writer is trying to achieve when Castle then declares in her final sentence, 'I couldn't help wanting to kill her.' Could this be a deliberate echo of the speaker of 'Daddy'? 'The Unbearable' might be fairly characterized as reactionary; as an example of the worst excesses of those pathology readings of Plath. In such readings, everything is a tautology leading to the poet's own death; Castle actually manages to take this to a further extreme – and a particularly cruel one – by including Plath's son.

'The Doom Myth of Sylvia Plath' is a narrative that was central to many of the early responses to Plath's writing and life, and it remains so for Castle.[87] Melissa Bradshaw captures the mood of the majority of the anniversary pieces, and their impulse to leave this behind. She writes, 'To move Sylvia Plath and her work in the way that it deserves, into the twenty-first century, and to hand her over in the best possible way to a new generation of readers, this narrative must be exorcised.'[88] One of Plath's contemporaries, another guest editor during the 1953 *Mademoiselle* summer of Plath's breakdown and attempted suicide, gives us a small – virtually revisionist – biographical anecdote. While Plath chose to interview Elizabeth Bowen for the magazine's special college edition, Laurie Levy's choice of interviewee was the 'composer Richard Rodgers'. Levy tells us, 'I had intended to break into song, once alone with him, at which he'd scream, "A star is born!" I didn't. Nor did he.' Plath's response to Levy's account of the experience was to say, 'You could've at least hummed a bit.'[89] Levy captures Plath's charm and humour when these were not the qualities for which she was famous.

The three biographies that were released to coincide with the anniversaries all try in their own ways to depart from previous accounts. In *American Isis: The Life and Art of Sylvia Plath* (2013), Carl Rollyson attempts 'to depict a joyous, triumphant side of her that is at odds with the legend of the doomed, suicidal poet'. Rollyson wants 'to show off the Sylvia who reveled in the sun and the sea, and who laughed every Sunday night while listening to Jack Benny's radio show'.[90] Andrew Wilson's *Mad Girl's Love Song: Sylvia Plath and Life Before Ted* (2013) also tries to approach its subject differently, countermanding the previously prevalent notion that her life and work began when she met Ted Hughes in February of 1956. In *Pain, Parties, Work: Sylvia Plath in New York, Summer 1953* (2013), Elizabeth Winder's slant is also unique and refreshing. She zeroes in on the same period as Laurie Levy. Like Wilson, she looks closely at the pre-Hughes Plath. Winder wants to bring to life the young woman in a 'bright and tangled real world that she still loved in spite of everything'. She wants to animate the Plath that became lost in the 'cult figure' of so many previous biographies.[91]

Terry Castle – somewhat hypocritically given the tone of 'The Unbearable' – asserts that the world of Plath biographers is 'rancorous'.[92] As Jane Shilling puts it in her own review essay, 'the story of [Plath's] short life has become so barnacled with angry proprietorial argument; so encrusted with the projected wishes and desires of her would-be champions and interpreters, that it is hard to discern the authentic lineaments of the young woman at the heart of the myth; and harder still to read her writing with the clarity that it demands'.[93] It is frustrating that even when Castle is on the threshold of terrain that is worth exploring, she must be grudging:

> it has to be said that Plath's writing captured the central and most disturbing psychic component in the lives of conventional middle-class American heterosexual women of the 1950s and early 1960s: a toxic, typically unconscious longing – sadomasochistic in structure – to be both adored and degraded, cherished and abjected, by a powerful man resembling one's father.[94]

Has to be said? The ambivalence and contradictory desires that the critic here finds in Plath's writing are powerful and real. One wonders why Castle must acknowledge it under sufferance, and what prevents her from going on to undertake a serious examination of the important questions she nearly raises. Something about Plath fascinates and enrages Castle. I would go so far as to say it critically incapacitates her; and the result is an oddly compelling, though disturbing piece of writing.

Anis Shivani provides a carefully considered attempt to address the question of what Plath means at the time of these anniversaries.

> *Ariel* is *not* ultimately about Plath's pathologies; it is about the pathologies that have pushed Plath into a kind of ferocious poetry that scars her yet leaves her untouched. The language in the best poems in *Ariel* is swift, uncomplicated, punchy, the words short and direct, the honesty of the assertive statements undiluted by hedging or excuses. Plath's poetry is so devastating half a century later because she doesn't excuse anyone or anything, least of all herself ... Plath, on the other hand, makes leaping connections which lead to refusal of self-pity ... In describing the feminine, dichotomies are always easily at hand. Radical poetry demolishes these binaries.[95]

By focusing on detail and technique, Shivani tackles the important point about ambivalent and contradictory desires that Castle neglects.

However contested 'The Unbearable' may deservedly be, the reactions against it reveal the aspirations of Plath's twenty-first-century readers and critics. Their insistence that biographies and literary criticism be measured, accountable and just. Their rejection of those which operate through reactionary and now-debunked methodologies. Their demand for responses to Plath's writing that open up new methods of reading it.

It is a privilege to be part of an ever-growing community of Plath scholars. There are of course disagreements, debates and differences of emphasis. But we have all, in our various ways, done our best to give Plath's poetry and prose the attentiveness and care they deserve. These anniversary pieces – and the new generation of talented researchers who have written them – demonstrate how far Plath's readers and critics have come in fifty years. And they show us, yet again, that there is still so much more to say.

Notes

1. Austin Allen, '"O My God, What Am I": Sylvia Plath's Miracle Month', *Big Think* (31 October 2012). Last accessed 9 October 2013. Available at: http://bigthink.com/book-think/o-my-god-what-am-i-sylvia-plaths-miracle-month
2. Clea Gibson, '50 Years Later, the Power of Plath Prevails'. *Lippy Magazine* (18 February 2013). Last accessed 12 October 2013. Available at: http://www.lippymag.co.uk/comment-50-years-later-the-power-of-plath-prevails
3. Tess Taylor, 'Reading Sylvia Plath 50 Years After her Death is a Different Experience', *NPR* (12 February 2013). Last accessed 3 October 2013. Available at: http://www.npr.org/2013/02/12/171837305/reading-sylvia-plath-50-years-after-her-death-is-a-different-experience
4. Anne Stevenson, 'On Sylvia Plath', *The New York Review of Books*, 60(15) (10 October 2013). Last accessed 13 October 2013. Available at: http://www.nybooks.com/articles/archives/2013/oct/10/sylvia-plath/
5. Emma Garman, 'Out of the Ash, Sylvia Plath's Legend Rises Anew', *Salon* (27 January 2013). Last accessed 6 October 2013. Available at: http://www.salon.com/2013/01/27/out_of_the_ash_sylvia_plaths_legend_rises_anew/
6. Brenda McKeon, 'Birthday Letter: Sylvia Plath and "Daddy"', *The Paris Review* (12 October 2012). Last accessed 7 October 2013. Available at: https://www.theparisreview.org/blog/2012/10/12/birthday-letter-sylvia-plath-and-%E2%80%9Cdaddy%E2%80%9D/
7. Sylvia Plath, *Ariel: The Restored Edition* (London: Faber & Faber, 2004), p. 12.

8. Sylvia Plath, *Ariel: The Restored Edition*, p. 14.
9. Philippa Hawker, 'Fifty Years Gone, Yet Plath Lives On', *The Sunday Morning Herald* (9 February 2013). Last accessed 12 October 2013. Available at: http://www.smh.com.au/entertainment/books/fifty-years-gone-yet-plath-lives-on-20130208-2e3nj.html
10. James Parker, 'Why Sylvia Plath Still Haunts Us', *The Atlantic* (June 2013). Last accessed 6 October 2013. Available at: http://www.theatlantic.com/magazine/archive/2013/06/why-sylvia-plath-haunts-us/309310/
11. Emma Garman, 'Out of the Ash, Sylvia Plath's Legend Rises Anew'.
12. Felicity Plunkett, 'Debate Continues to Rage Over Lady Lazarus, Sylvia Plath', *The Australian* (23 March 2013). Last accessed 14 October 2013. Available at: http://www.theaustralian.com.au/arts/review/debate-continues-to-rage-over-lady-lazarus-sylvia-plath/story-fn9n8gph-1226601837342
13. Jessica Ferri, 'Why Sylvia Plath Remains an Icon', *Dame Magazine* (11 February 2013). Last accessed 10 October 2013. Available at: http://www.damemagazine.com/2013/02/11/why-sylvia-plath-remains-icon
14. See the reading of 'Elm' in Tracy Brain, *The Other Sylvia Plath* (Harlow: Longman, Pearson Education, 2001), pp. 105–11.
15. Lavinia Greenlaw, quoted in 'Sylvia Plath: Reflections on her Legacy', *The Guardian* (8 February 2013). Last accessed 13 October 2013. Available at: http://www.theguardian.com/books/2013/feb/08/sylvia-plath-reflections-on-her-legacy
16. Sylvia Plath, *The Bell Jar* (1963) (London: Faber & Faber, 2005), p. 1.
17. Sylvia Plath, *Ariel: The Restored Edition*, p. 55.
18. Sylvia Plath, *The Bell Jar*, p. 154. For further discussion of Plath's use of the second person, see Tracy Brain, 'Story, Body, and Voice: Dating and Grouping Sylvia Plath's Poems', in William Buckley (ed.), *Critical Insights: Sylvia Plath* (Pasadena, CA, and Hackensack, NJ: Salem Press, 2013), pp. 70–91.
19. Kate Moses, quoted in 'Sylvia Plath: Reflections on her Legacy', *The Guardian*.
20. Marsha Bryant, 'Plath, Domesticity, and the Art of Advertising', in Janet McCann (ed.), *Critical Insights:* The Bell Jar (Pasadena, CA, and Hackensack, NJ: Salem Press, 2012), p. 180.
21. Sylvia Plath, *Ariel: The Restored Edition*, p. 11.
22. Sylvia Plath, *The Bell Jar*, p. 2.
23. Emily Temple, 'A Fifty-Year Visual History of Sylvia Plath's *The Bell Jar*', *The Atlantic* (16 January 2013). Last accessed 1 October 2013. Available at: http://www.theatlantic.com/entertainment/archive/2013/01/a-50-year-visual-history-of-sylvia-plaths-the-bell-jar/267227/
24. Edel Coffey, 'Sweet Out of the Jar: Sylvia's Masterpiece Still Shines Bright 50 Years On', *The Independent* (22 December 2012). Last accessed 10 October 2013. Available at: http://www.independent.ie/lifestyle/sweet-out-of-the-jar-sylvias-masterpiece-still-shines-bright-50-years-onedel-coffey-on-the-50th-anniversary-of-the-bell-jar-sylvia-plaths-famous-novel-about-a-woman-coming-of-age-in-1950s-new-york-28951023.html

25. Sylvia Plath, *The Bell Jar*, p. 6.
26. 'Designer du Jour: B. H. Wragge', *Past Perfect Vintage* (19 August 2011). Last accessed 14 October 2013. Available at: http://pastperfectvintage.blogspot.co.uk/2011/08/designer-du-jour-bh-wragge.html
27. Callie Beusman, 'Andrew Wilson on Plath Behind the Glass', *Interview* (April 2013). Last accessed 14 October 2013. Available at: http://www.interviewmagazine.com/culture/sylvia-plath-mad-girls-love-song/
28. Jessica Ferri, 'Why Sylvia Plath Remains an Icon'.
29. Megan Behrent, 'Trapped in the Bell Jar', *Socialist Worker* (25 March 2013). Last accessed 8 October 2013. Available at: http://socialistworker.org/2013/03/25/trapped-in-the-bell-jar
30. Sarah Churchwell, 'Who is Sylvia Plath?' *Financial Times* (5 April 2013). Last accessed 10 October 2013. Available at: http://www.ft.com/cms/s/2/b86e0e30-9b9d-11e2-8485-00144feabdc0.html#axzz2hAc8YDtM
31. Callie Beusman, 'Andrew Wilson on Plath'.
32. Mariella Frostrup, 'Ali Smith on the 50th Anniversary', *Open Book*, BBC Radio 4 (Broadcast Sunday, 10 February 2013).
33. Jennifer Egan, quoted in 'Sylvia Plath: Reflections on her Legacy'.
34. Margaret Drabble, quoted in 'Sylvia Plath: Reflections on her Legacy'.
35. Sylvia Plath, *The Bell Jar*, p. 80.
36. Mariella Frostrup, 'Ali Smith on the 50th Anniversary'.
37. Sylvia Plath, *The Bell Jar*, Chapter 4, p. 35.
38. Sylvia Plath, *The Bell Jar*, p. 53.
39. Sylvia Plath, *The Bell Jar*, p. 120.
40. Peter Orr, *The Poet Speaks: Interviews with Contemporary Poets Conducted by Hilary Morrish, Peter Orr, John Press and Ian Scott-Kilvert* (London: Routledge & Kegan Paul, 1966), p. 169.
41. Jaqueline Rose, quoted in 'Sylvia Plath: Reflections on her Legacy'.
42. Sharon Olds, quoted in 'Sylvia Plath: Reflections on her Legacy'.
43. Liesl Schillinger, 'Seeing Sylvia Plath with New Eyes', *The New York Times* (3 May 2013). Last accessed 3 October 2013. Available at: http://www.nytimes.com/2013/05/05/fashion/seeing-sylvia-plath-with-new-eyes-cultural-studies.html?pagewanted=all&_r=1&
44. Sarah Manguso, 'You'll Love Her! She's Crazy!' *The New Yorker* (11 February 2013). Last accessed 10 October 2013. Available at: http://www.newyorker.com/online/blogs/books/2013/02/youll-love-her-shes-crazy.html
45. Craig Morgan Teicher, 'On the 50th Anniversary of Sylvia Plath's Death, a Look at Her Beginning', *NPR* (11 February 2013). Last accessed 7 October 2013. Available at: http://www.npr.org/2013/02/11/171186656/on-the-50th-anniversary-of-sylvia-plaths-death-a-look-at-her-beginning
46. Dan Chiasson, 'Sylvia Plath's Joy', *The New Yorker* (12 February 2013). Last accessed 12 October 2013. Available at: http://www.newyorker.com/online/blogs/books/2013/02/ariel-and-sylvia-plaths-joy.html
47. Austin Allen, '"O My God, What Am I"'.
48. Felicity Plunkett, 'Debate Continues to Rage Over Lady Lazarus, Sylvia Plath'.

49. Sylvia Plath, *Letters Home: Correspondence 1950–1963*, ed. Aurelia Schober Plath (London: Faber & Faber, 1975), p. 437.
50. 'Sylvia Plath's *Ariel*'. Not attributed or dated, *Southbank Centre*. Last accessed 12 October 2013. Available at: http://www.southbankcentre.co.uk/whatson/sylvia-plaths-ariel-73622
51. James Parker, 'Why Sylvia Plath Still Haunts Us'.
52. Sylvia Plath, *The Bell Jar*, p. 23.
53. For a fuller discussion of 'Lesbos' see Tracy Brain, 'Medicine in Sylvia Plath's October Poems', *Plath Profiles: An Interdisciplinary Journal for Sylvia Plath Studies*, 6 (Summer 2013): 9–26.
54. Sylvia Plath, *Ariel: The Restored Edition*, p. 38.
55. Jacinta Le Plastrier, '"It was a place of force –" Re-reading the Poems of *Ariel*', *Cordite Poetry Review* (12 June 2013). Last accessed 9 October 2013. Available at: http://cordite.org.au/guncotton/it-was-a-place-of-force-re-reading-the-poems-of-ariel/
56. The cover can be seen on Faber & Faber's website. Last accessed 12 October 2013. Available at: http://www.faber.co.uk/catalog/the-bell-jar/9780571268863
57. Cathy Rentzenbrink, 'Don't Judge the Reader by the Book Cover', *Huffington Post* (12 February 2013). Last accessed 11 October 2013. Available at: http://www.huffingtonpost.co.uk/cathy-rentzenbrink/dont-judge-the-reader-by-the-book-cover_b_2670364.html
58. Alexandra Topping, '*The Bell Jar*'s New Cover Derided for Branding Sylvia Plath Novel as Chick Lit', *The Guardian* (1 February 2013). Last accessed 1 October 2013. Available at: http://www.theguardian.com/books/2013/feb/01/the-bell-jar-new-cover-derided
59. Tracie Egan Morrissey, '*The Bell Jar* Gets a Hideous Makeover', *Jezebel* (23 January 2013). Last accessed 1 October 2013. Available at: http://jezebel.com/5978457/the-bell-jar-gets-a-hideous-makeover/
60. Fatima Ahmed, 'Silly Covers for Lady Novelists', *London Review of Books Blog* (31 January 2013). Last accessed 1 October 2013. Available at: http://www.lrb.co.uk/blog/2013/01/31/fatema-ahmed/silly-covers-for-lady-novelists/
61. Jason Boog, '*The Bell Jar* Cover Inspires Online Parodies', *Storify* (February 2013). Last accessed 1 October 2013. Available at: http://storify.com/jasonboog/sylvia-plath-bell-jar-cover-inspires-online-parodi/preview
62. Grocott, Kirsty, '*The Bell Jar*'s New Cover is Just Perfect: No Chick-Lit in Sight', *The Telegraph* (7 February 2013). Last accessed 6 October 2013. Available at: http://www.telegraph.co.uk/women/womens-life/9854783/Sylvia-Plaths-The-Bell-Jars-new-cover-is-just-perfect-no-chick-lit-in-sight.html
63. Janet Badia, '*The Bell Jar* as Chick Lit?' *Ms. Blog* (5 February 2013). Last accessed 1 October 2013. Available at: http://msmagazine.com/blog/2013/02/05/the-bell-jar-as-chick-lit/
64. For a discussion of how these covers conflate autobiography and fiction, see Tracy Brain, *The Other Sylvia Plath*, Chapter 1.
65. Cathy Rentzenbrink, 'Don't Judge the Reader by the Book Cover'.

66. Jacqueline Rose, quoted in 'Sylvia Plath: Reflections on her Legacy'.
67. Elizabeth Winder, *Pain, Parties, Work: Sylvia Plath in New York, Summer 1953* (New York: HarperCollins, 2013), p. xi.
68. Cathy Rentzenbrink, 'Don't Judge the Reader by the Book Cover'.
69. Maeve O'Brien, '*The Bell Jar* Book Cover Discussion, *The Plath Diaries* (1 February 2013). Last accessed 1 October 2013. Available at: http://theplathdiaries.blogspot.co.uk/2013/02/the-bell-jar-book-cover-discussion.html
70. Sylvia Plath, *Ariel: The Restored Edition*, p. 35.
71. Sylvia Plath, *The Bell Jar*. p. 96.
72. Sylvia Plath, *Ariel: The Restored Edition*, p. 12.
73. Sylvia Plath, *Ariel: The Restored Edition*, p. 18.
74. Peter K. Steinberg, 'Textual Variations in *The Bell Jar* Publications', *Plath Profiles*, 5 (Summer 2012): 104–39.
75. Emily Temple, 'A Fifty-Year Visual History of Sylvia Plath's *The Bell Jar*'.
76. Kirsty Grocott, 'Sylvia Plath's *Bell Jar* Still Haunts Me', *The Telegraph* (11 January 2013). Last accessed 6 October 2013. Available at: http://www.telegraph.co.uk/women/womens-life/9793589/Sylvia-Plaths-Bell-Jar-still-haunts-me.html
77. Lena Dunham, quoted in 'Sylvia Plath: Reflections on her Legacy'.
78. Lesley McDowell, '*The Bell Jar*: by Sylvia Plath', *The Independent* (6 January 2013). Last accessed 9 October 2013. Available at: http://www.independent.co.uk/arts-entertainment/books/reviews/ios-book-review-the-bell-jar-by-sylvia-plath-8439627.html
79. Sarah Galo, 'Why Sylvia Plath's *The Bell Jar* is Still Relevant 50 Years Later, Especially for Millennials', *Policymic*. Last accessed 27 October 2013. Available at: http://www.policymic.com/articles/47265/why-sylvia-plath-s-the-bell-jar-is-still-relevant-50-years-later-especially-for-millennials
80. Sylvia Plath, *The Bell Jar*, p. 3.
81. Sylvia Plath, *The Bell Jar*, p. 98.
82. For a detailed discussion of *Bitter Fame*, see Jaqueline Rose, *The Haunting of Sylvia Plath* (London: Virago Press, 1991), pp. 92–101.
83. Beth Towle, 'Literary Slut-Shaming: Terry Castle and Sylvia Plath', *Actuary Lit* (25 June 2013). Last accessed 4 October 2013. Available at: http://www.actuarylit.com/?p=977
84. Anne Stevenson, 'On Sylvia Plath'.
85. Terry Castle, 'The Unbearable', *New York Review of Books*, 60 (11 July 2013). Last accessed 4 October 2013. Available at: http://www.nybooks.com/articles/archives/2013/jul/11/sylvia-plath-the-unbearable/?pagination=false
86. Beth Towle, 'Literary Slut-Shaming: Terry Castle and Sylvia Plath'.
87. Melissa Bradshaw, 'A Great Many Plathitudes: The Doom Myth of Sylvia Plath', *The Quietus* (10 February 2013). Last accessed 2 October 2013. Available at: http://thequietus.com/articles/11350-sylvia-plath-fifty-year-anniversary

88. Melissa Bradshaw, 'A Great Many Plathitudes: The Doom Myth of Sylvia Plath'.
89. Laurie Levy, 'My Summer with Sylvia Plath', *Chicago Tribune* (28 June 2013). Last accessed 8 October 2013. Available at: http://articles.chicagotribune.com/2013-06-28/features/ct-prj-0630-sylvia-plath-laurie-levy-20130628_1_mademoiselle-printers-row-journal-guest
90. Carl Rollyson, 'What You Don't Know about Sylvia Plath', *Huffington Post* (11 February 2013). Last accessed 14 October 2013. Available at: http://www.huffingtonpost.com/carl-rollyson/sylvia-plath-photos-_b_2648814.html
91. Elizabeth Winder, *Pain, Parties, Work*, pp. 238, 249.
92. Terry Castle, 'The Unbearable'.
93. Jane Shilling, 'Sylvia Plath's Secrets are Hidden in Plain Sight', *The Telegraph* (2 February 2013). Last accessed 12 October 2013. Available at: http://www.telegraph.co.uk/culture/books/9843847/Sylvia-Plaths-secrets-are-hidden-in-plain-sight.html
94. Terry Castle, 'The Unbearable'.
95. Anis Shivani, 'Sylvia Plath 50 Years Later: What Modern Feminism Can Learn from *Ariel*', *Huffington Post* (14 February 2013). Last accessed 7 October 2013. Available at: http://www.huffingtonpost.com/anis-shivani/sylvia-plath-death-anniversary_b_2672685.html

Further Reading

Axelrod, Stephen Gould, *Sylvia Plath: The Wound and the Cure of Words* (Baltimore, MD, & London: The Johns Hopkins University Press, 1990).

Badia, Janet, *Sylvia Plath and the Mythology of Women Readers* (Amherst and Boston, MA: University of Massachusetts Press, 2011).

Brain, Tracy, *The Other Sylvia Plath* (Harlow: Longman, Pearson Education, 2001).

Brain, Tracy, 'Dangerous Confessions: The Problem of Reading Sylvia Plath Biographically', in Jo Gill (ed.), *Confessional Writing* (London: Routledge, 2006), pp. 11–32.

Brain, Tracy, 'Hughes and Feminism', in Terry Gifford (ed.), *The Cambridge Companion to Ted Hughes* (Cambridge: Cambridge University Press, 2011), pp. 94–106.

Brain, Tracy, 'Medicine in Sylvia Plath's October Poems', *Plath Profiles: An Interdisciplinary Journal for Sylvia Plath Studies*, 6 (Summer 2013): 9–26.

Bayley, Sally and Kathleen Connors (eds), *Eye Rhymes: Sylvia Plath's Art of the Visual* (Oxford: Oxford University Press, 2007).

Bayley, Sally and Tracy Brain (eds), *Representing Sylvia Plath* (Cambridge: Cambridge University Press, 2011).

Buckley, William (ed.), *Critical Insights: Sylvia Plath* (Pasadena, CA, and Hackensack, NJ: Salem Press, 2013).

Bundtzen, Linda K., *The Other Ariel* (Amherst, MA: University of Massachusetts Press, 2001).

Butscher, Edward, *Sylvia Plath: Method and Madness* (Tucson, AZ: Schaffner Press, 1976, 2003).

Christina, Britzolakis, *Sylvia Plath and the Theatre of Mourning* (Oxford: Oxford University Press, 1999).

Clark, Heather, *The Grief of Influence: Sylvia Plath and Ted Hughes* (Oxford: Oxford University Press, 2011).

Ferretter, Luke, *Sylvia Plath's Fiction: A Critical Study* (Edinburgh: Edinburgh University Press, 2012).

Frostrup, Mariella, 'Ali Smith on the 50th Anniversary of *The Bell Jar*', *Open Book*, BBC Radio 4 (Broadcast Sunday, 10 February 2013). Accessed 15 October 2013. Available at: http://www.bbc.co.uk/iplayer/bigscreen/radio/episode/b01qhd10/Open_Book_Ali_Smith_on_the_50th_anniversary_of_The_Bell_Jar_Alex_Preston_on_innovation_in_the_novel

Gill, Jo (ed.), *The Cambridge Companion to Sylvia Plath* (Cambridge: Cambridge University Press, 2006).

Helle, Anita (ed.), *The Unraveling Archive: Essays on Sylvia Plath* (Ann Arbor, MI: University of Michigan Press, 2007).

Kendall, Tim, *Sylvia Plath: A Critical Study* (London: Faber and Faber, 2001).

Macpherson, Pat, *Reflecting on The Bell Jar* (London and New York: Routledge, 1991).

Malcolm, Janet, *The Silent Woman: Sylvia Plath and Ted Hughes* (New York: Alfred A. Knopf, 1993).

Middlebrook, Diane, *Her Husband: Hughes and Plath: A Marriage* (London: Little Brown, 2003).

Orr, Peter, *The Poet Speaks: Interviews with Contemporary Poets Conducted by Hilary Morrish, Peter Orr, John Press and Ian Scott-Kilvert* (London: Routledge & Kegan Paul, 1966).

Peel, Robin, *Writing Back: Sylvia Plath and Cold War Politics* (London: Associated University Presses, 2002).

Plath, Sylvia, *Letters Home: Correspondence 1950–1963*, ed. Aurelia Schober Plath (London: Faber & Faber, 1975).

Plath, Sylvia, *Ariel: The Restored Edition* (London: Faber & Faber, 2004).

Plath, Sylvia, *The Bell Jar* (London: Faber & Faber, 1963, 1966, 2008).

Plath, Sylvia, *Drawings* (London: Faber & Faber, 2013).

Rollyson, Carl, *American Isis: The Life and Art of Sylvia Plath* (New York: St Martin's Press, 2013).

Rose, Jacqueline, *The Haunting of Sylvia Plath* (London: Virago Press, 1991).

Stevenson, Anne, *Bitter Fame: A Life of Sylvia Plath* (London: Viking, 1989).

Van Dyne, Susan R., *Revising Life: Sylvia Plath's Ariel Poems* (Chapel Hill, NC, and London: University of North Carolina Press, 1993).

Wagner, Erica, *Ariel's Gift: Ted Hughes, Sylvia Plath, and the Story of Birthday Letters* (London: Faber & Faber, 2000).

Wilson, Andrew, *Mad Girl's Love Song: Sylvia Plath and Life Before Ted* (London: Simon & Schuster, 2013).

Winder, Elizabeth, *Pain, Parties, Work: Sylvia Plath in New York, Summer 1953* (New York: HarperCollins, 2013).

7

'You Asked Me to Sing Then You Seemed Not to Hear': African American Poetry since 1945

Lauri Ramey

Rita Dove raised the concern: 'We all understand the dangers of being put into one little box.'[1] From its origins, African American poetry has been more diverse and innovative than is commonly realized. In the past and present, a persistent bind for this genre has been the criterion of 'authenticity', which has relegated it to narrow stereotypes of how African American poetry should look, sound, and operate. The period from the end of World War II to the present has been an explosive time of poetic experimentation that extends the innovations of Modernism into the twenty-first century. This expanding body of new poetic styles equally builds on the genre's origins. Rather than signalling a departure or new direction, such exploratory and diverse practices are based on long-present trends, goals, and characteristics. These developments are an invitation to re-examine the canon, to speculate on why such dynamic, even difficult, writing has been systematically excluded, and to redraw the picture for a more accurate and richer view of the full range of African American poetry. Exposure to overlooked, under-appreciated, and forgotten voices produces a radically transformed perspective of the scope of recent African American poetry. When examined through the prospect of innovation, a hidden canon is revealed, putting to rest those stereotypes that African American poetry is autobiographical, vernacular, unitary, and exclusively about the theme of oppression. Its legacy of bold challenge to the status quo is a defining trait. This body of writing, whose founding texts are among the most original ever produced in America, proves that tradition and innovation are not mutually exclusive.

African American poetry is a unique and cohesive body of literature with its own tradition, worthy of study in its own right, and an integral component of American identity, literature, and culture. Although this body of poetry is as diverse and varied as its individual creators, some common themes and threads often appear which justify its consideration as a literary tradition: attention to both orality and print culture; themes and impacts of migration, diaspora, and transnationalism; the location and meaning of home and family; African survivals and the role of Africa; imagery of slavery and freedom; the purpose of art as social and political action; art as defining a relationship between the individual and the community; art as a bridge between the present and the past; the deep and spiritual significance of land and place; and concerns with assimilation and self-possession.

The African American poetry tradition is based on the anonymous spirituals, or slave songs. Of unknown origin, they were first transcribed in the nineteenth century. Early auditors described them as 'weird', 'wild', 'unique', 'strange', and 'different' in ways that were hard to define.[2] Even W. E. B. Du Bois, who called them 'the most beautiful expression of human experience born this side of the seas', referred to them as 'weird old songs' containing 'strange word[s]'.[3] Were these sung poems despairing or hopeful, sincere or ironic, primitive or uncanny? Though these spirituals were considered curiosities, critics disregarded their quality and originality. Some attributed their strangeness to being poor imitations of white hymns or verse. Others raised suspicions about the 'foreignness' of their unknown words, sounds, and phrases. Efforts were made to 'translate' these unfamiliar expressions into comprehensible messages. Observers were baffled by their semi-improvisatory, performative, and physical style of oral delivery and communal participation. These features contrasted with contemporaneous ideas of poems as fixed printed texts by sole authors.[4]

From its origins, African American poetry had to be inventive and cleverly subversive. Communication was an immediate challenge for kidnapped Africans, brought together on slave ships from multiple cultures, who needed to establish linguistic and social common ground. When arriving on plantations in America, the enslaved people were legally deprived of literacy. The spirituals needed to be transmitted orally, and serve diverse purposes efficiently. They offered the enslaved peoples a means of expressing their own theology, preserving African survivals, building community, keeping hope alive, communicating during work, relaxing with entertainment, sending messages of resistance to oppression, sharing local and political news, and carrying practical information. It is rare for a body of art to be called upon to mean so much for so many.

The perception of African American poetry as being unlike mainstream Anglo-American verse has been a double-edged sword that has followed the genre through the twentieth century and into the present. It is expected to be 'different' but only in particular ways. The peculiar criterion of 'authenticity' has gone hand in hand with 'otherness'. The more African American poetry is viewed as 'odd', the more it seems to be considered an 'authentic' expression of the language, ideas, and experiences of its creators. Yet, ironically, the demonstrable trajectory of poetries of challenge and change have not been widely embraced as part of the lyric poetry canon. African American poetry is a genre grounded in being thought of as the marked term, reflecting the circumstances of a population that has fought for equality for more than four centuries. Inevitably, the issue of racial discrimination in America is integrally related to perceptions of African American poetry. As Paul Robeson wrote in 'The Negro Artist Looks Ahead' (1951), America is a nation based upon oppression, where black artists in all fields have suffered discrimination, exploitation, and limited opportunities for success and recognition. In spite of the vast influence of African American artists on world culture, Robeson offered numerous examples to show how 'the fruits have been taken from us'.[5]

African American poetry has unquestionably played a unique rôle in identifiable moments in American history in chronicling particular kinds of national experience. For example, the spirituals had an indelible impact on the American character during the time of slavery. They provided a clarion call for the cause of abolition in the US and internationally, and offered community-building sustenance to the enslaved population. After Emancipation, the spirituals' position became more equivocal as they were seen as vestiges of plantation culture and the world of slavery. But perpetuated by organizations such as African American Methodist Churches and the newly established Historically Black Colleges and Universities (HBCUs), the spirituals continued to be an important articulation of African American voices, and a reminder that slavery did occur. They became an indelible part of American history, and evidence that African Americans had not been vanquished – in fact, they had produced works of eternal beauty under conditions of inhuman repression. The spirituals helped generate such uniquely American art forms as ragtime, gospel, blues, rhythm and blues, and jazz. In addition to their key role in musical history, they maintained a central place in religious services of different faiths, and remained potent during later eras of cultural turmoil, including the Civil Rights Movement. Today, they often are performed and recited in concerts, poetry readings, community events, schools, religious services, and political gatherings as symbols of such virtues as the human spirit's tenacity, the value of community, and the eventual conquest of evil by good. Ironically, in some of these primarily white contexts, audiences are unaware that songs such as 'Kumbaya' were authored by African Americans.

With the heyday of the Harlem Renaissance in the 1920s, and the drama of the Civil Rights Movement from about 1960 to 1975, mid-century African American writers have long been left in the position of 'poets between worlds', in the words of R. Baxter Miller.[6] Close examination makes it clear that some of the most extraordinary poets produced major work during a time that cannot be chronologically or stylistically affiliated with the Harlem Renaissance or the Black Arts Movement, although they may have links to both. The aesthetic sensibilities of poets born around the time of World War I were heavily influenced by the Harlem Renaissance but had a major impact on the Black Arts Movement. After World War II, disenfranchisement and alienation reached boiling points, and were in precarious tension with pressures to assimilate and accommodate. Early anthemic poetry by figures such as Ray Durem ('Take No Prisoners') and Raymond Patterson ('Black All Day') helped set the tone for the Black Arts / Black Power Movements to follow. This mid-century period also saw the emergence of two particularly important female voices, Margaret Walker and Gwendolyn Brooks. Poetry of the era displayed a continued expansion of formal possibilities and variety, from prose poems to sonnets to late modernist innovations signalling the coming explosion of postmodern experimentalism.

By 1945, more than a million African Americans had served with distinction in World War II in segregated units of the US military, an astonishing escalation from the few African American soldiers and officers enlisted in 1941. It is a widely acknowledged irony that the fight for Civil Rights continued on the home front while these soldiers risked their lives to represent America abroad. This dichotomy is represented in Gwendolyn Brooks's poem 'Negro Hero' (1945), the title of which interrogates what it means to be a hero as an African American. The poem is a long-lined, declamatory, dramatic monologue written from the perspective of an African American soldier who served abroad in combat. It opens with the line, 'I had to kick their law into their teeth in order to save them.'[7] The speaker explains how he was extolled for his success in battle, both in 'the Caucasian dailies / As well as the Negro weeklies'. This is a subtle commentary on the economic and informational disparities between those two worlds of publishing and readers. Double voicing is apparent in an ironic parenthetical aside, which is whispered editorially under the breath, as if to a different audience. These lines close the second stanza of this historically based persona poem: '(They are not concerned that it was hardly The Enemy / my fight was against / But them.)' Although the speaker is viewed by white society as heroic for fighting a foreign enemy to uphold Democracy, the tone suggests that his true heroism lies in the fight against the real enemy, American racism.

Extending the practices of racial separation in civilian life, the US Armed Forces did not adopt a policy of integration until 1948. While serving in Europe and the South Pacific, African Americans in the military were exposed to international standards and influences, while also spreading African American culture and arts. The prominence of African Americans honorably representing the US in World War II, and the ensuing cultural exchange, helped trigger the explosion of African American poetry from 1945 to the present. At the same time, pernicious discrimination created narrow perceptions of the genre and its creators, and limited the opportunities to disseminate this vibrant and incisive new poetry.

The mid-twentieth century's landmark African American literature anthology was *The Negro Caravan*, originally published in 1941, which summarized the situation of the time succinctly: 'Negro poets have concentrated upon protest poetry more than upon poetry of interpretation and illumination, but Negro poets have often had more to protest than others.'[8] Over the next thirty years, as 'Negro Poets' became 'Black Poets', progress was made to reflect hard-won rights. But in spite of steps forward, there remained a lack of understanding and appreciation of the full scope, variety, and unique value of African American poetry. Here is Stephen Henderson's mournful opening to *Understanding the New Black Poetry: Black Speech and Black Music as Poetic References* (1972), a later critical anthology of equally inestimable importance: 'Black poetry in the United States has been widely misunderstood, misinterpreted and undervalued ... an attempt should be made in which the *continuity* and the *wholeness* of the Black poetic tradition in the United States are suggested.'[9]

Extensive historical material addresses the tumultuous sociopolitical context of the post-war years in the struggle for equality for all Americans, and the slow dismantling of Jim Crow legislation. African American poetry of this period certainly reflects the lingering evils of bigotry, the power and agony of the Civil Rights Movement, the fight for educational and employment parity, and the demand for freedom and equal opportunity for all citizens. Progress has been slow and inconsistent, but steady, as indicated by some milestones among many that could be noted. In 1950, Brooks became the first African American to win the Pulitzer Prize, for *Annie Allen*. That same year, the literary journal *Free Lance*, which Conrad Kent Rivers called 'the oldest black-bossed magazine around', was founded by Russell Atkins.[10] This was the era of the landmark *Brown* v. *Board of Education* decision (1954), where the Supreme Court abolished the policy of segregated schools providing 'separate but equal' education. One year later, a fourteen-year-old African American boy called Emmett Till, accused of whistling at a white woman, was brutally murdered in Mississippi. In 1955, Rosa Parks refused to relinquish her bus seat to a white woman in Montgomery, Alabama. In 1962, Paul Breman, a young Dutchman in London, started the Heritage Series, the first press dedicated to publishing black poetry. Civil Rights activist Medgar Evers was assassinated in 1963. The Freedom Summer took place in 1964, the same year that three young Civil Rights workers – James Chaney, Andrew Goodman, and Michael Schwerner – were murdered in Mississippi. In 1965, *The Autobiography of Malcolm X* was published and Malcolm X was assassinated. In 1966, Robert Hayden's *A Ballad of Remembrance*, the first volume in the Heritage Series, won first prize at the First World Festival of Negro Arts in Dakar, Senegal. The studio album *A Love Supreme* by John Coltrane was released in 1965, the same year as the Watts Riots in Los Angeles. Martin Luther King, Jr. was assassinated in 1968. From 1976 to 1978, Robert Hayden was the first African American Librarian of Congress, the post that later became the US Poet Laureate. From 1993 to 1995, Rita Dove was the first African American woman to be appointed Poet Laureate. The first African American President of the United States, Barack Obama, was elected in 2008, later taking a second term of office in 2012.

Based on these major milestones, beginning with the spirituals, the African American experience – in its full diversity – has progressively developed a body of texts, figures, concepts, events, and experiences that serve as allusions and direct reference points. The spirituals have become ubiquitous as direct references and allusions, and appear in a constellation of poetries with drastically differering goals and styles, including some of the most *avant-garde*. They have been an irresistible resource for postmodern experimentation from mid-century to now because of their identity as a gnostic source, amenability to deconstruction, double voicing, metaphysical and ethical questioning, use of language as an inherently creative material, and semiotic ontology.

Russell Atkins, a member of the older generation of post-WWII *avant-garde* poets, produced an astonishing – and still too little known – body of theoretical writing that pre-dated Deconstruction.[11] Following in the footsteps of predecessors including Paul Laurence Dunbar, Langston Hughes, Melvin B. Tolson, Sterling A. Brown, and countless others, Atkins often uses folk materials to link current practices to African American origins. Since the start of the African American literary tradition, there was a critical split – the repercussions of which are still felt today – between the diasporic 'oral' or 'folk art' and 'literary' or 'high art' verse. This perspective of dualism was exemplified by Paul Laurence Dunbar at the turn of the twentieth century, who famously produced two styles of verse: standard diction and vernacular. While this perspective of dualism has been perpetuated – Ishmael Reed has even produced a poem by this name – there are greater benefits in recognizing that most poets integrate these traditions. Figures such as Atkins, Reed, Langston Hughes, Harryette Mullen, and Amiri Baraka (formerly LeRoi Jones), among many others, have worked in the interstices joining oral and written language.

Written during the period of the Black Arts Movement, Atkins's poem 'Spyrytual' (1966), exemplifies this motive.[12] Contrary to misconceptions of homogeneity, this poem also suggests the wide array of verse that was produced during this politically mobilized era. 'Spyrytual' displays how foundational materials can be inventively repurposed as a living legacy for postmodern readers. This concrete poem reflects the international influences of Guillaume Apollinaire's Calligrammes – in particular, the poem 'Il Pleut', which spatially and typographically depicts the image of a heavy rainstorm. By changing the 'i' in 'spirituals' to 'y', Atkins extends the experiments of the historical *avant-garde* by defamiliarizing this word visually, auditorally, and semantically. By doing so, he liberates this product of slavery, releasing 'spirit' and 'spiritual' from a possible state as frozen signifiers into new realms of re-animated meanings. Instead of a rhyme with 'ear' – and evocations of the oral tradition which birthed the spirituals – the 'y' repositions readers in a later era of technological advances. Oral and textual frames are mapped over each other and coexist, as the past is thrust into the present.

The first syllable can be broken into refreshed lexical units: 'pyre', 'spy', and 'spire'. 'Pyre' guides the eye to see the word clusters in the poem's layout as piles of combustible agents at a funeral, lighting the fires that the poem's renewing rain has the power to extinguish. 'Spy' – suggesting a political game of cat and mouse – implies the surreptitious role of the spirituals as subterfuge and hidden messages.

'Spires', the architectural structures forming the pyramidal roofs of churches, cleverly evokes the religious dimension of the spirituals. The contemporary poet, in a sense, is raising the roof as an integral participant in the continuous process of building on these folk products. The poem is structured as call-and-response, but one between the oral and textual domains, the past and the present. The call alludes to the spiritual 'Oh Didn't It Rain?', but the response echoes back from the textual world of the future. The sets of quotation marks, mimicking the appearance of raindrops, can be read visually, but have no oral or aural equivalents. The poem cannot be wholly 'read' or wholly 'recited'; rather, both actions are needed for its full comprehension.

From 1945 to 1975, a tradition of diverse and difficult African American poetry was formulated, though it may have been marginalized from most collections of black and white verse. From 1975 to the present, building on powerful precursors, this tradition has solidified and is moving forward. Douglas Kearney, a younger generation intermedia experimentalist, also shows the continuing presence of the oral and folk traditions in *avant-garde* African American poetry. Kearney frequently incorporates folk materials in his writing, often positioning them, both rhetorically and spatially, as alternately familiar and precarious. Similarly to Atkins, he problematizes water as a fraught symbol in African American history, in his poem 'Floodsong 2: Water Moccasin's Spiritual' (2009). Water is essential to life, yet it is also the medium of the Middle Passage, in which Africans were transported to enslavement. Drowning at sea while in transit – due to illness, murder, or suicide – was the fate of untold captives.

The spiritual that forms the allusive frame of this poem is called 'Wade in the Water' or 'God's a-Gwineter Trouble the Water'. It is a powerful anthem of retributive justice. The reference to the snake in the poem's title foreshadows the presence of evil in this Edenic scene. Kearney's poem opens with a virtually classic evocation of the spiritual's lyrics: 'wade in the water / wade in the water, children / wade in the water / god's gon' trouble the water'.[13] The spiritual expresses faith in God. In Exodus, God drowned the Pharoah's army, delivering the enslaved Hebrews to safety in the Promised Land, and the spiritual conveys a belief in God's power to comparably intervene once again, and free the enslaved African Americans. After eight lines that echo the original spiritual, Kearney's poem cannot manage to continue in that vein of optimism. The salvaged text begins to break down and stutter: 'wade in / wade in / wade in', lemming-like, or a broken record stuck on an ominous note. Is this an invitation or a warning about wading in? Where is God? What has become of the central metaphor of God as the protective parent of children? The mid-section of this one-stanza poem breaks down even more as the original components keep going awry: 'trouble / in the water' devolves further still into the pronouncement at the end: 'god's gon', with a lower case 'g' for the deity. 'Gon' in the spiritual, meaning 'going to', implying intended action, transforms phonetically into 'gone', an absence of action, in Kearney's bleaker retelling for current times.

Literary criticism typically has regarded 'black' and '*avant-garde*' writing as unrelated, even antithetical, bodies. There are extensive studies of the innovators of white modernism and postmodernism, but surprisingly little attention paid to the long legacy of African American experimentalism. Formally exploratory poetics is 'normative' for white *avant-garde* poets who are interested in decentring and re-conceptualizing identity, examining literary connections across metaphysical boundaries with others who have engaged in experimental practices, transcending the restrictions of genre and form, and interrogating language as a system of discourse. Why have African American poets working in similar terrain not had comparable attention and impact? The goal of 'destabilizing' or 'interrogating' boundaries, and the power that derives from a position of providing critique to the cultural centre, are mentioned by many African American poets whose writing is associated with stylistic innovation. That includes older figures such as Reed, Atkins, Baraka (Jones), Jayne Cortez, Bob Kaufman, Ted Joans, Lloyd Addison, Tom Weatherly, Stephen Jonas, Percy Johnston, N. H. Pritchard, Oliver Pitcher, De Leon Harrison, Elouise Loftin, Ed Roberson, and A. B. Spellman.

The next generations of progressive and visionary African American poets working in related modes include Mendi Lewis Obadike, Dawn Lundy Martin, Will Alexander, Claudia Rankine, Ron Allen, Erica Hunt, John Keene, Kearney, Tracie Morris, Julie Patton, Harryette Mullen, C. S. Giscombe, and Nathaniel Mackey. As white experimental writing has been mined for a century – since the time of T. S. Eliot, Hart Crane, Ezra Pound, and William Carlos Williams – or even a century earlier with the innovations of Emily Dickinson and Walt Whitman – it is clear that history has not evaluated poetry solely on the basis of style and quality, but also on the basis of who wrote it.

African American poets associated with practices of stylistic innovation often show great inventiveness by drawing on a variety of formally innovative trends associated with the historical *avant-gardes*, and blending them with African American references and racial signifiers. Their work contains numerous and varied references to writers, artists, musicians, activists, and political figures and events, both within and outside of African American culture and traditions. They purposely incorporate and slyly signify on the dual levels of meaning-making encompassed in Du Bois' concept of double consciousness. Much of this writing explores the uses of unconventional forms: prose poems, collages, fragments, inter-media forms, and mixed forms. The poetry also displays other features that are normative in *avant-garde* practices from Modernism to the present: the absence, questioning, or decentring of unitary speaking subjects or identities; breakdowns of conventional genre boundaries and expectations; play with absurd or ironic juxtapositions taken from widely contrasting realms of information and language uses; contrasting discourses coming from inside and beyond African American reference points; intermingling of allusions, imagery and dictions from American and international high and low art and culture, and diverse fields of knowledge; use of the double entendre, punning, wit, humour, signifying, and parody; compositional styles reflecting cross-genre and cross-media artistic practices; and reliance on engaged readers to actively construct meaning from these challenging poems.

Experimental poetry and African American poetry are often viewed as separate worlds – meaning that innovative poetry was considered to be white, and African American poetry was considered to be predictable. In the 1980s and 1990s, the majority of anthologies and scholarship on experimental writing focused almost exclusively on white poets. Anthologies and scholarship on African American poetry has rarely discussed innovative and *avant-garde* practices. Why was little or no attention paid to formally innovative African American poetry? Also, if this diverse body of poetry were available and better known, how might it change the African American poetry canon – and even the canons of American and Anglophone poetry?

Coupled with its stylistic diversity, many African American poems address a body of recurring themes, figures, events, and experiences that still provide cohesion as a canon. This lineage of direct references and allusions reveals an African American literary identity that is inextricably connected to the history of America – including themes, people, and events that have had to fight to rise to the surface of mainstream national consciousness, beginning with slavery and progressing through the fight for human rights. Poetic tributes to African American literary precursors and role models offer an alternative pantheon to those usually revered in the Anglo-American tradition. This poetry provides a line of sight on to the figures and events that have had lasting impact on African Americans. This implied narrative may be part of American and world history, but its function and impact have particular weight and meaning in the context of the African American experience.

Some of the most formally progressive and innovative African American poetry serves as a repository to name, honour, perpetuate, and preserve the major figures, influences, events, products, and experiences of African American history. The Middle Passage is the central theme of Lucille Clifton's 'Slaveship', Robert Hayden's 'Middle Passage', and Kearney's 'Swimchant for Nigger Mer-folk (An Aquaboogie Set in Lapis)'. Literary figures are extolled in poems such as 'To Richard Wright' and 'On the Death of William Edward Burghardt Du Bois by African Moonlight and Forgotten Shores' by Conrad Kent Rivers; 'Paul Laurence Dunbar' by Robert Hayden; 'Booker T. and W.E.B.' by Dudley Randall; 'Paul Laurence Dunbar in the Tenderloin' by Ishmael Reed; and 'The Rhetoric of Langston Hughes' by Margaret Esse Danner.

Countless poems are dedicated to figures and movements referring to the African American musical tradition. One of the defining traits of this poetic genre is the use of themes, structures, and compositional procedures of spirituals, blues, ragtime, gospel, jazz, soul, rhythm and blues, and rap. Examples of such poems include 'On Listening to the Spirituals' by Lance Jeffers; 'I've Got a Home in that Rock' by Raymond Patterson; 'Cross Over the River' by Sam Cornish; 'To Satch' (Louis Armstrong) by Samuel Allen; 'Homage to Paul Robeson' by Robert Hayden; 'Paul Robeson' by Gwendolyn Brooks; 'Yardbird's Skull (For Charlie Parker)' by Owen Dodson; 'John Coltrane' by A. B. Spellman; *leadbelly* by Tyehimba Jess; and 'Here is Where Coltrane Is', 'Last Affair: Bessie's Blues Song', 'Dear John, Dear Coltrane', and 'To James Brown' by Michael S. Harper.

Major activists, events, and political figures are frequent poetic subjects. A few examples of many include 'Nat Turner' by Samuel Allen; 'Frederick Douglass', 'The Ballad of Nat Turner', and 'El-Hajj Malik El-Shabazz (Malcolm X)' by Robert Hayden; 'Medgar Evers' and 'Malcolm X' by Gwendolyn Brooks; 'Malcolm's Blues' by Michael S. Harper; 'Possibilities: Remembering Malcolm X' by Haki Madhubuti; 'Saint Malcolm' by Johari Amini; 'Malcolm X – An Autobiography' by Larry Neal; 'For Malcolm: After Mecca' by Gerald W. Barrax; 'Portrait of Malcolm X' by Etheridge Knight; 'Harriet Tubman' by Samuel Allen; 'Harriet Tubman' by Margaret Walker; 'Malcolm Spoke / who listened?' by Haki Madhubuti; 'Harriet Tubman' by Sam Cornish; 'For Malcolm X' by Julia Fields; 'Assassination' by Don L. Lee (Haki Madhubuti) on the murder of MLK; 'The Last Quatrain of the Ballad of Emmett Till' by Gwendolyn Brooks; 'In Memoriam: Martin Luther

King, Jr.' by June Jordan; 'The Funeral of Martin Luther King, Jr.' by Nikki Giovanni; 'Emmett Till' by James A. Emanuel; 'After MLK' by Lloyd Addison; 'Elegy (for MOVE and Philadelphia)' by Sonia Sanchez; and 'The Summer After Malcolm' by Larry Neal.

The concepts of lineage, heritage, family, and home – as well as Africa, as an imagined ancestral homeland – are resonant themes for this diasporic population that was unnaturally separated from its roots. Examples are 'Heritage' by Gwendolyn Bennett; 'Far from Africa: Four Poems' by Margaret Danner; 'The Idea of Ancestry' by Etheridge Knight; 'African Dream' by Bob Kaufman; 'Legacy: My South' by Dudley Randall; 'For My People' by Margaret Walker; and 'The Still Voice of Harlem' by Conrad Kent Rivers.

'O Daedalus, Fly Away Home', by Robert Hayden, combines many of these traits and references as a veritable contemporary spiritual. This poem is replete with diction of the spirituals ('Fly away home'), references to African origins ('Do you remember Africa?'), diasporic diction ('Night is juba'), diasporic survivals, such as the invocation of ancestors as spirit guides ('My gran, he flew back to Africa, / just spread his arms and / flew away home'), and commonplaces of plantation culture ('Pretty Malindy, dance with me'), including references to music ('coonskin drum and jubilee banjo').[14] The spirituals' call-and-response structure is reproduced in the alternation of verses and italicized refrains from the spirituals, all playing on phrasal variants of 'fly away'. It uses such baseline phrases and ideas from the spirituals as 'O cleave the air', with 'cleave' in its polysemous sense of divide and cling. The imagery of 'wings' and 'fly away home' brings together the classical myth of Icarus and Daedalus with the equally classical imagery of the spirituals in African American culture.

The poetry of protest created during the Black Arts Movement of the 1960s and 1970s, by writers such as Baraka, Sonia Sanchez, Haki Madhubuti, Nikki Giovanni and Carolyn Rodgers, radically shaped the political texture of America with lasting impact during a time of national turmoil. These poets, and this movement, foregrounded even more emphatically two major historical themes and technical operations of African American poetry: its integral relationship with music and musicality, and its implicit goal to achieve social benefit. During this period of the Civil Rights and Black Arts Movements, Sonia Sanchez was publishing love poems, LeRoi Jones became Amiri Baraka, and, under Hoyt Fuller, *Negro Digest* became *Black World* and then was discontinued. Jazz poetry intertwined with the Beat and

Black Arts writers. The cross-sections and dialogues of this tumultuous time are less clear-cut than conventional representations may have it, allowing excellent opportunity to imagine a revised and more nuanced perspective.

The period from approximately 1960 to 1975 was highly political, openly dissident, and characterized by artistic self-determination and independence, ranging from issues of style to ownership to production to audience. New York, Chicago, DC, London, and Detroit were some of the dynamic social, political, and creative centres leading to a wealth of poetic production. Yet this era of broadsides and manifestos also generated certain kinds of aesthetic repression – for example, of stylistic divergence and the voices of women – alongside its political and creative productivity and progress.

This period still afforded relatively few publication and review opportunities in mainstream venues for African American poets. Hayden's first full-length collection was published in the London-based Heritage Series, as were early collections by other disparate and experimental poets such as Reed, Atkins, Lloyd Addison, Audre Lorde, Clarence Major, Samuel Allen, and Ray Durem. Other links and lines of communication must be remembered and represented. Dudley Randall – the US distributor of Heritage Press – was able to publish a collection of his own love poems, *Love You* (1971), with the Heritage Series rather than with his own more militant Broadside Press. Jones' resounding 'Preface to a Twenty-Volume Suicide Note' was published in 1961 by Eli and Ted Wilentz's Beat-oriented Corinth Books. In a two-year period, Major published *Symptoms & Madness* with Corinth (1971), two collections with Black presses (*Private Line* with Heritage Press in 1971 and *The Cotton Club* with Broadside Press in 1972), and a fourth collection under a mainstream imprint (*Swallow the Lake*, with Wesleyan University Press, 1970). A number of African American poets (Reed and Lorde as two important examples, in addition to Major) exhibited this level of ingenuity, originality, and a nuanced approach to individual literary artistry during a time of perceived ideological dogmatism.

In addition to the Black Arts Movement as the aesthetic wing – so imagined – of the Black Power Movement, key issues of the era include the relationships of both of those movements to the Civil Rights Movement; to other literary/artistic movements and organizations including Umbra, Free Lance, and Dasein; and to questions of American nationalism/self-empowerment and Pan-African internationalism, separatism, and diasporic consciousness. Little magazines and presses – many Black-owned – rose to particular prominence during this era, notably the literary magazines of HBCUs, and journals such as *Black World* (formerly *Negro Digest*), *Journal of Black Poetry*, *Phylon*, *Umbra*, *Black Dialogue,* and *Soulbook*, along with the advent of Black presses (Broadside, Third World, Heritage, and Lotus) to create an expanding readership for African American poetry.

From approximately the mid-1980s to the present, African American postmodernism has reflected trends of neo-realism, verbal jazz improvisation, L=A=N=G=U=A=G=E Poetry-inspired textual innovation, and hiphop-inflected performance poetries. With the full-blown emergence of performance poetry, spoken word, rap, and poetry slams, performance and orality reach a pinnacle of importance in the 1980s and become organically re-connected to the genre. Organizations such as the Black Took Collective, Cave Canem, and Dark Room Collective have provided support and training, and produced some of today's most prominent young African American poets. M.F.A. programmes in creative writing have become more aesthetically and culturally receptive to the presence and aesthetic goals of African American poets. There have been many artistic advances in the last twenty years, but progress does not signify erasure of memory. African American poetry has become increasingly influential nationally and internationally, though mainly the more conservative manifestations. It is clear that this genre has fully articulated its identity as a body of writing with distinctive features and provenance, which has the capacity to evolve meaningfully. Music soars in the poetry of Harper; slave songs are ironically reformulated in Kearney's *The Black Automaton*; Evie Shockley's *The New Black* is a volume of postmodern self-articulation coupled with close connection to a true family history in the ancient depths of plantation culture. Baraka's 'The Changing Same' sets the tune for the way contemporary African American poetry connects to its past.

Critical race theory grows in relevance in the context of a contemporary environment of racial mixing and 'post-racialism', and in conjunction with issues of American nationalism, ownership, migration, and identity. The ever-present role of music is another important strand carried on from the beginning of the tradition, including the increasing synthesis of African beats with Latin inflections as well as the authentic American products of jazz and blues, and their omnipresent influence on African American poetry and poetics. With the increasing ease of travel and development of the Internet, the international influence of African American poetry and its traditions continues as a topic of strengthening importance. This theme connects to developments in Modernism through the massive strides in technological developments in the early decades of the twentieth century. Previously, the ability to record and distribute poetry by Paul Laurence Dunbar and the spirituals sung by the Fisk Jubilee Singers resulted in international prominence for African American cultural products. Those early developments relate to the recent world-shaking advances and their influence on poetic form, style, production, and reception, including the ease of dissemination and access afforded by technology (examples include the inter-media poetry and sound environments of mendi + keith obadike, the textual innovations of giovanni singleton and Julie Ezelle Patton, among many others), and the impact of digitization and the Internet on diasporic dialogue and contact, including the spread of rap.

This is an auspicious moment for African American poetry to be recognized as an indispensable contribution to the American and Anglophone canon. African American poetry has maintained its traditional role by articulating both individual and communal concerns; using music, language, and performance to convey resistance; and creating unity and self-determined expression. It also has expanded in a wide array of styles and forms. A constant in African American poetry has been a belief that art can produce social change and challenge. African American poetry holds an inextricable role in reflecting and defining American identity, in addition to its ability to inspire world poetry, and serve as a source of literary and cultural inspiration. The last seventy years of African American poetry are the extension of a sophisticated, bold, and brilliantly *avant-garde* legacy once it has been perceived. Formally innovative poetry and black poetry do not have to be divergent bodies of writing. The future will most beneficially incorporate the full range of African American poetry in all of its stylistic, formal, thematic, and conceptual manifestations – including the most 'different' – in order to properly delineate the truth and brilliance of this field. The genre's diversity is now truly staggering; yet it retains a strong and recognizable core of character, concerns, values and manifestations carried along by a gifted cadre of unique and indispensable poetic voices.

Notes

1. Joanne M. Gabbin (Producer) (2015), *Furious Flower* III, DVD. Episode 1, California Newsreel.
2. Some of the early important collections and commentaries on the poetry known as Negro spirituals, slave songs, or plantation verse are William Francis Allen, Charles Pickard Ware, and Lucy McKim (eds), *Garrison Slave Songs of the United States* (1867); William E. Barton (ed.), *Old Plantation Hymns* (1899); E. P. Christy (ed.), *Christy's Plantation Melodies* (1851); and Thomas Wentworth Higginson, *Army Life in a Black Regiment and Other Writings* (1870).
3. W. E. B. Du Bois, Section XIV of 'The Sorrow Songs', in *The Souls of Black Folk*, 'Call & Response', in Patricia Liggins Hill (ed.), *The Riverside Anthology of the African American Literary Tradition* (Boston, MA, and New York: Houghton Mifflin, 1998), p. 749.
4. See, for example, *Methodist Error Or, Friendly, Christian Advice to Those Methodists, who Indulge in Extravagant Religious Emotions and Bodily Exercises* (1819), authored anonymously by 'A Methodist', and later attributed to John F. Watson. See further discussion of the early reception of the spirituals in the Preface and Introduction to Lauri Ramey, *Slave Songs and the Birth of African American Poetry*, 2nd edn (New York: Palgrave Macmillan, 2010), pp. xii–xviii, 1–15.
5. Manning Marable and Leith Mullings (eds), *Let Nobody Turn Us Round: Voices of Resistance, Reform, and Renewal* (Lanham, Boulder, New York, and Oxford: Rowman & Littlefield, 2000), p. 353.
6. R. Baxter Miller (ed.), *Black Poets Between Worlds, 1940–1960* (Knoxville, TN: University of Tennessee Press, 1988).
7. Elizabeth Alexander (ed.), *The Essential Gwendolyn Brooks* (New York: The Library of America, 2005), pp. 16–18.
8. Sterling A. Brown, Arthur P. Davis, and Ulysses Lee (eds), *The Negro Caravan* (New York: Arno Press and *New York Times*, 1970), p. 282.
9. Stephen Henderson, *Understanding the New Black Poetry: Black Speech and Black Music as Poetic References* (New York: William Morrow, 1973), p. 3.
10. Eugene B. Redmond, *Drumvoices: The Mission of African American Poetry: A Critical History* (New York: Anchor Press/Doubleday, 1976), p. 328.
11. Aldon Lynn Nielsen is one of the first and still most astute critics to call attention to Atkins' writing; Paul Breman similarly recognized his value by publishing Atkins' early collection, *Heretofore* (1968), in the Heritage Series. Nielsen discusses Atkins' work in *Black Chant: Languages of African American Postmodernism* (Cambridge: Cambridge University Press, 1997) and *Integral Music: Languages of African American Innovation* (Tuscaloosa, AL: University of Alabama Press, 2004).
12. Russell Atkins, *Spyrytual* (Cleveland, OH: 7 Flowers Press, 1966). This poem is reprinted in Aldon Nielsen and Lauri Ramey (eds), *Every Goodbye Ain't Gone: An Anthology of Innovative Poetry by African Americans* (Tuscaloosa, AL: University of Alabama Press, 2006), p. 14.

13. Douglas Kearney, *The Black Automaton* (Albany, NY: Fence Books, 2009), p. 60.
14. Robert Hayden, *Collected Poems*, ed. F. Glaysher (New York and London: W.W. Norton, 2013), p. 55.

Further Reading

Baker Jr., Houston A., *Afro-American Poetics: Revisions of Harlem and the Black Aesthetic* (Madison, WI: University of Wisconsin Press, 1988).

Benston, Kimberley W., *Performing Blackness: Enactments of African-American Modernism* (New York and London: Routledge, 2000).

Gladman, R. and Giovanni Singleton (eds), 'Expanding the Repertoire: Continuity and Change in African American Writing', *tripwire: a journal of poetics*, Issue 5 (Fall 2001).

Harper, M. S. and A. Walton (eds), *Every Shut Eye Ain't Asleep: An Anthology of Poetry by African Americans Since 1945* (Boston, MA, and New York: Little Brown, 1994).

Henderson, Stephen, *Understanding the New Black Poetry: Black Speech and Black Music as Poetic References* (New York: William Morrow, 1973).

Mackey, N., *Discrepant Engagement: Dissonance, Cross-Culturality, and Experimental Writing* (Tuscaloosa, AL, and London: University of Alabama Press, 1993; Rpt. Cambridge: Cambridge University Press, 2000).

Mullen, Harryette, *The Cracks Between What We Are and What We Are Supposed to Be* (Tuscaloosa, AL, and London: University of Alabama Press, 2012).

Nielsen, Aldon Lynn, *Black Chant: Languages of African-American Postmodernism* (Cambridge: Cambridge University Press, 1997).

Nielsen, Aldon Lynn and Lauri Ramey, *Every Goodbye Ain't Gone: An Anthology of Innovative Poetry by African Americans*, Volume 1 (Tuscaloosa, AL, and London: University of Alabama Press, 2006).

Nielsen, Aldon Lynn and Lauri Ramey, *What I Say: Innovative Poetry by Black Writers in America*, Volume 2 (Tuscaloosa, AL, and London: University of Alabama Press, 2015).

Rampersad, Arnold (ed.), *The Oxford Anthology of African-American Poetry* (Oxford: Oxford University Press, 2006).

Redmond, Eugene B., *Drumvoices: The Mission of Afro-American Poetry: A Critical History* (New York: Anchor/Doubleday, 1976).

Thomas, Lorenzo, *Extraordinary Measures: Afrocentric Modernism and Twentieth-Century American Poetry* (Tuscaloosa, AL, and London: University of Alabama Press, 2000).

Thompson, Gordon E. (ed.), *Black Music, Black Poetry: Blues and Jazz's Impact on African American Versification* (Farnham, Surrey, and Burlington, VT: Ashgate, 2014).

Part II
Form and Genre

8

The Great Divide? Post-confessional and Language Poetry

Paul Batchelor

'Not a *group* but a *tendency*'[1] is how Ron Silliman announced, in 1975, what has since come to be known as Language poetry. Similarly, we should see confessional poetry as a tendency, rather than as a group or movement. The term 'confessional poetry' was coined by M. L. Rosenthal in a review in 1959: the poets most directly associated with the tendency – Robert Lowell, John Berryman, Sylvia Plath, and Anne Sexton, with W. S. Snodgrass and Stanley Kunitz in supporting roles – did not consider themselves a group, and produced no manifesto. As only some of their work can be called confessional, it is misleading to refer to them as the 'confessional poets'. Furthermore, the confessional tendency was only one of several post-war reactions to the supposedly 'impersonal' poetics of Eliot and Pound, which seemed discredited after having proved compatible with fascist sympathies and anti-Semitism. Other avowedly 'personal' poetic movements included Projectivism, with its emphasis on the poet's breath; Frank O'Hara's 'I-do-this-I-do-that' poems and mock-manifesto 'Personism'; poetries of witness that asserted the political identity of the poet; and Beat poetry. Readers familiar with such movements may find it difficult to appreciate the extent to which confessional poetry represented, to many of its initial readers, a radical, decisive break with the high modernist tradition. Today it is more likely to appear timely, or else of its time, in the way it embodies the paradoxes that characterized the Cold War period in the US. The paranoia and insularity that accompanied the country's emergence as the dominant economic global force find a corollary in confessionalism's swaggering vulnerability and theatrical narcissism.

If 'confessional poetry' is a problematic label, 'post-confessional poetry' risks adding a further layer of vagueness, as it must be defined as 'a tendency formed in response to the confessional tendency'. The range of styles that can now be said to have derived something from confessionalism is vast, and would include the work of such diverse poets as Ai, Frank Bidart, Philip Levine, Sharon Olds, Adrienne Rich, and James Wright. To reflect this range, while also providing a more specific focus, this essay will look at some of the ways in which three poets – C. K. Williams, Robert Pinsky and Louise Glück – qualify and develop aspects of the confessional legacy. It will then consider Language poetry, particularly the work of Lyn Hejinian, Bob Perelman, and Rae Armantrout, and the extent to which such work is defined by its rejection of confessionalism.

C. K. Williams' often histrionic and formally sloppy early poetry, collected in *Lies* (1969) and *I Am the Bitter Name* (1972), displays many of the excesses associated with confessionalism at its most self-indulgent. The breakthrough Williams achieved in *With Ignorance* (1977) coincides with his adoption of a long, flexible line that sometimes runs to more than twenty syllables. His poems are now written in complete, punctuated sentences, and alongside newfound syntactical strategies he develops narrative skills, such as how to observe whilst acknowledging the observing self. His tone quietens and intensifies, and a great variety of subject matter becomes available to him. One of Williams' best poems of this period, 'Bob', is about a Vietnam veteran turned contract killer. While the speaker is uncertain whether to believe Bob's story ('If you put in enough hours in bars, sooner or later you get to hear every imaginable kind of bullshit'), the reader might wonder how reliable the speaker is.[2] The surface control of the long, grammatically correct lines subtly suggests that irrational, violent forces have been – perhaps only temporarily – mastered; and the speaker may have more in common with Bob than he realizes.

'Combat' describes Williams' youthful sexual yearning in the kind of excruciating detail that characterized confessionalism: aged twenty-one, Williams had a girlfriend who would not go all the way; eventually she left him. What defines the poem as post-confessional is Williams' self-consciousness about the extent to which the narrative he offers is a construction. His perspective has changed over time, and how the girl perceived him is doubly lost; but he suspects that his place in her narrative had something to do with his being Jewish, and her being German. The poem ends with a baffled, awed address to memory itself. Another self-consciously post-confessional poem is 'Gas Station', in which Williams describes getting a blowjob from a prostitute. Williams accuses himself of confessing to this mechanically, much as the prostitute mechanically fellated him: '*Why am I doing this? / I still haven't read Augustine.*'[3] In contrast, 'One of the Muses', the long final poem in *Tar*, disavows any confessional impulse: the poem is written not because the poet wants to suffer, nor for nostalgic reasons, nor to atone for or expiate guilt, nor to save, salvage or come to terms with anything. 'Why bother then?' the poet asks himself, and answers, 'It's to be accounted for, that's all. Something happened, the time has come to find its place.'[4] The poem then describes the convulsions his mind underwent in trying to understand a woman with whom he had a brief, unhappy relationship. In pointed contrast to Lowell's notorious use of personal correspondence in *The Dolphin* (1973), which quotes from Elizabeth Hardwick's letters, Williams' gaze is turned inwards, and he discloses few concrete details and minimal biographical information.

Throughout his work, Williams' eye is drawn to images of bodies, buildings, and communities in states of decay and degradation. Such imagery functions as both confessional psychic landscape and social commentary. In part, this is because his long line is always potentially in dialogue with Walt Whitman, allowing Williams to weigh present-day America against the country that was forming during the Civil War. The late-twentieth-century details of dilapidated housing, homeless alcoholics, vandalized parks, and diseased dogs are so gruesome, and the observing eye so unflinching, that the reader is likely to seize gratefully on the moments when the poems switch to the opposite pole, as when they end with a rhapsodic address to time, youth, or innocence: having depicted so much ugliness, the poems seem to have earned a little sentimental respite. Later, Williams would overplay this technique: a decline becomes apparent in *The Vigil* (1997), which contains a particularly mawkish villanelle and ends with 'Old Man', a poem that offers such banal observations as 'Sex and death: how close they can seem.'[5] Williams' subsequent books are vulnerable to such complacency; intriguingly, this has coincided with his return, in approximately half of the poems in each book, to a shorter line. That said, these books also contain impressive poems that show his powers of observation, and his capacity for candour, undiminished: 'The Cup', from *Repair* (1999), simply describes the poet's mother drinking coffee, and yet conveys intense, complex feelings of devotion, resentment, intimacy, and loathing. In adapting and broadening the confessional legacy, Williams continues to find ways of portraying a contemporary subjectivity that is uncomfortably aware of its constructed, provisional, and possibly self-deceiving condition.

Whereas Williams began his career brandishing his confessional credentials, Robert Pinsky took a more cautious approach, establishing his name with formally achieved, discursive poems that billed themselves as explanations, histories, essays, and ceremonies. Of Pinsky's first book, *Sadness and Happiness* (1975), Lowell said: 'it is refreshing to find a poet who is intellectually interesting and technically first-rate. Robert Pinsky belongs to that rarest category of talent, a poet-critic'.[6] The appellation 'poet-critic' may be one of Lowell's backhanded compliments, but it alerts us to the public, accountable nature of Pinsky's poetry and career. His criticism, such as *The Sounds of Poetry* (1998), addresses not the academy but the intelligent, interested reader; from 1997 to 2000 he was a notably energetic Poet Laureate, and he has even appeared on high-profile television shows like *The Colbert Report* and *The Simpsons*. In both his poetry and his advocacy, Pinsky has attempted to rehabilitate the role of the poet in the civic sphere.

Lowell's public aspect was largely inherited with his family name, leaving him free to disavow it, default on it, or treat its burden as a useful irritant to prompt poems. In contrast, Pinsky had to earn a public role, and did so by making more reasonable and temperate pronouncements. He praises such qualities in *An Explanation of America* (1980): 'to embrace a limit might show courage'.[7] The grand ambition trumpeted by the book's title poem is softened by its subtitle, 'A Poem for my Daughter', though this address is further qualified in the poem itself: 'I mean to write to my idea of you.'[8] The address (and the wry admission: 'Compulsive explainer that I am') gives the poem a note of tenderness and humility, and stresses its would-be practical aspect. One section, 'Local Politics', is concerned with the 'necessary evil' of voting, its possible futility, and the compromises inherent in any political action. Such reasonableness is in stark contrast to Lowell's more theatrical political pronouncements, such as volunteering for World War II and then later declaring himself a conscientious objector, or writing open letters to the president. Maturity, Pinsky argues, is what the age now demands. Speaking of the Vietnam War, he says: 'I think it made our country older, forever.'[9]

Although the self-expressive lyric has always had a place in Pinsky's work, for example in the title sequence of *Sadness and Happiness*, it is only relatively recently that he has had regular recourse to it. He describes 1996's 'Poem with Refrains' as 'unusual for me in its specific, autobiographical material. All of the remembered material is as accurate as I can make it."[10] In this poem, Pinsky intersperses italicized quotations from Renaissance-era English poets with fragmentary memories of his emotionally undemonstrative mother, who mysteriously refused to visit her own mother when she was dying:

They lived on the same block, four doors apart.
'*Absence my presence is; strangeness my grace;*
With them that walk against me is my sun.'[11]

The quotations are presented without comment, but here Fulke Greville's beautiful cadences reflect ironically on the flatly stated fact of the preceding line, and their emotional directness contrasts with the inarticulacy and repression Pinsky describes. Similarly, the elegiac poem 'Impossible to Tell' collages personal detail with jokes and reflections on the renga tradition; the 'cuts' are abrupt, but there are not too many of them, and the stately pace ensures that the reading experience is not one of disorientation, but rather of having our attention pointedly directed. Pinsky used to play the saxophone (his poem 'Ginza Samba' recounts the history of the instrument), but when his work evokes jazz, then it has tended to be the slower, bluesy, more conventionally structured variety. The cuts, however, speed up in his outstanding recent book, *Gulf Music* (2007), and the title poem begins with nonsense phrases inspired by Henry "Professor" Longhair:[12]

Mallah walla tella bella. Trah mah trah-la, la-la-la,
Mah la belle. Ippa Fano wanna bella, wella-wah.

The hurricane of September 8, 1900 devastated
Galveston, Texas. Some 8,000 people died.

The Pearl City almost obliterated. Still the worst natural
Calamity in American history, Woh mallah-walla.[13]

Longhair's idiosyncratic, oddly compelling nonsense jars against the impersonal list of facts, as two kinds of chaos, the personal and the historical, are tested against each other. Pinsky is always also aware of the danger of respect for the individual coarsening into self-interest, or self-regard. 'Poem of Disconnected Parts' begins with an especially pointed juxtaposition that glances at the confessional tendency:

At Robben Island the political prisoners studied.
They coined the motto *Each one Teach one*.

In Argentina the torturers demanded the prisoners
Address them always as *"Professor"*.

Many of my friends are moved by guilt, but I
Am a creature of shame, I am ashamed to say.[14]

Pinsky broadened his tonal palette by incorporating non-rational elements into his poetry, and we see several such self-correcting gestures in the career of Louise Glück, who describes the completion of each collection of poems as being accompanied by a 'conscious diagnostic act, a swearing off'.[15] Several commentators drew comparisons between Glück's first collection, *Firstborn* (1968), and Sylvia Plath's *Ariel* (1963). Both collections are characterized by emotional intensity, and a nervy, flinty rhythm; and both direct an acerbic wit towards the opposite sex (for example, Glück's 'Hesitate to Call', which ends with the line 'Love, you ever want me, don't').[16] More significantly, both write poems that combine dramatic monologue and candour. Glück's 'Seconds', spoken by a woman in an abusive relationship, refuses conventional sentiments and conclusions: 'I'd let my house go up in flame for this fire.'[17] 'La Force' concerns a female speaker's relationship with her mother. Still living in her mother's house, and by extension her mother's world, the speaker describes herself as 'Gray, glued to her dream / Kitchen' ('her' refers to the mother).[18] As in many of her early poems, the incisive line-break establishes Glück's tone as deadpan rather than neutral.

The House on Marshland (1975) marks a clearer demarcation between autobiographical and persona poems, and 'Gretel in Darkness' announces the dramatic monologue as one of Glück's signature forms. Whereas this collection is otherwise a steady development of her first, Glück's subsequent progression from book to book can be seen as a series of part-willed, part-intuitive imaginative leaps. This arc takes Glück far from Plath's influence, though it could be argued that self-reinvention is itself a Plath-like impulse. With *Descending Figure* (1980), Glück reverts to autobiographical material, but does so in poem-sequences that allow her to explore multiple aspects of her experience. In one such sequence, 'Dedication to Hunger', we see a young girl laugh because 'she's realized / that he never touches her'.[19] 'He' is the girl's father, and by never touching her he acknowledges the non-sexual nature of the relationship. The respected boundary enables the girl's happiness, and perhaps even her identity (the line-break allows us to read 'she's realized' as 'she *is* realized'). Later in the sequence, a grandmother is shown to have accepted, in her youth, a marriage that silenced her:

> his kiss would have been
> clearly tender –
>
> Of course, of course. Except
> it might as well have been
> his hand over her mouth.[20]

Glück does not voice anger on the grandmother's behalf ('I do not question / their happiness'), rather, she explores the idea that refusals and repudiations may be sources of comfort and identity. The theme of *anorexia nervosa* becomes apparent in the fourth section. By refusing food, the speaker feels that she has gained a sense of selfhood. Whereas Plath felt able to blame family members in the starkest terms, for example casting her father as a Nazi and herself as a Jew, Glück's argument is more nuanced, though the poem contains an unmistakable echo of Plath's 'Edge' in the lines 'I felt / what I feel now, aligning these words – / it is the same need to perfect, / of which death is the mere byproduct.'[21]

The material in Glück's next collection, *The Triumph of Achilles* (1985), is less obviously autobiographical, dramatizing figures from mythology and the Bible, and striking a more strident and rhetorical note. Glück later criticized the book as 'a concession ... to conventional imagination, or the conventional definitions of ambition', and with *Ararat* (1990) she returns to a more candid, plain-spoken style.[22] Line-breaks now coincide with sense pauses, rather than opening new perspectives or possible readings, and the relaxed, sometimes prosy effect can seem at odds with the material. This is partly due to a deliberately acquired tic: Glück now uses many contractions, as in the opening lines of 'A Fantasy': 'I'll tell you something: every day / people are dying. And that's just the beginning.'[23] These poems strike a chatty tone, yet deal with personal subject matter, and offer precise, considered observations. The effect is unsettling, like hearing someone over-share in a monotone.

In *The Wild Iris* (1992), which brought Glück a wider readership when it won the Pulitzer Prize, the voices that we hear are even more disembodied. While the project of writing in the language of flowers may sound genteel, many of the poems narrate experiences of returning from death or winter to 'the raw wind of the new world'.[24] The speakers often sound surprised to have survived, though not especially pleased to have done so: rather, they appear to have been emptied of such frivolous feelings. And it is as a voice – proclaiming, inveigling, pleading – that they have returned:

I cannot go on
restricting myself to images

because you think it is your right
to dispute my meaning:

I am prepared now to force
clarity upon you.[25]

These lines from 'Clear Morning' recall George Oppen's statement of his own aesthetic ambitions in 'Route', from *Of Being Numerous*:

> Clarity, clarity, surely clarity is the most beautiful thing in the world,
> A limited, limiting clarity
>
> I have not and never did have any motive of poetry
> But to achieve clarity[.][26]

In a penetrating essay on Oppen and John Berryman, Glück says that she finds it 'valuable, though nearly impossible' to read two such different poets side by side.[27] Glück's willingness to admit that other, antithetical kinds of poetry exist, and her more unusual ability to engage meaningfully with them, have helped guard her work against the risk of a 'limited, limiting clarity' degenerating into mannerism. That she was aware of this danger from the start, and able to counter it via a programme of deliberate stylistic variety, bespeaks an acute self-awareness.

Glück's attempt to draw on distinct poetic traditions will strike some readers as sensible, refreshing, and democratic; others will find it naïve and ahistorical. Charles Bernstein has referred to Language poetry as 'nonabsorbable' writing, that is, writing driven by disruptive techniques that prevent an 'initial / "illusionistic" reading'. That its primary characteristics should begin with negative prefixes is significant, for Language poetry is rooted in opposition. Most obviously, it opposes confessionalism, which it sees as staid, repetitive, and complacent in its belief that poetry can offer the reader untrammelled access to the poet's experience; but Language poetry also rejects Charles Olson's self-valorizing Projectivist verse, as well as poetry that would comment on politics rather than enact politicization through poetic form. To distinguish their work from such individualist poetries, the Language poets utilize depersonalizing disjunctive procedures, prefer parataxis to hypotaxis, write poems in collaboration, and insist on the social or dialogic context of each poem's creation and publication.[28] The reader is required to participate, to a greater extent than in other poetries, in the construction of meaning.

The poets associated with Language poetry include Bruce Andrews, Carla Harryman, Susan Howe, Bernadette Mayer, and Ron Silliman, but it is a porous grouping: Clark Coolidge, for example, might be claimed as a Language poet or a second generation New York poet. Language poetry took its name from *L=A=N=G=U=A=G=E*, a magazine that ran for 13 issues from 1978 to 1980, and which published not poetry but writing about poetics; however, *L=A=N=G=U=A=G=E* was only the most public manifestation of the Bay Area poetry scene. Charles Bernstein describes the early days of the movement:

> We shared a very strong dislike of the Official Verse Culture of that time, which seemed to favor poems so crippled by their formulas for personal epiphany that personal epiphany was shed at the starting line in favor of a highly mannered voicey voice 'indicating' (like they used to say in Method Acting) rather than expressing the poet's feelings, the so-called feelings of the so-called poet. In contrast, we tried to focus our work more on an acknowledgement of the structures of language, forms, styles, and also the relationship of ideology to syntax, you might say, ideology to grammar, ideology to rhetoric, with the recognition that language is never neutral but also that language always has an unconscious or nonrational dimension to it.[29]

To define yourself in opposition to something as nebulous as 'Official Verse Culture' is to give a hostage to fortune. Language poetry is now widely taught in universities, many of its practitioners are tenured professors, and Rae Armantrout's *Versed* (2009) won the Pulitzer Prize: today's Official Verse Culture, however it is defined, includes Language poetry.

The principal antecedents of Language poetry are Gertrude Stein, John Ashbery at his most experimental (as in his 1962 volume *The Tennis Court Oath*) and the Objectivists (particularly Louis Zukofsky). The Language poets take the Objectivist tendency to foreground the materiality of the word to an extreme, insisting that language and syntax enact, rather than critique, material conditions. Bruce Andrews describes how Language poetry offers '[A] conception of writing *as* politics, not writing *about* politics', and 'emphasizes a spectrum of writing that places attention primarily on language and ways of making meaning, that takes for granted neither vocabulary, grammar, process, shape, syntax, program, or subject matter'.[30] Many early Language essays are charged with a utopian left-wing rhetoric, such as Ron Silliman's 'For Open Letter', which claims that '[A Language-centered poem] … is the first step (and only that) of the return of the poem to the people.'[31]

A key text in the theoretical basis of Language writing is Lyn Hejinian's provocative essay 'The Rejection of Closure', which posits 'the conjunction of form with radical openness' as the '"paradise" for which writing often yearns'.[32] Hejinian draws a distinction between 'closed' and 'open' texts:

> We can say that a 'closed text' is one in which all the elements of the work are directed toward a single reading of it. Each element confirms that reading and delivers the text from any lurking ambiguity. […] The

> 'open text,' by definition, is open to the world and particularly to the reader. It invites participation, rejects the authority of the writer over the reader and thus, by analogy, the authority implicit in other (social, economic, cultural) hierarchies. It speaks for writing that is generative rather than directive. The writer relinquishes total control and challenges authority as a principle and control as a motive. The 'open text' often emphasizes or foregrounds process, either the process of the original composition or of subsequent compositions by readers, and thus resists the cultural tendencies that seek to identify and fix material and turn it into a product; that is, it resists reduction and commodification.[33]

Influential as it was, Hejinian's essay was no more universally accepted than any other single theory of Language poetry. Steve McCaffery, for example, questioned whether such 'open' texts could represent a significantly new direction, as they appeared to replace one site of meaning-production (the writer) with another (the reader), without challenging the underlying capitalist paradigm. Less sympathetic readers are likely to have many more questions. Can Hejinian cite any poem that exhibits 'total control'? How can Language poems be 'open' when they implicitly demand a poststructuralist, deconstructive reading? How are Shakespeare's sonnets (which the essay quotes in its concluding paragraphs) 'closed' to the world and the reader, when thousands of readers have offered conflicting interpretations?

Ironically, Hejinian's most celebrated work seems to promise confessional material. *My Life* was originally written as thirty-seven paragraphs of thirty-seven sentences, after the poet's age. Eight years later a revised version appeared, consisting of forty-five paragraphs of forty-five sentences. Upon its most recent appearance, the revised version was supplemented by another sequence, 'My Life in the Nineties'. Throughout the sequence, Hejinian jumps from memories to philosophical reflections ('If reality is trying to express itself in words it is certainly taking the long way around'); literary asides ('The work is probably a good deal wiser than the horny old doctor he was', aimed at Carlos Williams presumably); old wives' tales ('If you cut your fingernails they will grow back thick, blunt, like a man's'); and self-reflexive statements such as 'If it is personal, it is most likely fickle' or 'The obvious analogy is with music.'[34] It is a distinctly female story, partly because of the nature of the self-images that are entertained and cast aside ('It seemed natural to her to confuse the romantic with the motherly'), and partly because of the passionate intensity with which domestic experience is described and encrypted ('The refrigerator makes a sound I can't spell'), recalling Stein's *Tender Buttons*.[35]

As in her earlier poems such as 'Resistance', Hejinian takes each paragraph to represent 'a single moment of time, a single moment in the mind, its content all the thoughts, thought particles, impressions, impulses – all the diverse, particular, and contradictory elements – that are included in an active and emotional mind at any given instant. For the moment, for the writer, the poem *is* a mind.'[36] The difference in *My Life* is that the poem is a *remembering* mind. Self-expression and self-representation have not been abandoned but attempted afresh, and the poem draws attention to the paradoxes and ambiguities inherent in any attempt we might make to tell our story. As Lisa Samuels has noted, the fact that Hejinian's formal procedures are innovative but not entirely arbitrary gives the poem a broader appeal than many other Language poems, and explains why it is frequently taught.[37] Even a reader unconvinced by Hejinian's theories may appreciate the rich ambiguities of *My Life*, and the ways in which the poem formally enacts the shifting understandings of self that constitute memory and consciousness.

Many of Bob Perelman's poem titles similarly tease the reader with promises of personal revelations: 'Autobiography by Aphorism', 'My One Voice', 'An Autobiography' (which collages quotations from Mozart, Shackleton and Stendhal), 'Confession' (which begins 'Aliens have inhabited my aesthetics for / decades. Really since the early 70s),[38] and 'The Story of My Life', which ends: 'So, in conclusion, give me a society of smashed-in cubes, a place to / stand, and a head of pre-owned words, and I will move the / earth, write my name, do the dishes, and be myself.'[39] Perelman has said that what he took from Language poetry was 'an appetite for poetic techniques – *avant* or not, as long as they're useful for trying to write the present'.[40] His most compelling work combines arbitrary writing procedures with playful wit, as in 'China', which consists of seemingly random sentences, and concludes:

> You look great in shorts. And the flag looks great too.
>
> Everyone enjoyed the explosions.
>
> Time to wake up.
>
> But better get used to dreams too.[41]

While it is possible to find oblique references to Chinese history and politics in the poem, any unifying argument will be of the reader's own making, for the poem originated in a series of captions that Perelman wrote to accompany a book of photographs he found in Chinatown. In denying the reader access to these photographs, Perelman ensures that the poem's authority lies not in its own aesthetic coherence, but in the reader's subjective response.

A more complex interaction of procedural technique and reception-context is staged in 'Chronic Meanings'. The poem is written in quatrains. Each line is five words long, and is end-stopped. It begins:

> The single fact is matter.
> Five words can say only.
> Black sky at night, reasonably.
> I am, the irrational residue.[42]

The poem is dedicated to Lee Hickman, who edited the poetry magazine *Temblor*, where 'Chronic Meanings' was first published as the final poem in the tenth and final issue in 1989. Many of the poem's first readers would have known that Hickman had AIDS, and would have read Perelman's abrupt, incomplete sentences as an attempt to, in his words, 'register time's evanescence'.[43] Such a personal dimension might not occur to the reader encountering the poem in the collection *Virtual Reality* (1993), or in Perelman's selected poems, *Ten to One* (1999). Perelman has said that poetry must 'resist the tyranny of elemental words', which he defines as 'words that brook no argument, that are intended to be outside of syntax and thus outside of history'.[44] As 'Chronic Meanings' illustrates, the contexts of publication and reception determine a poem's meaning: all meaning is chronic, in the sense that it is time-bound.

Ron Silliman has described Rae Armantrout's work as 'poems that at first glance appear contained and perhaps even simple, but which upon the slightest examination rapidly provoke a sort of vertigo effect as element after element begins to spin wildly toward more radical (and, often enough, sinister) possibilities'.[45] Armantrout's early poems tend to be less richly textured than this, and many are content to stage a language joke, or depict, albeit with elegance and economy, irksome aspects of contemporary life. 'Dusk', from 1979, consists of a four-line description of a spider, before exclaiming: 'I'm not like that!'[46] The poem refuses the too-easy identification with which a product of Official Verse Culture would presumably conclude. Of course, a reader of Armantrout would not *expect* such an identification, and by pointedly refusing it, Armantrout offers such a reader much the same gratification that a reader of, say, C. K. Williams would derive from a sense of epiphanic closure. While many of Armantrout's early poems feel like preparatory sketches for the more achieved work that begins with *Necromance* (1991), her characteristic note is struck in 'Anti-Short Story', which reads in full:

> A girl is running. *Don't* tell me
> 'She's running for her bus.'
>
> All that aside![47]

The crash-zoom urgency, the dialogic standoff, and the ambiguously gestural final line that activates multiple assumptions and contexts whilst simultaneously dismissing them, will all become familiar in Armantrout's later work.

As 'Writing' pithily observes, 'I, myself, was always a forwarding address,' and by inviting the reader to contemplate alienated fragments of reality, Armantrout ensures that her poetry reflects our autobiographical impulses as much as her own.[48] The third and final section of 'As One', from her 2004 collection *Up to Speed*, reads as follows:

> 'There are really only two
> ideas.'
>
> A) We can be represented,
> someone can take our place or suffer
> in our stead.
>
> B) This has happened already, in the distant past,
> and all we need do is recall it.[49]

'A' may refer to a Christian world-view, in which a redeemer suffers on our behalf, and 'B' to the philosophical concept of eternal recurrence; but other pairings would apply. As in many of Armantrout's poems, a premise and a choice are presented, and the poem arises from a moment of paralysed indecision, as though it suspected a hidden agenda. Rather than presenting a speaker with which we may identify, Armantrout's poems require us to follow a fugitive subjectivity as it picks its way between competing discourses, all of which seem plausible but not entirely convincing. She often enhances this effect by presenting her poems in numbered sections, insisting on their constructed, decentred, and perhaps provisional state. As she asserts in 'Veil': 'I too / am a segmentalist.'[50]

The title poem of Armantrout's recent collection, *Money Shot* (2012), is a poem of artistic self-assessment. By way of gauging the distance between seemingly antithetical poetic traditions, it may be compared with Lowell's 'Epilogue', which begins:

Those blessèd structures, plot and rhyme –
why are they no help to me now
I want to make
something imagined, not recalled?[51]

Lowell goes on to criticize his poetry as often seeming 'lurid, rapid, garish, grouped, / heightened from life, / yet paralyzed by fact', before executing an abrupt about-turn: 'Yet why not say what happened?' Initially, this question may sound naïve or artless; but Lowell knew perfectly well how difficult, and how costly, it is to 'say what happened', whether 'say' is taken to mean 'know' or 'express'. The question is rhetorical, and by asking it he reaffirms his commitment to his established poetic process (to 'say what happened' is precisely what he had done) whilst offering the challenge to which post-confessional poetry would have to rise. The opening section of Armantrout's poem reads in full:

IndyMac:

Able to exploit pre-existing.
Tain.

Per. In. Con.
Cyst.[52]

'IndyMac' is the name of one of the first mortgage banks to fail in the financial crisis that began in 2008, and 'tain' is a rare word for the foil backing of a mirror. The fragmented words appear to be some combination of 'pertain', 'contain', 'sustain', 'persist', 'consist', and 'inconsistency'; or they may be, as Armantrout has suggested, 'free-floating prefixes and suffixes ready to be recombined, reshuffled'.[53] The reader must, in the words of the poem, 'exploit' these pre-existing fragments in order to construct meaning. Armantrout's method here is characteristic of her approach throughout *Money Shot*: a lyric subjectivity collides with various destabilizing, invasive voices and contexts, resulting in a fragmented, elliptical poem.

Lowell's poem asks 'Yet why not say what happened?', and the second, final section of 'Money Shot', which I will once again quote in full, builds to a seemingly similar question:

I'm on a crowded ship
and I've been served the wrong breakfast.

This small mound
of soggy dough
is not what I ordered.

'Why don't you just *say*
what you mean?'

Why don't I?[54]

Where Lowell's question is rhetorical, Armantrout's appears genuine, and presumably put to her by the waiter to whom she has complained. She is unable to answer, and the poem ends either by internalizing the question silently, or by appealing to the reader. Either way, there is a greater vulnerability here. Armantrout, in Hejinian's neat formulation, 'discovers not epiphanies but dilemmas'.[55] Nevertheless, the similarities between the poems are striking: both stage a lyric engagement with inimical 'structures', and both question the validity of their own poetic processes even as they exploit them.

The title of this essay referred to a great divide, and discussion of post-1945 poetry often employs dichotomies such as 'formal versus free', or 'mainstream versus *avant-garde*', or, slightly earlier, Lowell's distinction between 'raw' and 'cooked' poetry.[56] Some of the poets under discussion here would endorse such dichotomies, but in practice their work has progressed by extending itself towards an 'other'. Those who started out with the most confessional assumptions came to question and qualify such impulses; while many of the poets associated with Language reconciled themselves to the idea of using autobiographical material, and manipulating the fiction of a coherent subjectivity. Williams learns to express powerful and sometimes violent emotions through a carefully manipulated syntax; Pinsky incorporates the non-rational into his naturally eloquent voice; principled risk-taking allows Glück to develop Oppen's legacy in symbolist, mythological terms that would have been anathema to the Objectivists; Hejinian's verse autobiography reconciles the polarities upon which her criticism is based; Perelman's work marries depersonalizing procedure and immediately identifiable wit; and Armantrout asks us to identify with a lyric subjectivity even as it unravels before us. In their different ways, all of these poets question, adapt, and sometimes violate the aesthetic principles of the movement with which they are primarily associated.

Notes

1. Ron Silliman, 'Preface and Notes' to 'The Dwelling Place: 9 Poets', in *Alcheringa*, New Series, 1(2) (1975): 104.
2. C. K. Williams, *Collected Poems* (Tarset: Bloodaxe Books, 2006), p. 129.
3. C. K. Williams, *Collected Poems*, p. 196.
4. C. K. Williams, *Collected Poems*, p. 201.
5. C. K. Williams, *Collected Poems*, p. 483.
6. Robert Lowell, blurb quote for *Sadness and Happiness* (Princeton, NJ: Princeton University Press, 1975).
7. Robert Pinsky, *The Figured Wheel: New and Collected Poems 1966–1996* (Manchester: Carcanet, 1996), p. 185.
8. Robert Pinsky, *The Figured Wheel*, p. 158.
9. Robert Pinsky, *The Figured Wheel*, p. 191.
10. Robert Pinsky in *P.N. Review 100: A Calendar of Modern Poetry*, 21(2) (November–December 1994): 94.
11. Robert Pinsky, *The Figured Wheel*, p. 7.
12. Jeremy Bass, 'Impossible to Tell: On Robert Pinsky', *The Nation* (16 July 2012).
13. Robert Pinsky, *Gulf Music* (New York: Farrar, Straus & Giroux), p. 6.
14. Robort Pinsky, *Gulf Music*, p. 3.
15. Louise Glück, 'Education of the Poet', *Proofs and Theories: Essays on Poetry* (New York: Ecco, 1994), p. 17.
16. Louise Glück, *Poems 1962–2012* (New York: Farrar, Strauss & Giroux, 2012), p. 9.
17. Louise Glück, *Poems 1962–2012*, p. 30.
18. Louise Glück, *Poems 1962–2012*, p. 37.
19. Louise Glück, *Poems 1962–2012*, p. 124.
20. Louise Glück, *Poems 1962–2012*, pp. 124–5.
21. Louise Glück, *Poems 1962–2012*, p. 126.
22. Louise Glück, author's note to *The First Five Books of Poems* (Manchester: Carcanet, 1997).
23. Louise Glück, *Poems 1962–2012*, p. 204.
24. Louise Glück, *Poems 1962–2012*, p. 250.
25. Louise Glück, *Poems 1962–2012*, pp. 251–2.
26. George Oppen, *New Collected Poems*, ed. Michael Davidson (New York: New Directions, 2002), p. 193.
27. Louise Glück, 'Disruption, Hesitation, Silence', *Proofs and Theories*, p. 78.
28. See, for example, 'The Grand Piano: An Experiment in Collective Autobiography', a collaboration between Rae Armantrout, Bob Perelman, Barret Watten, Steve Benson, Carla Harryman, Tom Mandel, Ron Silliman, Kit Robinson, Lyn Hejinian, and Ted Pearson (San Francisco, 1975–80).
29. Charles Bernstein, interview with Romani Freschi, *Green Integer Review*, 1 (December 2006). Last accessed 24 September 2015. Available at:

http://www.greeninteger.com/green_integer_review/issue_1/Charles-Bernstein-interview.htm
30. Bruce Andrews, 'Poetry as Explanation, Poetry as Praxis', in Paul Hoover (ed.), *Postmodern American Poetry* (New York: W. W. Norton, 2013); the essay is also reproduced in Bruce Andrews, *Paradise and Method: Poetry and Praxis* (Evanston, IL: Northwestern University Press, 1996).
31. Ron Silliman, 'For Open Letter', *Open Letter*, Third Series, No. 7 (Summer 1977): 93.
32. Lyn Hejinian, 'The Rejection of Closure', quoted in Dana Gioia, David Mason and Meg Schoerke (eds), *Twentieth-Century American Poetics: Poets on the Art of Poetry* (New York: McGraw-Hill, 2004), p. 368.
33. Lyn Hejinian, 'The Rejection of Closure', p. 369.
34. Lyn Hejinian, *My Life and My Life in the Nineties* (Middletown, CT: Wesleyan University Press, 2013), pp. 91, 43, 47, 44, 17.
35. Lyn Hejinian, *My Life and My Life in the Nineties*, pp. 64, 29.
36. Lyn Hejinian, 'The Rejection of Closure', p. 369.
37. Lisa Samuels, 'Eight justifications for canonizing Lyn Hejinian's *My Life*'. Last accessed 24 September 2015. Available at: http://wings.buffalo.edu/epc/authors/samuels/mylife.html
38. Bob Perelman, *Ten to One: Selected Poems* (Hanover: Wesleyan University Press, 1999), p. 205.
39. Bob Perelman, *Face Value* (New York: Roof Books, 1988), p. 70.
40. Bob Perelman, Introduction to *Ten to One: Selected Poems*, p. xiii.
41. Bob Perelman, *Ten to One: Selected Poems*, p. 33.
42. Bob Perelman, *Ten to One: Selected Poems*, p. 166.
43. Bob Perelman, in Mark Strand (ed.), *The Best American Poetry 1991* (New York: Collier Books, 1991).
44. Bob Perelman, Introduction to *Ten to One: Selected Poems*, p. xvi.
45. Ron Silliman, 'Foreword: "Aloha, Fruity Pebbles": The Poems of Rae Armantrout', in Rae Armantrout, *Veil: New and Selected Poems* (Hanover: Wesleyan University Press, 2001), p. ix.
46. Rae Armantrout, *Veil*, p. 22.
47. Rae Armantrout, *Veil*, p. 12.
48. Rae Armantrout, *Veil*, p. 93.
49. Rae Armantrout, *Up to Speed* (Hanover: Wesleyan University Press, 2004), p. 52.
50. Rae Armantrout, *Veil*, p. 131.
51. Robert Lowell, *Collected Poems*, ed. Frank Bidart and David Gewanter (London: Faber, 2003), p. 838.
52. Rae Armantrout, *Money Shot* (Middletown, CT: Wesleyan University Press, 2011), p. 5.
53. Rae Armantrout, in an interview with Ben Lerner. Last accessed 24 September 2015. Available at: http://yaleunion.org/rae-armantrout-currency/
54. Rae Armantrout, *Money Shot*, p. 5.
55. Lyn Hejinian, blurb quote to *Veil*.

56. Robert Lowell, acceptance speech for the 1960 Poetry Award (for *Life Studies*) at the National Book Award. A longer excerpt: 'Two poetries are now competing, a cooked and a raw. The cooked, marvelously expert, often seems laboriously concocted to be tasted and digested by a graduate seminar. The raw, huge blood-dripping gobbets of unseasoned experience are dished up for midnight listeners. There is a poetry that can only be studied, and a poetry that can only be declaimed, a poetry of pedantry, and a poetry of scandal. I exaggerate, of course.' Last accessed 24 September 2015. Available at: http://www.nationalbook.org/nbaaccept speech_rlowell.html

9

The Art of Exclusion: Form and Prosody in American Poetry since 1970

David Caplan

The latest edition of *The Princeton Encyclopedia of Poetry and Poetics* contains 1639 pages and 1100 articles. At more than one million words, it is roughly four times the length of *Ulysses* and five times the length of *Moby-Dick*.[1] It is a book meant to be consulted, not read whole. This hefty text, though, addresses only a portion of the nearly countless forms and prosodies that the contemporary moment offers. The Internet presents an even more massive, swiftly expanding resource that dwarfs any print volume, regardless of how comprehensive it seeks to be.

In an era that presents such abundant poetic choices, too many exist for any poet to try, let alone master. To write a poem, then, is also *not* to pursue nearly countless options and opportunities. 'In the Renaissance', Northrop Frye observed, 'anyone who wanted to be a serious poet ... was supposed to be what Gabriel Harvey called a "curious universal scholar" as well as a practical expert in every known rhetorical device.'[2] As Frye implies, no contemporary poet claims a comparable status. No matter how learned, none is a 'universal scholar'; no matter how devoted to the art, none claim expertise 'in every known rhetorical device'. In a culture generally suspicious of universalizing claims, some observers might object to the very notion of all-encompassing expertise and knowledge, seeing its partiality and biases. They place 'universal', as Stuart Hall urged, 'always in quotation marks'.[3]

Faced with developments, contemporary American poets remain mindful of what their poems are not. Inspired by this knowledge, some forthrightly announce their ambition in negative terms. When writing an epistolary poem, Robert Hass first distinguishes it from earlier examples of the genre; 'This is a letter of apology, unrhymed / Rhyme belongs to the dazzling couplets of arrival. / Survival is the art around here.'[4] Hass defines his poem against potential models. The absence of rhyme, the poem contends, marks an essential difference. The versification clarifies what the poem is not. Even more forcefully, Charles Wright's manifesto, 'The New Poem', proclaims a negative *ars poetica*. The poem consists of nine lines, each beginning with, 'It will not'. 'It will not resemble the sea', the poem opens, and ends, 'It will not be able to help us.'[5] The anaphora repeats the poem's essential charge; 'the new poem' is known by the functions it does not perform. Such examples are hardly unusual. Indeed, some of the most famous lines written by American poets over the last several decades return to this theme, adding different emphases, 'You can't say it that way any more'; 'This poem is not addressed to you'; 'Wherever I am / I am what is missing'; and 'it will not be simple, it will not be long'.[6]

Such works encourage a certain kind of reading, a particular type of attentiveness. To understand this kind of poem, a reader must recognize what it excludes: what is not addressed, missing, and not articulated. In this respect, reading follows the act of composition. As Peter Gizzi describes it, the process of writing a poem involves 'tracking what is not said': 'As if there are always two poems in my ear. What amazes me is how specific the "other" or phantom poem can be.'[7] Other poems encourage readers to 'track' multiple phantom alternatives. The conceptualist poet Kenneth Goldsmith hardly resembles Hass, Wright, or Gizzi in temperament or style, yet the advice he offers also broadly applies to their poems: 'I've found that the way to deal with the most perplexing of texts is not to try to figure out what they are but instead to ask what they are not.'[8] In this essay, I will investigate the different ways American poets have practised these strategies of exclusion. I will move from considering this issue in its most limited sense – in rather focused examples such as parodies and minimalist verse, which devote considerable attention to this task – to a more expansive consideration of how form and prosody gain force and power by excluding alternatives. While precedents certainly exist for this tendency, increasingly it marks contemporary practice as new works implicitly propose a certain definition of the field: poetry as the art of exclusion.[9]

As has been widely noted, the proliferation of creative-writing programmes distinguishes American poetic culture. Few American poets have not taken classes in poetry writing and many leading poets make their living teaching these classes. Amidst the debates over whether the creative-writing discipline exerts a beneficial or detrimental influence on the field of American poetry, one of its effects has received relatively little attention. Poets realize that the poetic training they receive constitutes only one of a large number of possible options. It is neither inevitable nor comprehensive.

In her fascinating memoir, *The Middle Room*, Jennifer Moxley ruminates on this situation's implications. After her mother faced treatments for cancer, Moxley took a leave of absence from the university where she studied. As a consequence, she missed taking 'a very charged poetry workshop being given that quarter by Charles Bernstein':

> Helena, Chuck, Steve, Douglas, and Bill were all enrolled, and under the Language poet's influence every one of them, to the last, had abandoned their habit of writing short lyrics in favor of long systematic works. Steve began 'Oust,' his erasure of Proust, and Helena started a serial poem that would eventually win her a university prize. Though I have, after many years, learned to accept *most* of the 'things I cannot change,' I've wasted little time wondering what might have happened to me that winter if there had not been a 'large carcinogenic mass' inside my mother's breast and, instead of spending hours at Kaiser, I had, along with my friends, been a student of Charles Bernstein. Would I too have written a long and systematic poem? Or would I have, as I had in Michael Davidson's class, thundered against the strictures of another's poetic agenda? Was the whole history of my life rewritten when I missed that crucial workshop?[10]

Moxley claims to have 'wasted little time wondering what might have happened to me' had she taken the class with Bernstein. Her detailed ruminations, however, betray her deep interest in the subject. She considers a number of possibilities. Like her friends, she might have been moved by 'the Language poet's influence' to change the length, style, and form of her writing. Unlike them, she might have rebelled against 'another's poetic agenda' (as she had in an earlier class with Michael Davidson). The missed workshop vividly demonstrated how many options exist for aspiring poets to pursue. To pick one – consciously or not – is to exclude others.

For Moxley, 'the whole history' of her 'life' was potentially 'rewritten' when she 'missed' a 'crucial workshop'. To consider what their work excludes, other poets contemplate other aspects of their identity. In a recent poem, Mark Strand daydreams about how a poet might claim an alternative nationality. Strand's 'Poem of the Spanish Poet' opens with a prose meditation on this issue:

> In a hotel room somewhere in Iowa an American poet, tired of his poems, tired of being an American poet, leans back in his chair and imagines he is a Spanish poet, an old Spanish poet, nearing the end of

> his life, who walks to the Guadalquivir and watches the ships, gray and ghostly in the twilight, slip downstream. The little waves, approaching the grassy bank where he sits, whisper something he can't quite hear as they curl and fall. Now what does the Spanish poet do? He reaches into his pocket, pulls out a notebook, and writes ...[11]

America exists almost in a single detail: 'Iowa', the home of the famed Iowa Writers' Workshop, where Strand both studied and served on the faculty. Though not specified, the depicted poet appears to be a vising writer or faculty, living a rootless existence '[i]n a hotel room'. As presented in the poem, a national poetic identity is similarly unfixed; it can be changed through an act of imagination. The 'American' poet first 'imagines he is a Spanish poet' then becomes 'the Spanish poet' as '[h]e reaches into his pocket, pulls out a notebook, and writes'. Whereas Strand describes national poetic identity largely as a matter of imagination and style, Adrienne Rich presents it as the product of a lived historical consciousness, a particular 'truth and dread' that a nation's citizens experience. Describing an archetypal Russian scene of a poet picking mushrooms, Rich cautions, 'I've walked there picking mushrooms at the edge of dread, but don't be fooled, / this isn't a Russian poem, this is not somewhere else but here, / our country moving closer to its own truth and dread.'[12] Rich's poem resists the process Strand encourages. In 'North American Time', Rich dismisses the idea 'that you are simply you / that the imagination simply strays / like a great moth'. In 'What Kind of Times Are These', she similarly refuses to imagine herself as 'standing outside history', that is, as a poet of another nationality, 'somewhere else.'[13] In essence her earlier lines anticipate and chastise Strand's. However, even Strand's itinerant imagination recognizes certain restrictions. While the poem suggests that the poet can change his national artistic identity, it also acknowledges this strategy's limits. A poet can be an 'American poet' or a 'Spanish poet', but not both simultaneously. To put this idea in slightly different terms, to be an 'American poet' is to be *not* a 'Spanish' or 'Russian' poet. One poetic identity excludes the other.

Parody offers a genre for the more pointed expression of this idea. Rae Armantrout's 'Traveling through the Yard' invokes a specific poetics in order to reject it: 'So thinking hard for all of us, / I scooped it up, heaved it / across the marriage counselor's fence.'[14] As its title and the dedication, 'For Willard Stafford', suggest, 'Traveling through the Yard' recasts William Stafford's 'Travelling through the Dark'. In particular, Armantrout focuses on the most famous parts of the poems, the opening and closing lines:

> Travelling through the dark I found a deer
> dead on the edge of the Wilson River road.
> ...
>
> I thought hard for us all – my only swerving –,
> then pushed her over the edge into the river.[15]

'Poems like this ["Travelling through the Dark"] have often been attacked by language writers', observes Bob Perelman, but it is more accurate to say that Language poets have attacked Stafford's poem with particular vehemence for what it seems to represent.[16] Perelman, for instance, has notably criticized it twice. In 1980, Perelman discussed the poem in a talk attended by many leading figures in Language writing including Robert Grenier, Ron Silliman, Tom Mandel, and Barrett Watten, several of whom criticized the poem, as well as the readers who enjoy it, in the ensuing discussion ('People like that poem', Mandel observed, 'because it makes them feel shitty'[17]). Perelman subsequently published a transcript of the talk and discussion in the journal *Hills*. A decade and a half later, Perelman returned to 'Travelling through the Dark' in *The Marginalization of Poetry: Language Writing and Literary History*, in order to disparage it a second time. Citing his earlier essay, he tellingly notes, 'I discuss (attack) this poem.'[18] As the parenthetical aside suggests, for a certain kind of reader to discuss Stafford's poem is to attack it. Perelman's denunciations hardly stood by themselves. In a group manifesto published in 1988, Ron Silliman, Carla Harryman, Lyn Hejinian, Steve Benson, Bob Perelman, and Barrett Watten also singled out the poem as 'a prime example' of 'the confessional verse poem', 'in which the specifics of experience dissolve into the pseudo-intimacy of an overarching authorial "voice"'.[19]

The publication history of 'Travelling through the Dark' partly inspired this reaction; it made Stafford's poem into an attractive target. 'Travelling through the Dark' is the first poem in Donald Hall's anthology *Contemporary American Poetry*, one in a series of anthologies that drew lines within American poetry between '*avant-garde*' and 'traditional' work. Donald M. Allen's *The New American Poetry 1945–1960* featured poems that, as its editor famously announced, share 'one common characteristic: a total rejection of all those qualities typical of academic verse'.[20] Starting with *New Poets of England and America* (1957) co-edited with Robert Pack, Hall's anthologies seemed to promote the opposing aesthetic. While more recent scholarship has called into question the neat distinction between these poetic schools, emphasizing, for instance, the commerce between the allegedly antagonistic positions,[21] Armantrout's 'Traveling through the Yard' insists on the essential difference between her and Stafford's work and the two movements they represent. To mock 'Travelling through the Dark' is to discredit one poetics in order to promote another.

The prose critiques of 'Travelling through the Dark' and Armantrout's poem share a similar logic. Published six years after Perelman's original talk, Armantrout's poem concentrates on the same lines he analyses. She nearly quotes Stafford's culminating insight, the line Perelman identifies as 'the climax of the poem' and Silliman, Harryman, Hejinian, Benson, Perelman and Watten also contemptuously analyse, 'I thought hard for us all', revising it only slightly, 'So thinking hard for all of us'.[22] Analysing Stafford's poem, Perelman disparages him for being 'firmly in control of meaning', instead of accepting the instability of language and insisting on the reader's more active participation.[23] 'I', Robert Creeley more politely observed, 'shy from the generalizing "we" of his [Stafford's] poems.'[24] Armantrout, like Perelman, ridicules 'the generalizing "we"' in order to promote nearly the opposite effect: a poetics of fissure and rupture, of multiple 'conflicting voices', qualities which, despite their other differences, her work shares with other writers associated with Language poetry.[25] She replaces Stafford's dead deer with a dead dove, a traditional symbol of peace, as if rejecting any possibility of reconciliation, and 'heaved it / across the marriage counselor's fence', a gesture that also suggests defying authority ('the marriage counselor') and limits (the 'fence'). Presented as idiosyncrasies, such revisions also advance a shared poetic agenda. In this respect, 'Travelling through the Dark' offers the perfect foil, a contrast to a common ambition. Armantrout's poem turns Stafford's into a negative example, an example of what she and other like-minded authors believe poetry should not do.

Other poems announce what they omit more literally: they lay bare their exclusions. Donald Justice's 'The Thin Man', for instance, boasts of its 'rich refusals': 'Nothing suffices. / I hone myself to / This edge.' [26] The poem's meticulously lean rhetorical style matches its form. 'The Thin Man' consists of six short verse lines, each comprised of five syllables and two stresses: a skeletal structure to define an 'edge'. No sentence extends for more than six words. The brief poem foregrounds what it excludes.

Justice's poem is classified as 'minimalist', committed to what Marjorie Perloff calls 'the principle of intentional reduction', 'a poetics that holds that sparseness, tautness, understatement, and reduction constitute poetic authenticity'.[27] Just as all short poems are not minimalist, though, a minimalist poem need not be short. As its title suggests, Paul Muldoon's 'Kissing and Telling' recounts a casual sexual encounter. The poem's last line withholds the awaited salacious details, the 'telling'. 'I could name names. I could be indiscreet,' the speaker notes, keeping those particulars private.[28] Teasingly the poem ends before it fulfils half of the title's promise. Both Justice's and Muldoon's poems share an anti-confessional impulse; they refuse to participate in the chattiness and self-disclosure of a certain strain of contemporary poetry and culture. They do not over-share. Instead, they make a virtue of what they are not, of their pointed refusals.

The contrary impulse – what might be called 'maximalism' or a principle of intentional expansion – is more common. It serves as both a poetic style and a rallying cry. A number of recent poetic movements and critical statements announce their ambitions in these terms. They seek to broaden the art, to introduce new experiences, composition techniques, and influences: 'opening the field', 'enlarging the temple', and 'pushing the limits' with 'forms of expansion'.[29] Eager for new material and techniques, they dramatize a sense of speed and openness, of their own voracious appetites.

Given such sweeping claims and the counter-claims that greet them, it is easy to mistake poems written in this style for something other than what they are: poems that employ one style among countless others. Reviewing Albert Goldbarth's collection *Everyday People*, Stephen Burt praised Goldbarth's poetic style but offers a reservation about what he perceives to be its limitations. Burt writes:

> Goldbarth's hunger for information as such, his gleeful drive toward more and more parts in each sentence, his near indifference to the acoustic properties of single words prevent him from representing stillness or peace.[30]

Burt describes Goldbarth's 'drive' as more a compulsion than an artistic choice. Yet Goldbarth's previous collection, *Kitchen Sink: New and Selected Poems 1972–2007*, opens with a poem that exhibits the very qualities Burt finds missing in Goldbarth's work. 'Shawl' describes a long bus ride across the American Midwest. Eight hours into the trip, a particular passenger experiences speed as an intimate slowness, a 'stillness or peace'. A phrase from another of Goldbarth's poems best describes 'Shawl': it might be called 'a sonnety fourteen lines'.[31] 'Shawl' departs from some of the sonnet's historic conventions. It lacks patterned end-stopped rhyme and a consistent meter, and it moves the turn from the start of the ninth line to the start of the tenth.

At the same time, 'Shawl' rewards the procedures that attentive readers developed to analyse sonnets. In *The Art of Shakespeare's Sonnets*, Helen Vendler identifies what she calls 'the Couplet Tie', words appearing in the body of the sonnet (ll. 1–12) and repeated in the couplet (ll. 13–14), and the 'Key Word', a word whose root appears in each section of the sonnet.[32] Goldbarth's less schematically organized poem revises these structures. The first four lines of 'Shawl' introduce the poem's key word, 'see', emphasizing it through repetition: 'He could **see** himself now / in the window, **see** his head there.'[33] The next quatrain repeats the word in homonym form: 'Darkness outside; darkness in the bus – as if the **sea** / were dark.' The quatrain also emphasizes the key word through partial and full rhyme: 'He was **twenty**: of course his eyes returned, **repeatedly**, / to the **knee**,' a strategy which the sonnet's second half continues, rhyming the key word, 'see', but not including the word itself: 'Now his, the **only** / overhead turned on' and '**only** him, and the book, and the light thrown over his shoulders / as **luxuriously** as a cashmere shawl'. Revising Shakespeare's method, partial and full rhyme repeat the key word in sonic form. It advances the poem's central argument: reading redefines deprivation into luxury.

'Shawl' stands roughly midway between the two poles I have sketched, between 'minimalist' and 'maximalist' styles. Skilfully it adapts familiar lyric techniques, which is why it rewards Vendler's method. To use an anachronistic metaphor, it plays a 33 rpm record at 33. The poem creates a certain experience of language familiar to much lyric poetry: private and enclosed, its words quietly work by implication. They gain meaning and force when readers pay sufficient attention, when they enter the poem's 'silence or peace', its 'silence and slow time' (in Keats's classic phrase).[34] Language turns erotic. In an embedded metaphor, the bus's dim reading light, 'Now his, the only / overhead turned on' casts a seductive glow. With such gestures and invitations, the poem encourages the kind of reading it depicts.

More often, though, Goldbarth's poems feature an almost jarring swiftness, a refocus and disorientation, a 33 played at 78. Goldbarth's remarkable poem '1400', for instance, achieves such force and velocity it is easy to miss its delicacy, wit, and precision. The poem consists of twenty-seven lines:

> Saps, and the anal grease of an otter, and pig's blood,
> and the crushed-up bulbous bodies of those insects
> that they'd find so thickly gathered on barnyard excrement
> it makes a pulsing rind, and oven soot, and the oil
> that forms in a flask of urine and rotting horseflesh,
> and the white of an egg, and charcoal[.][35]

Goldbarth overhauls the poetic genre most susceptible to preciousness and pedantry: ekphrastic verse. '1400' does not offer what 'vivid description of art objects' provides.[36] The art object is barely mentioned, let alone detailed and analysed. Redefining the invention involved, Goldbarth praises the ingredients the painters use with a startling specificity.

The opening line's lurid details establish the method. I cannot recall another poem which mentions 'anal grease', let alone 'the anal grease of an otter'. '1400' gives the impression that it can describe nearly anything: 'the liquid pearl of fish scales stirred in milt', 'spit-in-charcoal', and 'human milk', to cite only three more examples of the more than forty ingredients that the poem mentions. Its wide-ranging vocabulary and syntax certainly delight in its powers of naming, but such virtuoso effects also honour the industry and ingenuity of the late medieval artists who made art out of such seemingly unpromising material, out of carefully extracted waste and filth.

The poem also features several formal restrictions. It consists of one sentence, whose grammar the final three verse lines clarify; 'and so from these / they made their paints: and then / their Gods and their saints'. In that final movement, the poem's loose iambics tighten into an embedded trimeter couplet, complete with a fastening final rhyme. Expanding the effect, the couplet also features an easily avoidable metrical substitution. Where Goldbarth writes 'and so from these / they made their paints: and then / their Gods and their saints', an extra unstressed syllable appears in the least common location, the final metrical foot. '[A]nd their saints', he writes, not 'and then / their Gods and saints'. Just as the poem clarifies its sentence structure, and a rhyme clinches the final movement, it adds a moment of metrical hesitancy. Twice the poem mentions 'their': their Gods and their saints, emphasizing a contrast. But what exactly is being compared? Most obviously, the reference to 'their Gods and their saints' distinguishes between the contemporary moment's understanding of the sacred and the medieval period's, between what we and they believe. Complicating this distinction, Goldbarth follows the depicted artists' methods; he creates a poem out of their materials. More than six hundred years separate Goldbarth and the painters whose work he describes. However, Goldbarth, a secular, Jewish-American writer, reveals a surprising affinity.

With this poem limited to one sentence, the grammatical restriction animates Goldbarth's rush of words and the large theological and historical concerns they explore. Justice's 'The Thin Man' forms a telling contrast. Justice's much shorter poem consists of four sentences, three more than '1400'. The one-sentence limit encourages Goldbarth's expansiveness, the long list he crafts of one ingredient following another. As it suggests, maximalist poems need forceful restrictions. They do not expand all aspects of poetry; they contract certain elements in order to expand others. They gain such force from their exclusions.

I began this essay by noting how a certain recognition marks the contemporary moment: that no universal knowledge of an art form or other subject is possible. Propelled by familiar technologies, the unrelenting rush of information across computers, smartphones, and the Internet intensifies this sensation as language and data overwhelm our ability to follow it. Robert Fitterman describes the opportunities that these pressures offer:

> I think that the web and other language-based technologies have changed the landscape considerably – the language landscape and the landscape for poets. All of a sudden we have this excess and daily deluge of language and text. I think that appropriation strategies are really interesting to reflect that, rather than to make some kind of a comment on it. I think that in order to have commentary on it, you have to use it directly. So that's what interests me. It doesn't even have to be from the web – this kind of radical appropriation can also be, like, textbooks. The material really doesn't matter so much to me as the interest in those strategies. There are strategies that we continue to echo – it is the culture of language.[37]

Faced with the 'excess and daily deluge of language and text', the poet needs to develop a method of selection and appropriation. In Fitterman's terms, then, the material matters less than the poetic strategy.

Fitterman's collection *Holocaust Museum* is composed entirely of captions cut and pasted from the Holocaust Museum's website. It excludes all the images and does not add any of the poet's own descriptions. The reader experiences an odd sensation: three hundred captions evoke what is not present: both the photographs, which the reader does not see, and the victims whose lives they document and turn into a narrative about the Holocaust and its meaning. (As their titles suggest, the last two sections emphasize 'American Soldiers' and 'Liberation'.) Relentlessly caption follows caption and the great mass of material can persuade even expert readers to overlook its formal properties. In a blurb that adorns the collection's back cover, Al Filreis praises *Holocaust Museum* for its all-inclusiveness: 'To the extent that the holocaust encompassed everything, *Holocaust Museum* responds to the problem of representation by making precisely everything its object.'[38] *Holocaust Museum*, however, very carefully selects what it represents. As it suggests, in art inclusion requires an equally powerful exclusion. No matter how generous, a poem must define what it is not.

Notes

1. See p. vii and back cover.
2. Northrop Frye, in Troni Y. Grande and Garry Sherbert (eds), *Northrop Frye's Writings on Shakespeare and the Renaissance* (Toronto: University of Toronto Press, 2010), p. 98. I would like to thank my colleague Zack Long for directing me to this reference.
3. Stuart Hall, 'Old and New Identities, Old and New Ethnicities', in Anthony D. King (ed.), *Culture, Globalization and the World-System: Contemporary Conditions for the Representation of Identity* (Minneapolis, MN: University of Minnesota Press, 1997). p. 68. For a paradigmatic expression of a related stance, see Michel Foucault, in Paul Rabinow (ed.), *The Foucault Reader* (New York: Pantheon Books, 1984), p. 73, where he observes, 'The intellectual is not "the bearer of universal values".'
4. Robert Hass, *Praise* (New York: Ecco Press, 1979), p. 43.
5. Charles Wright, *Country Music: Selected Early Poems* (Middletown, CT: Wesleyan University Press, 1991), p. 17.
6. John Ashbery, *Selected Poems* (New York: Penguin, 1985), p. 235; Donald Justice, *Collected Poems* (New York: Alfred A. Knopf, 2004), p. 160; Mark Strand, *New Selected Poems* (New York: Alfred A. Knopf, 2007), p. 10; and Adrienne Rich, *Adrienne Rich's Poetry and Prose* (New York: W. W. Norton, 1993), p. 160.
7. Peter Gizzi, 'An Open Letter of Poetics to Steve Farmer', September 1999. Last accessed on 29 August 2015. Available at: http://www.petergizzi.org/assets/an-open-letter-of-poetics-to-steve-farmer-(1999)-revised.pdf
8. Kenneth Goldsmith, *Uncreative Writing* (New York: Columbia University Press, 2011), p. 168.
9. For example, William Wordsworth famously declares in 'Observations Prefixed to Lyrical Ballads' (1800):

    > It is supposed, that by the act of writing in verse an Author makes a formal engagement that he will gratify certain known habits of association; that he not only thus apprises the Reader that certain classes of ideas and expressions will be found in his book, but that others will be carefully excluded.

    See William Harmon (ed.), *Classic Writings on Poetry* (New York: Columbia University Press, 2003), p. 280.

10. Jennifer Moxley, *The Middle Room* (Berkeley, CA: Subpress, 2007), p. 277.
11. Mark Strand, *Almost Invisible: Poems* (New York: Alfred A. Knopf, 2012), p. 22.
12. Adrienne Rich, *Later Poems Selected and New: 1971–2012* (New York: W. W. Norton, 2013), p. 247.
13. Adrienne Rich, *Adrienne Rich's Poetry and Prose*, p. 115.
14. Rae Armantrout, *Veil: New and Selected Poems* (Middletown, CT: Wesleyan University Press, 2001), p. 30.
15. William Stafford, 'Travelling through the Dark', in Donald Hall (ed.), *Contemporary American Poetry*, 2nd Edition (New York: Penguin Books, 1972), p. 39.
16. Bob Perelman, *The Marginalization of Poetry: Language Writing and Literary History* (Princeton, NJ: Princeton University Press, 1996), p. 113.
17. Bob Perelman, 'The First Person', *Hills*, 6/7, Talks issue (1980): 163.
18. Bob Perelman, *The Marginalization of Poetry: Language Writing and Literary*, p. 178.
19. Ron Silliman, Carla Harryman, Lyn Hejinian, Steve Benson, Bob Perelman and Barrett Watten, 'Aesthetic Tendency and the Politics of Poetry: A Manifesto', *Social Text*, 19/20 (Autumn 1988): 264–65.
20. Donald M. Allen, *The New American Poetry 1945–1960* (New York: Grove Press, 1960), p. xi.
21. See, for example, David Caplan, *Questions of Possibility: Contemporary Poetry and Poetic Form* (Oxford: Oxford University Press, 2004), pp. 7–8; and Cole Swensen and David St John (eds), *American Hybrid* (New York: W. W. Norton, 2009).
22. Bob Perelman, 'The First Person': 162.
23. Bob Perelman, 'The First Person': 156.
24. Robert Creeley, in Rod Smith, Peter Baker and Kaplan Harris (eds), *The Selected Letters of Robert Creeley* (Berkeley, CA: University of California Press, 2014), p. 276.
25. Rae Armantrout, 'Poetic Statement: Cheshire Poetics', in Claudia Rankine and Juliana Spahr (eds), *American Women Poets in the 21st Century: Where Lyric Meets Language* (Middletown, CT: Wesleyan University Press, 2002), p. 26.
26. Donald Justice, *Collected Poems*, p. 88.
27. Marjorie Perloff, 'Minimalism', *The Princeton Encyclopedia of Poetry and Poetics*, 4th edition, p. 866. My next point is also indebted to her entry.
28. Paul Muldoon, *Quoof* (Winston-Salem, NC: Wake Forest University Press, 1983), p. 33.
29. See, for example, Robert Duncan, *The Opening of the Field* (New York: Grove Press, 1960); Charles Altieri, *Enlarging the Temple: New Directions in American Poetry During the 1960s* (Lewisburg, PA: Bucknell University Press, 1980); and Lynn Keller, *Forms of Expansion: Recent Long Poems by Women* (Chicago, IL: University of Chicago Press, 1997).
30. Stephen Burt, 'Poetry in Review', *The Yale Review*, 100(2) (April 2012): 186.

31. Albert Goldbarth, *The Kitchen Sink: New and Selected Poems* (Saint Paul, MN: Graywolf Press, 2007), p. 22.
32. Helen Vendler, *The Art of Shakespeare's Sonnets* (Cambridge: Belknap Press, 1997), pp. xiv–xvi.
33. Albert Goldbarth, *The Kitchen Sink: New and Selected Poems*, p. 5.
34. John Keats, *Complete Poems*, ed. Jack Stillinger (Cambridge, MA: Harvard University Press, 1982), p. 282.
35. Albert Goldbarth, '1400', *Poetry*, 189(2) (November 2006): 88.
36. Alastair Fowler, 'Genre and Tradition', in Thomas A. Corns (ed.), *The Cambridge Companion to English Poetry: Donne to Marvell* (Cambridge: Cambridge University Press, 1993), p. 91.
37. Bree Davies, 'Conceptual Writer Robert Fitterman on his New Book, *Holocaust Museum*', Denver Westward Blogs (21 November 2013). Last accessed on 29 August 2015. Available at:http://blogs.westword.com/showandtell/2013/11/conceptual_writer_robert_fitte.php?page=2
38. Robert Fitterman, *Holocaust Museum* (Denver, CO: Counterpath, 2013), back cover. I would like to thank Julie Carr for bringing *Holocaust Museum* to my attention.

Further Reading

Allen, Donald M., *The New American Poetry 1945–1960* (New York: Grove Press, 1960).

Armantrout, Rae, *Veil: New and Selected Poems* (Middletown, CT: Wesleyan University Press, 2001).

Ashbery, John, *Selected Poems* (New York: Penguin, 1985).

Caplan, David, *Questions of Possibility: Contemporary Poetry and Poetic Form* (Oxford: Oxford University Press, 2004).

Fitterman, Robert, *Holocaust Museum* (Denver, CO: Counterpath, 2013).

Goldbarth, Albert, *The Kitchen Sink: New and Selected Poems* (Saint Paul, MN: Graywolf Press, 2007).

Goldsmith, Kenneth, *Uncreative Writing* (New York: Columbia University Press, 2011).

Hass, Robert, *Praise* (New York: Ecco Press, 1979).

Justice, Donald, *Collected Poems* (New York: Alfred A. Knopf, 2004).

Moxley, Jennifer, *The Middle Room* (Berkeley, CA: Subpress, 2007).

Muldoon, Paul, *Quoof* (Winston-Salem, NC: Wake Forest University Press, 1983).

Perelman, Bob, *The Marginalization of Poetry: Language Writing and Literary History* (Princeton, NJ: Princeton University Press, 1996).

Rich, Adrienne, *Adrienne Rich's Poetry and Prose* (New York: W. W. Norton, 1993).

Rich, Adrienne, *Later Poems Selected and New: 1971–2012* (New York: W. W. Norton, 2013).

Silliman, Ron, Carla Harryman, Lyn Hejinian, Steve Benson, Bob Perelman and Barrett Watten, 'Aesthetic Tendency and the Politics of Poetry: A Manifesto', *Social Text*, 19/20 (Autumn 1988): 261–75.

Strand, Mark, *New Selected Poems* (New York: Alfred A. Knopf, 2007).

Strand, Mark, *Almost Invisible: Poems* (New York: Alfred A. Knopf, 2012).

The Princeton Encyclopedia of Poetry and Poetics, 4th Edition, editor in chief Roland Greene (Princeton, NJ: Princeton University Press, 2012).

Wright, Charles, *Country Music: Selected Early Poems* (Middletown, CT: Wesleyan University Press, 1991).

10

The Art of Losing: American Elegy since 1945

Stephen Regan

American poets writing about death and mourning since the middle years of the twentieth century have faced severe challenges, both philosophical and linguistic, in composing an elegiac art for modern readers. In the aftermath of two world wars and the accompanying assault on religious belief, it became increasingly difficult for poets to perform the traditional elegiac rites of honouring the dead and consoling the living. The classical myths and ceremonies that had been carried over into Christian elegy, helping to sustain belief in immortality, were now likely to appear hollow and ineffective. What ideas and what words might sustain a sceptical post-war generation in the midst of massive personal and public loss? Since 1945, attitudes to death have altered dramatically and so, too, have artistic responses. Peter Sacks notes how death has 'tended to become obscene, meaningless, impersonal', an event either 'stupefyingly colossal in cases of large-scale war or genocide' or 'clinically concealed behind the technology of the hospital'.[1] The consequences for the writing of elegy have been profound, with modern American authors wilfully renouncing traditional elegiac codes and conventions, or else treating them ironically, while flagrantly disputing the comforting, consoling function of earlier poetry. However, if modern American poetry has sometimes displayed 'a drying up or a deliberate termination of the familiar expressions of grief', it has also been astoundingly inventive in its artistic exploration of death and mourning.[2]

From the outset, American elegy was radically innovative in its handling of the traditional myths and rituals of the genre, and strongly assertive in its declaration of individuality and distinctiveness. The classical, pastoral settings and motifs associated with elegy did not lend themselves easily to American poetry, and consequently the

American elegist often appears displaced or marginalized. At the same time, compared with its English counterpart, the American elegy is likely to appear unusually intense and direct in its expression of loss. Sacks claims that the 'severe repression and rationalization of grief' in Puritan America perhaps prompted in poetry a 'nakedly expressive style' and an insistent focus on the 'unique and isolated self' of the griever.[3] Walt Whitman's great elegy for Abraham Lincoln, 'When Lilacs Last in the Dooryard Bloom'd', is in many ways a foundational American elegy, observing decorum but also following its own wayward path, and eloquently combining stunned bewilderment with a candid and fulsome declaration of love: 'O how shall I warble myself for the dead one there I loved?'[4] An elegy for the Civil War dead, as much as for the President of the United States, Whitman's poem became an exemplary model of personal grieving elevated to a public and national level. In much modern American poetry, this explicit and outspoken personal style is inclined to be volatile and tempestuous. Jahan Ramazani goes so far as to claim that the modern American elegy is not only intimate and immediate, but also aggressive and antagonistic to an unprecedented degree. Consequently, he draws attention away from elegy as a successful 'work of mourning' (in the Freudian sense), towards a concentration on the unresolved, traumatic and violent expression of grief in modern examples of the genre.[5] Within this broader precinct of fraught and rebellious grieving, a powerful and accumulated charge can be observed in the work of many post-war American poets, among them Robert Lowell, Elizabeth Bishop, John Berryman, Adrienne Rich, Sylvia Plath, Anne Sexton, and Amy Clampitt. Modern American poetry mourns the death of friends and family with an often surprising intimacy, and it mourns the death of poets with a searing intensity. At the same time, what gives this poetry an added poignancy is the intimation that it also mourns the lost structures of belief and value that once upheld the ideal of an afterlife and made consolation possible.

Wallace Stevens, more than any other American poet, explores the possibilities of a modernist poetics of grief. From *Harmonium* (1923) to *Auroras of Autumn* (1950), his poetry is fundamentally concerned with the metaphysics of loss and absence, repeatedly proffering its own aesthetic achievements as substitutes for an outmoded faith. If his poetry is often obscure and impersonal, seeming to repudiate the direct expression of deeply felt grief, along with the rituals, myths and ceremonies of traditional elegy, it is also habitually given to ceremonial lament, extending rather than simply rejecting the familiar conventions of the genre. As Ramazani notes, Stevens is not usually thought of as a major elegist, but he is a highly prolific and resourceful writer of 'anti-elegies, mock elegies, covert elegies, and self-elegies'. As his early, celebrated poem 'The Emperor of Ice Cream' demonstrates, Stevens 'satirizes the standard elements of the elegiac repertoire, yet he also reveals the surprising persistence of consolatory elegiac traditions within modernist poetry'.[6]

Stevens is also a writer of enigmatic war elegies, and those that emerge from the Second World War sustain his reputation and influence after 1945. Several poems in *Transport to Summer* (1947) reflect on the mental and emotional turmoil of the soldier in the face of death as a magnified instance of our common human predicament. 'Flyer's Fall' contemplates the death of an airman, finding nobility not in the conventional notion of sacrifice in war but in the man's alert and anguished consciousness, 'Knowing that he died nobly, as he died.' In this modern, secular vision, the flyer escapes 'the dirty fates' of a defunct mythology of death. The traditional elegiac yearning for transcendence and consolation is replaced by a stark recognition and admission of emptiness: 'Darkness, nothingness of human after-death, / Receive and keep him in the deepnesses of space.'[7] The striking compound 'after-death' is an abrupt and resolute refusal of the expected 'afterlife', while the plural 'deepnesses' effectively multiplies the imagined depth of space. Significantly, the verbal mood of 'Receive and keep' can be read as both simply indicative and prayerfully imperative, with a call to darkness displacing the usual address to gods and angels. The poem's closing perception of 'Profundum' plays with etymology in devastating ways, simultaneously registering the abyss of space, the lack of philosophical knowledge and insight, and the absence of belief in the efficacy of prayer, exemplified by the De Profundis (Psalm 130): 'Out of the depths have I cried to thee, O Lord.'[8] This is the dimension in which 'We believe without belief, beyond belief.' With a startling syntactical economy, Stevens acknowledges the incomprehensible and incommensurable nature of death, while exerting an existential awareness of our continuing human need for explanatory theologies.

'The Owl in the Sarcophagus' tests the resources of wisdom and imagination in confronting the stark reality and darkness of death. Written in 1947 after the death of Henry Church, to whom Stevens dedicated his 'Notes on a Supreme Fiction', the poem originally carried the epigraph 'Goodbye H.C.' A modernist elegy *par excellence*, it swoops through the underworld of classical antiquity, surveying 'the forms of dark desire' that initiate and sustain the genre, while also declaring an urgent need to make it new. With a nod to Shelley's elegy for Keats and to Whitman's elegy for Lincoln, Stevens introduces a ceremonial procession of the forms that 'move among the dead': two brothers ('high sleep' and 'high peace') followed by an earthly mother, 'she that says / Good-by in the darkness'. While dutifully observing the elegiac conventions of the past, 'The Owl in the Sarcophagus' is candid in its realization of how these fictions and fabrications are born out of human need and desire. It exposes the stitching by which the figure of peace has been robed and adorned across the years, and it shows the workings of imagination 'In the weaving round the wonder of its need'.[9]

Stevens is more intent than any other twentieth-century elegist in revealing 'the mythology of modern death', even to the point of decrying the familiar poetic personifications of death as 'monsters of elegy'.[10] As a 'goodbye', 'The Owl in the Sarcophagus' is strangely impersonal and obscure in its dark flittings of thought. As Angela Leighton has noted, it makes its way 'in an atmosphere of evasions and tangents, of weirdly displaced syntax and grammar, which seem hardly to bear upon the event in question'.[11] At the same time, it carries a profound awareness of the thoughts and desires that populate the grieving mind in need of consolation, locating that fundamental need in its delicate closing image of 'a child that sings itself to sleep'. It both invokes 'the forms of dark desire' and demythologizes death by understanding our common human rituals, including elegy itself, as 'inventions of farewell'.[12] If that resonant phrase acknowledges a deep and recurring impulse to find words and images that are somehow adequate to the predicament of loss, it also subtly intimates that loss is productive of new art, and that 'Death is the mother of beauty,' as Stevens writes elsewhere.[13]

Stevens is the most subtle theoretician of death and mourning in modern American poetry, a writer whose late poems are exemplary in their contemplation of emptiness and their calm reflection on 'The stillness of everything gone' ('Autumn Refrain').[14] The most powerful and prolific practitioner of the modern American elegy, however, is undoubtedly Robert Lowell, who announced his precocious talent for the poetics of loss with 'The Quaker Graveyard in Nantucket' in 1946. Ostensibly an elegy for Lowell's cousin, Warren Winslow, lost at sea when the Navy destroyer on which he was serving accidentally exploded in New York Harbor in January 1944, the poem expands geographically and historically to become a searing indictment of the abuse of political power and the corruption of religious belief. The epigraph from Genesis ('Let man have dominion over the fishes of the sea and the fowls of the air ...') casts an ironic shadow over the entire poem. The Quaker graveyard is a fitting setting for a poem that meditates on a lost sailor's body, imagined to be somewhere in the turbulent North Atlantic (though never recovered), but the inspired displacement from New York to Madaket, on the western tip of Nantucket, is indicative of a more general and profound dislocation that generates the elegy. The speaker of the poem is himself strangely dislocated, initially appearing as one of the crew recovering a drowned sailor (a representative or substitute for Winslow), and then later addressing the dead man in more formal, elegiac terms as 'my cousin'.[15] The imaginative excursion to Nantucket pays dividends in allowing Lowell to invert the usual peaceful associations of Quakerism (recalling Herman Melville's acknowledgement of fighting Quakers in *Moby-Dick*), and to employ the brutal imagery of whale fishing as emblematic of New England's inglorious exercise of power and pursuit of wealth. Ahab is depicted in the poem as a figurehead of destructive idealism in American culture, and Lowell does not flinch from including himself among Ahab's deranged and dangerous progeny.

Death at sea gives Lowell's poem a strong thematic link with John Milton's 'Lycidas', which it also emulates technically in its loose pentameter and occasional trimeter lines. Like its predecessor, it embraces both Classical and Christian archetypes and allusions. From the outset, though, 'The Quaker Graveyard in Nantucket' is resolute in its refusal of traditional ideas and images of consolation. It will ask for 'no Orphean lute / To pluck life back' (the neat musical pun here testifies to the poet's ironic and circumspect attitude), listening instead to the 'hoarse salute' of modern warfare in 'The guns of the steeled fleet'. Where Milton is decorously restrained in broaching the topic of death at sea, Lowell is violently explicit, depicting how 'the drowned sailor clutched the drag net' and 'grappled at the net / With the coiled, hurdling muscles of his thighs'. The energetic physicality of the poetry is so intense that the cold, wet corpse with 'matted head and marble feet' appears to be reanimated, only to be cast back into the sea, this time suitably weighted and without any solemn memorializing ('the name / Is blocked in yellow chalk').[16]

Like Stevens, Lowell is inclined to let the poetry of loss modulate into prayer, though with a greater sense of urgency. The 'troubled waters' of the Atlantic are a fitting place for the plangent strains of 'De Profundis': '*Clamavimus*, O depths', while Section V of the poem cries out to the composite figure of Jonas Messias in a pacifist plea against past and present violence: 'Hide / Our steel, Jonas Messias, in Thy side.' Section VI, 'Our Lady at Walsingham', acknowledges the deep instinct for penitence in Christian communities, though the image of pilgrims moving like 'cows to the old shrine' threatens to degrade that instinct. The shrine of Our Lady might well be Lowell's still point in the turning world, but there is a measure of scepticism in the poem's response to the 'expressionless' face of the statue. The poem distances itself from the spiritual transcendence with which Milton closes 'Lycidas'. The triumphant directive, 'Look homeward, angel,' is undermined in Lowell's sardonic 'upward angel, downward fish' (with mankind delicately poised between these categories), while the ethereal 'blue mantle' of Milton's pastoral swain is displaced by the 'blue-lung'd combers' of the sea, which throughout history have 'lumbered to the kill'. Despite the rhyming couplet that it forms, the closing line is enigmatic, unyielding, and unconsoling: 'The Lord survives the rainbow of His will.'[17]

'The Quaker Graveyard in Nantucket' came to be seen as a landmark in the history of the American elegy, appearing in the immediate aftermath of World War II and seizing the opportunity to give public voice and significance to personal loss. While still searching for a distinctive poetic voice, Lowell manages to give the elegy immense stature, ambitiously and provocatively connecting historical and contemporary events. In other respects, however, the poem has been read by Marjorie Perloff and others as one of a series of Winslow family poems. Perloff claims that Lowell's 'most characteristic and celebrated poems have been elegies, particularly elegies on his maternal or Winslow relatives', and she counts 'In Memory of Arthur Winslow' (published in *Lord Weary's Castle* in 1946) among 'Lowell's finest early poems'. At the same time, she concedes that the poem is 'an elegy that fails to fulfill the most basic requirements of the form: it contains no lament and a very dubious consolation'.[18] Indeed, Lowell the Catholic convert turns on his grandfather with contempt and disgust, berating him for his materialistic greed, and closing with a prayer to Our Lady. The elegy opens with an Easter setting, but 'The *resurrexit dominus* of all the bells' is muted.[19] The poem audaciously summons both Charon and the risen Jesus to Boston, and imagines Acheron beyond the Charles River, though its mood is pervasively ironic and mocking. Lowell shows great skill in adopting the familiar conventions of the classical elegy and its English imitations, including its redemptive water imagery, but all the signs are that Lowell and his forebears are still a long way from shore. The harshness of Lowell's elegy for his grandfather is matched only by the malice of the companion poem for his grandmother, 'Mary Winslow', in which the pampered imperious socialite regresses to sickly childhood until Charon comes from the frozen Charles River and 'stops her hideous baby-squawks and yells'. Boston Common provides an unlikely pastoral setting, while the elegiac declarations, 'Mary Winslow is dead' and 'Nothing will go again', sound hollow and ineffective.[20]

The Winslow family constitutes an imposing *tableau vivant*, ironically overshadowed by death, in 'My Last Afternoon with Uncle Devereux Winslow', widely regarded as the keystone achievement among many distinguished poems in Lowell's *Life Studies* (1959). Here, the family's foibles and failings are brilliantly refracted through the child's half-comprehending intelligence, and movingly offset against sudden moments of clarity and devastating simplicity: 'My Uncle was dying at twenty-nine.'[21] Even so, it was undoubtedly Lowell's elegy for his mother, 'Sailing Home from Rapallo', that sealed his reputation as the major elegist of his time and announced the arrival of so-called 'confessional' poetry. The euphemistic title of the poem, invoking both leisurely vacation and elegiac mythology, leads into caustic social satire, but only after the candid intimacy of the opening lines and an unabashed declaration of deep feeling:

> Your nurse could only speak Italian,
> but after twenty minutes I could imagine your final week,
> and tears ran down my cheeks. . . .

The ellipsis at the end of each verse section signals an uncontrollable welter of thoughts and feelings, while also seeking to establish the speaker's bearings in a world of 'lost connections'. The poem reconnects mother and son, at the same time as exploiting the striking contrasts between the 'fiery flower' of the *Golfo di Genova* and the dark, icy cemetery in Dunbarton. Any tendency towards sentimentality, or any further display of unchecked feeling, is held at bay by Lowell's fine sense of the intrusion of accident and incongruity in the realm of death and grief:

> In the grandiloquent lettering on Mother's coffin,
> *Lowell* had been misspelled *LOVEL*.
> The corpse
> was wrapped like *panettone* in Italian tinfoil.[22]

In a prose account of his mother's death, Lowell castigates the Italian undertakers for 'an ugly and tasteless error', but the poem manipulates that error for ironic effect, allowing just a glimpse of love in an otherwise discordant set of family relations.[23] The misnaming, along with the repeated italicization of names and foreign words, further testifies to Lowell's self-conscious handling, and perhaps even mistrust, of the very medium in which he conveys his loss. There is sweetness and a shimmer of light, as well as grotesquerie, in the *panettone* simile, but its purpose, for all the seeming confessionalism of the opening, is to lend the poem a final flourish of achieved objectivity and emotional detachment.

The first paperback edition of *Life Studies* (1960) closed with a new poem titled 'Colonel Shaw and the Massachusetts' 54th', which was later to become the title poem of Lowell's next volume, *For the Union Dead* (1964). One of the great public elegies of the post-war era, a poem about 'childhood memories, the evisceration of our modern cities, civil rights, [and] nuclear warfare', the work was read by Lowell at Boston Arts Festival in June 1960, close to the monument of Colonel Robert Shaw and his soldiers, from which it had taken its inspiration. 'For the Union Dead' opens, however, with a child's memories of 'the old South Boston Aquarium', now with windows 'broken' and 'boarded', symbolic of all that is being replaced by modernizing projects such as the underground car park being 'gouged' out of Boston Common. The memorial statue 'propped by a plank' during the excavations is emblematic of a lost sense of moral certitude and direction, though in other respects Colonel Shaw is seen as a type of the dangerous idealist, inflexible and unyielding: 'he cannot bend his back'. The sacrifice made by his regiment of black soldiers still awaits recognition in an era of continued racial segregation. The great achievement of the poem, however, is in its brilliant stylistic control of subtly modulated patterns of imagery. The monument 'sticks like a fishbone / in the city's throat', while the 'cowed, compliant fish' from the old aquarium are transformed into the more assertive and disturbing creatures of a changed social order: 'giant finned cars nose forward like fish'. A world of loss is encapsulated in the simple declaration, 'The Aquarium is gone,' while the 'savage servility' of modern American consumerism displaces the more honourable ideal of service ('Servare') represented by Shaw and his soldiers.[24]

Lowell's final book of poems, *Day by Day*, appeared just before his death in 1977, and it carries the imprint of his meditations on death and the afterlife. In finely poised elegies for his father, mother and grandfather, Lowell revisits his earlier poems of loss and mourning, and reconsiders his earlier harsh judgements in the soft, autumnal light of his own declining mortality. In 'Robert T. S. Lowell' (the name he shared with his father), the poet presents a dialogue between Son and Father, each wishing that they might have relived their lives. 'To Mother' signals a new, forgiving intimacy, even in its title. Lowell's mother is still regarded as a formidable Napoleonic spirit, '*Josephine*

Beauharnais, la femme militaire', but along with the familiar disdain for her domestic rule, there is also a tender admission of loss and regret: 'Your parlor was a reproach. I wish I were there with you, / the minutes not counted, but not forever –'. This is an altogether gentler portrait of his mother than the one Lowell painted in *Life Studies*. It closes with a confession of his own human failings, and with the unstable self split by the telling ellipsis: 'It has taken me the time since you died / To discover you are as human as I am . . . / if I am.'

Lowell was himself the subject of a fine elegy, 'North Haven', written by Elizabeth Bishop soon after his death. Returning to their 'favorite' island in Penobscot Bay, off the coast of Maine, Bishop speaks intimately and affectionately to Lowell while meditating on loss and renewal. The poem opens with a present-tense perception of stillness within nature, the italicized lines initiating the movement of the mind as it encounters space and time, distance and nearness: '*I can make out the rigging of a schooner / a mile off; I can count / the new cones on the spruce*'. Bishop's island pastoral seems ideally suited to the traditional conventions of elegy, being 'full of flowers' and populated by goldfinches and other birds that seem to guarantee nature's perpetual return. North Haven is perfectly placed to observe the interplay of land and water, and the mystical blue of sky and sea. The islands, of which it is one, are 'free within the blue frontiers of bay'.[25]

There is no hint of Lowell's death, other than the dedication '*In memoriam: Robert Lowell*', until the pleading call of the sparrow 'brings tears to the eyes'. Nature's process of repetition is now aligned with poetry's process of revision, the seasonal cycle of renewal with the artistic urge for perfection and permanence: 'Nature repeats herself, or almost does: / *repeat, repeat, repeat; revise, revise, revise*'. The work of mourning, in the Freudian sense, often calls for erotic arousal and sexual renewal, the urge for life, and in the closing two stanzas, which enter into more intimate conversation with Lowell, Bishop recalls him telling her that it was here, at North Haven, that he 'learned to kiss'. There is wry amusement, as well as sorrow, in her recollection of Lowell's personal struggles for fulfilment: '("Fun" – it always seemed to leave you at a loss . . .)', but the colloquial ease of the line prepares us for the terminal 'leave' and 'loss' of the ending. The elegant stanzas of iambic pentameter, sparsely rhymed, with a closing line of hexameter, are disrupted by words in parentheses or italics or quotation, in a style reminiscent of Lowell's *Life Studies*. The poem moves towards an elevation of Lowell, even subtly suggesting that it is the poet, not just North Haven, 'afloat in mystic blue'. Though it might court conventional elegy, however, 'North Haven' quietly asserts its own vision, gently replacing the usual gestures of consolation and resurrection with life's changefulness and art's completion beautifully balanced. There is satisfaction, as well as sadness, in knowing that Lowell is beyond derangement and rearrangement: 'The words won't change again. Sad friend, you cannot change.'[26]

Bishop had, of course, already established her credentials as a poet of intense elegiac sensitivity in poems such as 'Sestina' and 'First Death in Nova Scotia' in *Questions of Travel* (1965). In both poems, the intensity derives from the exploration of a child's innocent apprehension of absence and loss, and from the metrically controlled manipulation of the child's way of seeing the world. In 'First Death in Nova Scotia', the trimeter lines and the repetition of particular words and sounds give the poem the appearance of light verse ('In the cold, cold parlour / my mother laid out Arthur'), and that impression is reinforced by the collision of images, with a stuffed bird ('the red-eyed loon') comically relieving the arranged colonial formality of the royal family. The child sees the world in red and white: the red eyes of the loon against the 'white, frozen lake' of the marble-topped table, and the red maple leaf of the Canadian flag against a white background. Death is understood in metaphors and similes drawn from the child's local and immediate experience: cousin Arthur is 'all white, like a doll / that hadn't been painted yet', and his coffin is 'a little frosted cake'. The simplicity of vision, matched with a simplicity of technique, culminates in the poem's closing question, as the child imagines cousin Arthur being invited by the royal family to be a page at court:

> But how could Arthur go
> clutching his tiny lily,
> with his eyes shut up so tight
> and the roads deep in snow?[27]

If the child's way of seeing the world allows Bishop an obliquity and detachment in writing about death, it also suggests that death will never cease to be a mystery, and that the inventions of the mind are all that we have by way of understanding it.

'One Art', published in *Geography III* in 1976, employs the villanelle form with virtuosic skill, demonstrating the relentless struggle of art to embrace and order a world of contingency and loss. The tensions implicit in the form – those of repetition and variation – are deftly handled by Bishop in a poem that swells with an alarming and increasing sense of loss, while exerting control over its own linguistic medium. Slightly modifying the traditional villanelle with its two repeated refrains, Bishop follows the opening insistence that 'The art of losing isn't hard to master' with variations on the theme of 'disaster'. The poem opens out from lost door keys and lost time to lost cities and even 'a continent'. The comparison with Lowell is instructive, as Bishop's art is one that seeks to exercise, rather than violate, restraint and decorum where personal loss is invoked. Even so, it is difficult to ignore the corresponding losses in Bishop's own life: the loss of her mother to a psychiatric hospital when Bishop was a child, the loss of three houses in Brazil, and the loss (by suicide) of her partner, Lota, in 1967. The closing quatrain, with its dramatic dash, presents a new challenge: the prospect of losing a new and promising love: '– Even losing you (the joking voice, a gesture / I love) I shan't have lied.' Seeking to exert and maintain a stoical attitude, the poem brings 'master' and 'disaster' into even closer relationship, though it struggles to hold them together in a rhyming couplet. Mimetically and metrically the poem enacts disaster, inscribing and re-inscribing what it is 'like', and insisting on the efficacy of writing in a closing line that hesitates, then wills its own recovery: '(*Write* it!)'.[28]

The correspondence of Bishop and Lowell records the death by suicide ('so sad & awful') of John Berryman on 7 January 1972.[29] Although Berryman's work has been extensively studied as confessional poetry, rather less attention has been given to its elegiac qualities. Reading it alongside the work of Lowell and Bishop helps to illuminate some shared stylistic features among these poets, but also reveals what is most distinctive and peculiar in Berryman's poems of loss and mourning. Berryman thought of *The Dream Songs* as a title in 1955, though the volume of poems we have come to know by that name did not appear until 1969. John Haffenden claims that there are glimpses of *The Dream Songs* in Berryman's draft poems as early as 1948, and August Kleinzahler sees the style taking shape around the same time (1947–48).[30] Although the book was the product of a long imaginative process of accretion and amalgamation, of many and varied parts, Berryman liked to think of it as a single poem. It might even be considered as a single extended elegy, all of it emerging from the 'irreversible loss' suffered by its imaginary character, Henry. That loss is given prominence in the opening Dream Song. The world 'once did seem on Henry's side', but 'Then came a departure.'[31] The departure is signalled over and over in elegies for other poets, including W. B. Yeats, Delmore Schwartz, and Sylvia Plath, but the 'songs' for his father, John Smith, who shot and killed himself in Florida in 1926, are among the most powerful and disturbing elegies in modern American poetry.

'Dream Song 145', the closing song in Section V of the seven sections of *The Dream Songs*, moves towards 'forgiveness time' in Berryman's relationship with his father, opening abruptly and surprisingly, 'Also I love him.' The struggle for coherence and connection in the final stanza, however, suggests a deeper and darker stir of feelings:

> I cannot read that wretched mind, so strong
> & so undone. I've always tried. I – I'm
> trying to forgive . . .

Berryman, in his prefatory 'Note' to *The Dream Songs*, is adamant that Henry is 'not the poet, not me', but the poignancy of the poetry suggests otherwise. Here, there is a terrible, ironic recollection of the father having made his departure in the 'summer dawn', and having 'left Henry to live on'.[32] The tone is half pitiful, half accusatory. Any buoyant sense of *The Dream Songs* progressing from melancholia towards successful mourning is completely undermined by the penultimate poem in the collection, 'Dream Song 384'. Although the declining day conforms to elegiac expectations, the slanted grave marker and the absence of flowers do not bode well: 'The marker slants, flowerless, the day's almost done, / I stand above my father's grave with rage . . .'. The poem angrily flouts the usual tokens of decency, respect and consolation, scorning traditional rites of mourning, as well as the conventions of elegy: 'I spit upon this dreadful banker's grave / who shot his heart out in a Florida dawn.'[33] There is a Hamlet-like theatricality in Henry's moaning and raving around the grave, but the allusion serves to heighten, rather than diminish, the intense personal tragedy.

The death of Delmore Schwartz in July 1966 affected Berryman profoundly, and prompted a series of elegiac meditations (Songs 146–59) in Section VI of *The Dream Songs*, in which the New York poet becomes 'the new ghost / haunting Henry most'. As is often the case in elegies written by one poet for another, the surviving writer's own mortality and immortality are implicated in the mourning, and Berryman responds to that convention with calculated insouciance: 'I wait on for my own, / I dare say it won't be long.' The songs for Schwartz constitute 'one solid block of agony' and mix the fragments of an antiquated elegiac tradition ('dying O and O I mourn') with contemporary colloquial speech. 'Dream Song 155' opens urgently and alarmingly – 'I can't get him out of my mind, out of my mind' – invoking both senses of 'out of my mind', before showing without any trace of doubt that Schwartz, too, was out of his mind.[34]

Plath, like Berryman, lost her father when she was still a child (she was eight years old when he died), and her memories of him generate a poetry of intense melancholic mourning, in which anger and aggression vie with love and devotion. Otto Plath died from natural causes, but Plath's poetry responds to the loss with violently destructive urges. The emotional extremity perhaps explains why Plath's poems have not generally been read as elegiac. They appear anti-consolatory, volatile, and vindictive. Plath herself was inclined to see the relationship in terms of the Electra Complex – the unresolved psychosexual desire of a daughter for her father – and to dramatize the associated feelings of guilt and self-blame in her poems. According to Anne Stevenson, it was a visit to her father's grave for the first time, nearly twenty years after his death, that prompted 'Electra on Azalea Path'.[35] The poem opens with the speaker's confession of having descended into the darkness of the earth with her father – 'The day you died I went into the dirt' – and later emerging from her dreaming state to find herself in a cemetery: 'The day I woke, I woke on Churchyard Hill.' In a stubborn refusal of conventional floral tributes, and of the associated elegiac consolation and promise of renewal, the poem asserts that 'no flower / Breaks the soil'. Instead, there is a 'basket of plastic evergreens', with 'ersatz petals' dripping red. Plath's subversion of elegiac expectations is clearly pronounced here, and in other poems, but what distinguishes her writing in the genre most of all is the startlingly forthright mode of address, involving both self-conscious theatricality and a relentless talking to the dead, by turns adulatory and accusatory:

> I am the ghost of an infamous suicide,
> My own blue razor rusting at my throat.
> O pardon the one who knocks for pardon at
> Your gate, father – your hound-bitch, daughter, friend.
> It was my love that did us both to death.

The implications here are manifold and psychologically complex, but the overriding suggestion is that the loving daughter has been abandoned by the father; that the father was neglectful in caring for himself, perhaps even causing his own death; and that the resulting pain and struggle to survive will bring about the eventual suicide of the daughter. The measure of the poem's success, however, is not in the extent to which it corresponds to biographical fact, but rather in the style with which it creates a dramatic and arresting voice. The poem anticipates the later Plath of *Ariel* in its dizzying array of verbal registers, from the rhetorically mannered ('O pardon') to the casually devastating ('did us both to death').[36]

A daughter's disturbed and troubled grieving for her father shapes 'The Colossus' and 'Daddy', two of Plath's most accomplished poems. In both of these, the father is simultaneously elevated and derided, mourned and mocked. He is the lost and shattered Titan figure of the famed Colossus at Rhodes, and a 'Ghastly statue' that stretches head to toe across America. At the same time, he is a confining and restricting presence, with the speaker being compelled to 'squat in the cornucopia' of his 'left ear' in 'The Colossus' and live 'like a foot' in a 'black shoe' in 'Daddy'. The struggle for communication and resolution is powerfully conveyed through cultural references and registers that sweep alarmingly from the comic imitation of nursery rhymes such as 'Humpty Dumpty' and 'Old MacDonald's Farm' to classical tragedy and the Holocaust. 'The Colossus' closes in subdued light and shadow, but the signs of resignation and abandonment suggest that mourning has been overtaken by melancholia: 'No longer do I listen for the scrape of a keel / on the blank stones of the landing.' 'Daddy' is even more recalcitrant in its memorializing of the dead father, generating a violence that militates against elegiac consolation and reconciliation. The poem fiercely exploits the ambivalence of a single word, holding on desperately to the possibility of *getting through to* the dead while caustically declaring the finality of *being through with* them: 'Daddy, daddy, you bastard, I'm through.'[37] Plath explained in a BBC recording that the poem was 'spoken by a girl with an Electra complex', whose 'father died while she thought he was God'. She helpfully added that 'her father was also a Nazi and her mother very possibly part Jewish', these 'two strains' paralysing each other in the daughter.[38] Readings of 'Daddy' that seek to highlight the biographical circumstances of Plath's own life are apt to miss both the daring construction of a psychologically complicated persona and the brilliant theatricality of the poem.

If Plath creates a new kind of parental elegy that threatens in its emotional vehemence and parodic style to undo the familiar conventions of the genre, she also brings a chilling candour and clarity to the self-elegy, both anticipating what death might be like and trying to imagine its aftermath. In 'Sheep in Fog', written two weeks before she died, she creates a bleak pastoral in which all of the elegiac images conspire to portend her own imminent demise and point to 'a heaven starless and fatherless, a dark water'.[39] Her final poem, 'Edge', looks from the brink of existence at her own dead body with a macabre sense of accomplishment: 'The woman is perfected.' In a final flourish of ironic elegiac ceremony, the energy drained from the dead woman's body is transferred to her principal mourner, the moon: 'Her blacks crackle and drag.'[40] The combination of studied postures and startling performances produced a style that very few of Plath's contemporaries could equal. Anne Sexton's suicide poems, including 'Sylvia's Death', 'Wanting to Die', and 'Suicide Note', look desultory in comparison with Plath's stridently provocative poems on the same topic. Plath's poems gain in stature, not least because they engage so intensely with a strong and well-established set of elegiac images, myths, and conventions, even if they relentlessly flout and undermine them.

The intensity and extremity of Plath's elegiac art urged some of her contemporaries to follow a different direction in writing poems of mourning. Adrienne Rich, in a proleptic elegy for her father, written just a year after Plath's suicide, moves towards composure and a peaceful letting go. For all its troubling revelations of a daughter's contempt for her father, 'After Dark' chooses the open expanse of grass and water over the confinement of prison and the grave, and it ends with the pair sitting together, 'waiting till the blunt barge / bumps along the shore'.[41] 'A Woman Mourned by Daughters', published in 1963, is similarly composed, gently easing grief with wit. The description of the mother as 'swollen' and 'puffed up in death' has a physical immediacy, while testifying to her persistent authority.[42] The poem speaks collectively for the daughters, addressing their need to carry on with their own lives while still instinctively adhering to their mother's wishes.

Amy Clampitt's 'A Procession at Candlemas' records a daughter's journey by bus along Route 80 to visit her dying mother in hospital. For all its startlingly modern urban imagery, the poem is steeped in myth and history, drawing deeply on elegiac convention at the same time as it radically transforms it. The moving lights on the highway conjure up an elegiac procession, while the curtain in the intensive care ward becomes the veil that so often intervenes between the living and the dead in traditional elegy. The feast of Candlemas, associated with rites of purification, provides Clampitt with an opportunity to reassert the figure of the mother in a genre of writing so often dominated by patriarchal figures of authority. As Ramazani notes, the anger in the poem is directed not at a dead or dying parent, but at 'two religious traditions that have degraded mothers while seeming to celebrate them: the cults of Athena and of the Virgin Mary'. While gathering to itself a powerful symbolism drawn from classical and biblical myth, the poem roots its own personal sorrow in the larger losses of American history, alluding both to the sufferings of

Native Americans and to the violent destruction caused by modern warfare: 'for every carried flame // the name of a dead soldier'. The poem makes its impact most forcefully, however, in bringing its search for origins and meanings back to the female body and the physical realities of childbirth. The poem's intricately linked tercets urge the speaker forward, but the procession ends at nightfall, and in falling snow, with 'the stillness and sorrow / of things moving back to where they came from'.[43]

Not surprisingly, perhaps, the tradition of the American family elegy has been severely disrupted in the twenty-first century, especially in the aftermath of the violent atrocities that took place on 11 September 2001. The attacks on New York City and Washington D.C. prompted a stunned and bewildered silence among many writers, but they also led to an unprecedented outpouring of elegiac poetry by thousands of individuals not habitually given to poetic expression. The editors of *Poetry After 9/11*, an anthology of work by New York poets published in 2002, claimed that there were 'poems everywhere' in the city: 'Walking around the city you would see them – stuck on light posts and phone stalls, plastered on the shelters at bus stops and the walls of subway stations . . . Downtown, people scrawled poems in the ash that covered everything.'[44] Much of this writing was spontaneous and ephemeral, and unlikely to be recorded, but there were also some salient elegiac poems printed and preserved in the aftermath of the attacks. Martín Espada's 'Alabanza: In Praise of Local 100' is a tribute to the 43 employees who lost their lives while working at the Windows on the World restaurant in the World Trade Center.[45] If the poem gives elegiac dignity to the cook, the waitress, and the dishwasher caught up in the violence of international politics, it also gives a more general recognition to the chronic instability of immigrant workers subjected to the indignity of discrimination and marginalization in New York and elsewhere. Pervasive loss is countered with lyric praise and a profound acknowledgement of these workers as makers and creators.

In Frank Bidart's 'Curse', the positive associations of 'making' in poetry are undermined, as are the usual consolations and restorations expected in conventional elegy. In a hollow, violent inversion of prayer, Bidart wishes upon the perpetrators of violence a death that recalls the collapsing floors and falling masonry of the World Trade Center: 'May what you have made descend upon you.'[46] The poem ends with a troubled but unrepentant acknowledgement that the more beneficent powers of poetry have been displaced in the process: 'what I have made is a curse'. Lucille Clifton's 'September Song:

A Poem in Seven Days' offers a more conventional, elegiac response. Here, the speaker herself is 'cursed with long memory', but she invokes the spirit of forgiveness and reconciliation, aided by the birth of a grandchild.[47] The poem opens on 11 September 2011 and offers a daily meditation in the aftermath of the attacks, moving towards a reassuring Christian vision of paradise.

Anne Stevenson's 'New York is Crying' takes its title and its epigraph from words attributed to a New York policeman, Tyrone Dux: 'New York is crying. I didn't hear screaming, just dead, dark silence.' The poem sensitively registers its own discomfort as it moves between an appalled awareness of the enormity of the attacks and a sceptical apprehension of the media-manipulated response of politicians who 'Weep in the lens light of a billion eyes. / They want the world to notice they are crying.' At the same time as speaking eloquently to the needs of the present, it suggests that poetry itself, and its long tradition of resourceful and creative response to adversity, is faced with severe challenges and constraints: 'Is that Walt Whitman? Yes, but he is crying. / Hart Crane, in tears, is haunting Brooklyn Bridge.'[48] Stevenson's invocation of the spectres of poets past is a technique familiar to readers of her brilliant *Lament for the Makers*, one of the most ambitious elegiac works in recent contemporary poetry. Indeed, Stevenson has strong claims to being regarded as the exemplary elegist for a post-1945 generation of poets that came through confessionalism and emerged acutely conscious of its own survival. Stevenson's impeccably modulated 'Elegy' for her father, Charles Leslie Stevenson (1909–1979), takes its place in the gallery of American family elegies, but contrasts strongly with both Rich's 'After Dark' and Plath's 'Daddy' in its positive appraisal of the lasting musical connection between father and daughter. Stevenson's highly innovative 'Sonnets for Five Seasons' (also dedicated to her father) opens an In Memoriam section of her *Poems 1955–2005* that also includes the hauntingly beautiful 'Willow Song' for Frances Horovitz, the playfully confiding 'Waving to Elizabeth' (for Elizabeth Bishop), and the deceptively deferential 'Letter to Sylvia Plath'.

American elegy since 1945 has proved to be versatile and resilient, even when threatening to shatter completely under the pressures of a contemporary civilization habitually given to cynicism and disbelief. In the hands of a disillusioned post-war generation of writers, the elegy was subjected to an unprecedented degree of formal violation. It was as if the form was routinely stripped of the usual courtesies and consolations, and as if its main purpose was not to praise, but to provoke and humiliate, the dead. At the same time, however, the most powerful and memorable elegies have been those that have effectively reconfigured traditional codes and conventions of poetic mourning rather than simply abandoning them. Among poets themselves there has been a consoling sense of shared endeavour, a kind of salvific consciousness that poetry bestows upon its makers. After reading the last of *The Dream Songs*, Robert Lowell wrote one of his own last poems, 'For John Berryman', in which he confesses to his dead friend, 'I used to want to live / to avoid your elegy.' In pushing the elegy to its extreme existential and stylistic limits, American poets have effectively reinvented the genre, reconfiguring its myths and conventions, and forging their own modern poetics of death.

Notes

1. Peter M. Sacks, *The English Elegy: Studies in the Genre from Spenser to Yeats* (Baltimore, MD, and London: Johns Hopkins University Press, 1985), p. 299.
2. Peter M. Sacks, *The English Elegy*, p. 306.
3. Peter M. Sacks, *The English Elegy*, p. 313.
4. Walt Whitman, 'When Lilacs Last in the Dooryard Bloom'd', from *Inventions of Farewell: A Book of Elegies*, ed. Sandra Gilbert (New York and London: W. W. Norton, 2001), p. 343.
5. Jahan Ramazani, *Poetry of Mourning: The Modern Elegy from Hardy to Heaney* (Chicago, IL, and London: University of Chicago Press, 1994).
6. Jahan Ramazani, *The Poetry of Mourning*, p. xii.
7. Wallace Stevens, *The Collected Poems* (New York: Vintage, 1982), p. 336.
8. *Catholic Prayer Book*, compiled by Ruth Hannon (New York: Walker, 1991), p. 70.
9. Wallace Stevens, *The Collected Poems*, pp. 431–4.
10. Wallace Stevens, *The Collected Poems*, p. 435.
11. Angela Leighton, *On Form: Poetry, Aestheticism, and the Legacy of a Word* (Oxford: Oxford University Press, 2007), p. 195.
12. Wallace Stevens, *The Collected Poems*, pp. 432–6.
13. Wallace Stevens, 'Sunday Morning', *The Collected Poems*, p. 69.
14. Wallace Stevens, *The Collected Poems*, p. 160.
15. Robert Lowell, *Collected Poems*, ed. Frank Bidart and David Gewanter (New York: Farrar, Straus and Giroux, 2003), pp. 14–15.
16. Robert Lowell, *Collected Poems*, p. 14.
17. Robert Lowell, *Collected Poems*, pp. 17–18.
18. Marjorie G. Perloff, *The Poetic Art of Robert Lowell* (Ithaca, NY, and London: Cornell University Press, 1973), pp. 131–3.
19. Robert Lowell, *Collected Poems*, p. 23.
20. Robert Lowell, *Collected Poems*, p. 28.
21. Robert Lowell, *Collected Poems*, p. 166.

22. Robert Lowell, *Collected Poems*, pp. 179–80.
23. Robert Lowell, *Collected Prose*, ed. Robert Giroux (New York: Farrar, Straus and Giroux, 1987), p. 350.
24. Robert Lowell, *Collected Poems*, pp. 376–8.
25. Elizabeth Bishop, *Complete Poems* (London: Chatto & Windus, 2004), p. 188.
26. Elizabeth Bishop, *Complete Poems*, pp. 188–9.
27. Elizabeth Bishop, *Complete Poems*, pp. 125–6.
28. Elizabeth Bishop, *Complete Poems*, p. 178.
29. Thomas Travisano with Saskia Hamilton (eds), *Words in Air: The Complete Correspondence Between Elizabeth Bishop and Robert Lowell* (London: Faber, 2008), p. 696.
30. John Haffenden and August Kleinzahler, 'All the girls said so', review of John Berryman, *The Dream Songs*, *London Review of Books*, 37(13) (2015): 9–12.
31. John Berryman, *The Dream Songs* (London: Faber, 1990), p. 3.
32. John Berryman, *The Dream Songs*, p. 162.
33. John Berryman, *The Dream Songs*, p. 406.
34. John Berryman, *The Dream Songs*, pp. 165, 176, 174.
35. Anne Stevenson, *Bitter Fame: A Life of Sylvia Plath* (Boston, MA: Houghton Mifflin, 1989), p. 152.
36. Sylvia Plath, *The Collected Poems*, ed. Ted Hughes (New York: Harper & Row, 1981), pp. 116–17.
37. Sylvia Plath, *The Collected Poems*, pp. 129–30, 222–4.
38. Sylvia Plath, *The Collected Poems*, p. 293.
39. Sylvia Plath, *The Collected Poems*, p. 262.
40. Sylvia Plath, *The Collected Poems*, pp. 272–3.
41. Adrienne Rich, *Collected Early Poems, 1950–1970* (New York: W. W. Norton, 1993), pp. 227–9.
42. Adrienne Rich, 'A Woman Mourned by Daughters', from *Inventions of Farewell: A Book of Elegies*, ed. Sandra Gilbert (New York and London: W. W. Norton, 2001), p. 200.
43. Amy Clampitt, 'A Procession at Candlemas', *New England Review*, 4(2) (1981): 185–9.
44. Dennis Loy Johnson and Valerie Merians (eds), *Poetry After 9/11: An Anthology of New York Poets* (New York: Melville House, 2002), Foreword.
45. Martín Espada, 'Alabanza: In Praise of Local 100', *Alabanza: New and Selected Poems 1982–2002* (New York and London: W. W. Norton, 2003), p. 231.
46. Frank Bidart, 'Curse', *Star Dust* (New York: Farrar, Straus and Giroux, 2005), p. 25.
47. Lucille Clifton, 'September Song: A Poem in Seven Days', *Mercy*, American Poets Continuum Series 86 (Rochester, NY: BOA Editions, 2004), p. 43.
48. Anne Stevenson, 'New York is Crying', *Michigan Quarterly Review*, XLI(3) (2002).

Further Reading

Gilbert, Sandra (ed.), *Inventions of Farewell: A Book of Elegies* (New York and London: W. W. Norton, 2001).

Johnson, Dennis Loy and Valerie Merians (eds), *Poetry After 9/11: An Anthology of New York Poets* (New York: Melville House, 2002), Foreword.

Leighton, Angela, *On Form: Poetry, Aestheticism, and the Legacy of a Word* (Oxford: Oxford University Press, 2007).

Ramazani, Jahan, *Poetry of Mourning: The Modern Elegy from Hardy to Heaney* (Chicago, IL, and London: University of Chicago Press, 1994).

Sacks, Peter M., *The English Elegy: Studies in the Genre from Spenser to Yeats* (Baltimore, MD, and London: Johns Hopkins University Press, 1985).

Part III
Movements and Moments

11

'Singularly rich': Donald Allen's *The New American Poetry 1945–1960*

Rory Waterman

In 1958 and 1959, when Donald Allen was laboriously putting together *The New American Poetry: 1945–1960*, he could have had no idea that by the end of the century his assemblage of poems mainly by marginalized and unfavoured poets would have achieved canonical status, or that many of the poets he included would have the reputations he wished for them.[1] He could not have expected the volume to be reprinted after four decades with a blurb advertising 100,000 sales, or that it would come to be widely regarded as the most influential *avant-garde* American poetry anthology of the twentieth century. It was the 'Bible of American counterpoetics', in the words of Mark Scroggins[2] – a book that, as Marjorie Perloff points out, is 'still acknowledged by all later anthologists as the fountainhead of radical American poetics'.[3]

But Allen did know he was doing something of considerable cultural significance. As he states in his 'Afterword' added to the 1999 edition, the idea for the book arrived in 1957 when 'it occurred to me that an anthology might be an effective way to introduce the new generation of poets I'd become increasingly aware of', but that the wider poetry-reading public had not. That same year – though Allen does not stoop to acknowledge it in his 'Preface' or 'Afterword' – a poetry anthology had been published in the US with the title *New Poets of England and America*, edited by Donald Hall, Robert Pack, and Louis Simpson.[4] Despite its title, however, this was a fairly traditional and largely formalist volume, ostensibly paying little attention to the younger poets continuing very actively to engage with the modernist revolutions that had altered poetry in the preceding four or five decades. The book made it into a lot of homes across America, and apparently also made its way right up the nose of Allen, who saw something very different occurring in mid-century American poetry and going largely unnoticed. His resulting *The New American Poetry* was at no point motivated by a desire to represent the status quo, only to challenge and change it: he focused solely on America (though some British ex-patriots also make it into his book) and did not include any of the poets in the Hall, Pack, and Simpson volume.

Befitting any anthology predicated on a desire to alter public perceptions, *The New American Poetry* opens with a strong justification for its *raison d'être*. The 'Preface' begins:

> In the years since the war American poetry has entered upon a singularly rich period. It is a period that has seen published many of the finest achievements of the older generation: William Carlos Williams' *Paterson, The Desert Music and Other Poems*, and *Journey to Love*; Ezra Pound's *The Pisan Cantos, Section: Rock-Drill*, and *Thrones*; H.D.'s later work culminating in her long poem *Helen in Egypt*; and the recent verse of E. E. Cummings, Marianne Moore, and the late Wallace Stevens. A wide variety of poets of the second generation, who emerged in the thirties and forties, have achieved their maturity in this period: Elizabeth Bishop, Edwin Denby, Robert Lowell, Kenneth Rexroth, and Louis Zukofsky, to name only a few very diverse talents. And we can now see that a strong third generation, long awaited but only slowly recognized, has at last emerged.[5]

'A strong third generation' of what, exactly? Not of poetry since the war, surely, since so many of that first generation wrote a lot of their most influential work before Hitler had come to power, let alone invaded Poland. Rather, Allen is identifying the 'generations' since modernism fundamentally altered the range and scope of poetry – with an eagerness for somewhat loose and baggy groupings that he also demonstrates in the anthology proper. As such, he is putting the 'third generation' in highly exalted company. None of the poets Allen mentions in this opening paragraph of his introduction to the book actually appear in its pages, even though he is keen to point out that they are the dominant figures in this 'singularly rich' poetic age. Instead, the anthology concentrates wholly on the 'third generation': apparent successors to the great, long-established, and often still active poets of this golden age, rather than alternatives to them. Allen is putting his poets into the tradition – not as an annexe to the big names on the programme, but as the brand new main event.

It is manifestly a bold claim. Though many of the poets collected in *The New American Poetry* had by 1960 achieved literary reputations to greater or lesser extents, the vast majority certainly had not. In fact, most of the work Allen collected had not previously had much of an audience at all. As he notes in the 'Preface', 'only a fraction of the work has been published, and that for the most part in fugitive pamphlets and little magazines. The field is almost completely uncharted; there is, not very surprisingly, very little first-rate criticism of any of the new poetry, and that little has been written by the poets themselves. Consequently, I have had to go directly to the poets for manuscripts.'[6] This third generation of a singularly golden age is in general barely known about, and barely wanted by most of the poetry presses, but apparently deeply necessary.

Allen's shoehorning of poets into distinct generations is a little too convenient. The first poet in the anthology, Charles Olson, was born in 1910, which made him older than several poets Allen names as belonging to the 'second generation' such as Elizabeth Bishop (born 1911) and Robert Lowell (born 1917) – though it should be noted that Olson had come to poetry late and had only published his first collection, *In Cold Hell, In Thicket*, in 1953. However, some of the other poets were older still: Helen Adam, born in 1909, had been publishing since her late teens; and Madeline Gleason was born in 1903, had seen her poems in print since the 1930s, and had published her first poetry book in 1944. There is no good reason to regard them as members of a later generation other than to give them a further chance of gaining a wider readership and some critical acclaim. And of course that is Allen's intention: to lay the ground so that these poets might get the attention he keenly believes they deserve, and to match them up with promising poets who genuinely are of a younger set. Omitting obvious elders gave the book a radical air (it makes it clear that they are not needed), but including neglected ones gave the impression that the book demonstrates a natural progression (they are not a flash in the pan either). *In Cold Hell, In Thicket* might have been around for seven years, but it had been published by a tiny imprint, Cid Corman's Origin Press. In the twenty-first century, the Internet age, it is sometimes easy to forget that in the mid-twentieth century access to new poetry could be extremely restricted; Allen's anthology became the one-stop shop where readers could find out what was going on with the Black Mountain Poets, the San Francisco Renaissance, the Beats, the New York School, and others. For poets such as Olson, Robert Creeley, Denise Levertov, Frank O'Hara, and Robert Duncan, Allen intended increased recognition, an end to perceived relative neglect; for others, the plan was to provide a first wide national and international airing in a book published by Grove Press, which might actually find its way into the main bookshops and libraries.

All anthologies must have an organizing principle of one kind or another. Allen takes the unusual and radical decision to divide his forty-four poets into five groups: they are the four groups mentioned above, in that order – three of which are aligned manifestly with a particular city or institution – and a fifth 'group' of other poets not identified with a specific school or movement. This organizational system comes freighted with problems, of course, mainly because some of the poets could really have been placed in two or more categories. Robert Duncan, for example, who is given more page space in the book than anyone other than Olson, is presented in the Black Mountain section, though he was also one of the most influential poets of the San Francisco Renaissance and it was there that he had come to prominence. In fact, partly because he had briefly taught at Black Mountain College in the mid-1950s, shortly before it closed, he had been instrumental in involving Black Mountain poets in the San Francisco Renaissance – in uniting the two, in other words. Moreover, the groupings were in themselves somewhat nebulous. It seems customary for most artists aligned with any movement to deny it really exists, so perhaps we should not read too much into John Ashbery's assertion that the New York School was a name 'foisted upon' the writers associated with it, and comprised 'a bunch of poets who happened to know each other' but who had 'vast differences between' their work,[7] or Allen Ginsberg's claim that the Beat Generation were just 'a group of friends who had worked together on poetry, prose and cultural conscience'.[8] But certainly most of Allen's groups do not indicate poets writing under a shared manifesto. They are largely disparate writers with a partially shared background that is often as geographical as it is theoretical or stylistic. Even Allen provides the caveat in his 'Preface' that 'these divisions are somewhat arbitrary and cannot be taken as rigid categories',[9] and in the 1999 'Afterword' he notes that, within two decades, 'the divisions had become obviously irrelevant'.

So, what was the point in the divisions? Why group the poets this way at all? The answer is simple enough: it is useful for readers, and it assists in the promotion of unfamiliar writers. The other organizing principle of the book is by date of birth from oldest to youngest (within each of the five sections), which naturally tends to place the more established poets near the beginning of each of the book's parts.[10] As such (to make an example of the Black Mountain section), readers are guided through the work of better-known poets such as Olson, Duncan, and Denise Levertov before they reach selections of work by younger and less well-known writers including Edward

Dorn, Jonathan Williams, and Joel Oppenheimer – all of whom had been students at Black Mountain College. Williams in particular had enjoyed some success, being the recipient of a Guggenheim Fellowship in poetry in 1957, but readers who had barely read Olson or Creeley were hardly likely to know much about these younger, less established poets, and Allen's organizing principle gave them a helping hand, firstly by linking them directly with more notable figures, and secondly by putting them in a clear cultural context. Comparably, the shorter Beats section of the book included parts I and II of Ginsberg's 'Howl', which had already become infamous as the result of a 1957 trial for obscenity, even if many of Allen's readers had not previously been able to get their hands on a copy; and following Jack Kerouac and Gregory Corso, the last of the four designated Beats was the twenty-seven-year-old Peter Orlovsky, Ginsberg's lover, who had only taken up writing poetry at Ginsberg's behest three years previously. Thanks to Allen, Orlovsky met readers on a near-equal footing with the most prominent poets of mid-century American Beat counterculture. The groupings may have been 'occasionally arbitrary' and 'justified finally only as a means to give the reader some sense of milieu', as Allen's otherwise terse 'Preface' goes on almost apologetically to explain, but it helped his poets to find their readers: the book not only indicated *which* poets of the 'third generation' Allen thought particularly worthy of readers' attention, but it also gave some indication *how* they might be approached and conceived of by an otherwise uninitiated readership.[11]

The layout of this anthology, then, is very consciously egalitarian, as well as being organized so systematically that it might make a fastidious library curator blush. In addition to the poets being sorted into five categories and listed within each by date of birth, their poems (and most poets are represented by several) are then ranked by date of composition. It is a methodology that gives the impression of putting the poets' work before the anthologist's role as compiler: points of connection between poems and poets, beyond the broad categorizations at least, are not highlighted for us. It is also a methodology that implies a completeness to the task, a temporal thoroughness, as though no sizeable stone has been left unturned. This is, after all, *the* new American poetry. And moreover, it is a methodology that eschews individual greatness in favour of collectivism(s). In *The New Poetry* edited by Al Alvarez, for example, a prominent British anthology from the same era, the two American 'confessional' poets Robert Lowell and John Berryman are held up as something of an example for British poets to follow.[12] This is partly as a result of Alvarez's polemical introduction, and partly because he puts these two Americans at the front of the book, before a slew of British poets, in what was otherwise a British anthology. Though it is far less ostensibly judgemental, however – between the poets it includes, at least – Allen's anthology does favour the more established for the simple reason that they tend to be the oldest and the oldest go first. More to the point, he has to begin the book somewhere, with the poets of one of his five categories, and opts for those poets associated with Black Mountain College in North Carolina, where Olson, Creeley and others had taught (but which had closed in 1956).

It is a decision that makes some sense, in that the Black Mountain poets were perhaps the central of Allen's four groups, with clear links to the Beats and San Francisco poets. This was partly due to the efforts of Creeley, who had edited *Black Mountain Review* for two years, publishing several of the Beat poets before moving to San Francisco in 1957. But it was also partly due to the overwhelming influence on modernist poetry of Olson's essay 'Projective Verse', first published in 1950. This advocated 'open field' poetic composition, in which each line is predicated on the breath and the single utterance, and each perception immediately and directly is followed by the next perception. 'Projective Verse' effectively became a manifesto for the poets directly or tangentially associated with the Black Mountain College, and also influenced poets as ostensibly different from Olson as Ginsberg. What is more, the Black Mountain or 'Projectivist' poets created a fertile environment for the re-emergence of the Objectivist poets such as Louis Zukofsky: a then-neglected part of Allen's 'second generation'.[13]

Of the four schools, or nexuses, presented in the book, the poets aligned with Black Mountain are also given twice as much page space as any other group, and the first among them, Olson, takes up at least twice as much room as anyone else. Moreover, the sixth section of the book, which contains statements on poetics by several contributors and which does not follow the established pattern of ranking by date, begins by reprinting 'Projective Verse', and of the other fifteen contributions to this final section, Creeley's 'Olson and Others: Some Orts for the Sports' is essentially a favourable discussion of Olson, his methods and his significance. As such, and in spite of the anthology's very deliberate pluralism, Olson is quite subtly presented as both a central figurehead and a doyen to not only the poets associated with Black Mountain College, but the new American poets as a whole. Allen did almost as much as Olson had done to make Olson the Pound of his generation.

The first poem with which readers of *The New American Poetry* are confronted is Olson's ambitious, tumultuous 'The Kingfishers'. This poem was in fact not especially 'new', as it had originally appeared in 1949, but it was in a sense an exemplar of Olson's nascent ideas that would feed into 'Projective Verse', and was self-consciously 'major' in terms of both scope and length. It begins with a maxim that is circular, almost tautological, followed instantly by an apparent manifestation of Olson's demand in 'Projective Verse' that a poem 'must, at all points, be a high-energy construct and, at all points, an energy-discharge'.[14] With its heady enjambements, its charged lines throwing one impression directly on top of another, it goes off from that first line and strophe like a pressurized spring:

What does not change / is the will to change

He woke, fully clothed, in his bed. He
remembered only one thing, the birds, how
when he came in, he had gone around the rooms
and got them back in their cage [...][15]

'The Kingfishers' is in part a post-Second World War response to Eliot's *The Waste Land*, with its own fragmented vision of a society in crisis. And it is on some level a response to the same idea touched on by Theodor Adorno (also in 1949) in his often misunderstood statement that 'To write a poem after Auschwitz is barbaric.' It is also a challenge to Olson's contemporaries, to match that expressed in his 'Projective Verse'; it ends by whittling down to an arid, Eliotian statement:

Despite the discrepancy (an ocean courage age)
this is also true: if I have any taste
it is only because I have interested myself
in what was slain in the sun

I pose you your question:

shall you uncover honey / where maggots are?

I hunt among stones[.][16]

With its sense of a culture in disarray, its fractured narrative and unapologetic allusiveness, this owes a huge debt to Olson's modernist forebears – just as 'Projective Verse' in many ways rehashed notions central to Louis Zukofsky's Objectivist manifestos, and built directly upon William Carlos Williams' concept of the poem as a 'field of action'[17] – and of course upon Pound's earlier instruction in 'A Retrospect' to 'compose in the sequence of the musical phrase'.[18] But in Olson, Allen had a central figure for his new American poets, one determined to make it new but also developing out of the modernism of the earlier twentieth century.

Following the Black Mountain poets, the section dedicated to the poetry of the San Francisco Renaissance is an apparently far more catholic selection. The San Francisco poets are given half the page space of the Black Mountain poets, but the section includes work by thirteen authors: three more than the book's opening part. However, none of them is given more than a handful of pages each, and there are no obvious central figures – partly because of Allen's decision to place Robert Duncan amongst the Black Mountain poets.

The 'San Francisco Renaissance' fitted somewhere between the Black Mountain School and the Beats – just as it does in Allen's anthology. The term 'Renaissance' completely lacks the neutrality of 'school' or 'movement', of course, and proudly proclaims a rebirth or return to consciousness. Defining it, however, is especially tricky, because the San Francisco Renaissance was many things. It might be regarded as a revival not so much of Renaissance aesthetics as of Romanticism, albeit in the context of the freedoms afforded by modernism and a burgeoning mid-twentieth-century counterculture in the San Francisco Bay Area. What connects the writing of poets associated with the San Francisco Renaissance, though, is less apparent than for any of Allen's groupings apart from the fifth; they were less a nexus of thought and feeling than a very disparate group of poets with a time and a place somewhat in common, many of whom naturally associated with one another, and often shared a preoccupation with writing about the natural world. Some of the poets adopted a surrealist approach, such as Jack Spicer:

> The moon is God's big yellow eye remembering
> What we have lost or never thought. That's why
> The moon looks raw and ghostly in the dark.[19]

This is a fitting enough sentiment for a writer who equated the poet to a radio receiving transmissions from space. Others, such as Lawrence Ferlinghetti, often wrote in a fragmented style manifestly influenced by Eliot, Pound and other earlier modernists. But some San Francisco Renaissance poets, including Helen Adam (and Duncan, of course), worked as much as anything in traditional 'closed' forms and with traditional tropes.

The first poem in this section of the anthology, Adam's 'I Love My Love', is a far cry from anything in the first section – though it begins with an epigraph from Duncan, pulling the Black Mountain into San Francisco in the context of the anthology. The entire poem is in strict ballad stanzas, replete with a refrain, and tells an unbroken narrative. And it is anything but an example of Olsonian open form:

> There was a man who married a maid. She laughed as he led her home.
> The living fleece of her long bright hair she combed with a golden comb.
> He led her home through his barley fields where the saffron poppies grew.
> She combed, and whispered, 'I love my love.' Her voice like a plaintive coo.
> Ha! Ha!
> Her voice like a plaintive coo.[20]

Adam had come to San Francisco from her native Scotland, where she had made a name for writing in the ballad tradition, and in America she continued to compose in this vein. Allen's comment in his 'Preface' that she 'helped establish the ballad made new' is disingenuous; he is characteristically loath to explain what he means by this, but the truth is that Adam wrote firmly from within a long-established tradition even if she ended up living outside of it.[21] Her models and forebears were Rossetti, Hardy, the oral traditions she had grown up with, and so forth. Allen wanted to find a way to include her without admitting her evident lack of concern with the need to 'make it new'. 'I Love My Love' has more in common with the work of the occasional balladeer Charles Causley, a British contemporary, than with any other contributor to *The New American Poetry*. She might have been more of a model for the New Formalists, an American poetic movement about as far removed from the bulk of Allen's *avant-garde* New American poetry as it is possible to get, were it not for her inclusion in this overwhelmingly modernist *mélange* encouraging unaware Formalists to overlook her.

Adam's link to the San Francisco poets, then, was one of personal association more than aesthetic unity: in San Francisco she had become a member of Spicer's 'Magic Workshop' and had come to know Duncan and others. In a sense, this demonstrates the inclusiveness of the San Francisco Renaissance – the need for Allen's section, once he had decided to include the San Francisco Renaissance as a category, to demonstrate plurality by including many poets and many styles, and thereby implying that the category is not a particularly useful one from a reader's perspective. However, this in turn renders it hard to say exactly what the Renaissance stood for *other* than plurality. Adam is fairly consistently written out of histories of the San Francisco

Renaissance, no doubt because her style irritates those most likely to want to write about it. But Allen not only decides to include her, he puts her first, uniquely adjusting his organizational system (i.e. putting Adam before the older Madeline Gleason, as mentioned earlier) in order to do so. He seems intent on emphasizing in no uncertain terms that this balladry is going on too, that the new American poets are not necessarily divorced from their non-modernist forebears.

The San Francisco Renaissance had a lot in common with the Beat or 'Beatnik' Generation. The poets associated with the latter tended to be more concertedly bohemian, and originally they had been associated with New York – a fact that hardly seems all that important, especially to a twenty-first-century reader. At any rate, the poets of the San Francisco Renaissance were not at the time particularly clearly separated from the Beats: Ferlinghetti, for example, published Ginsberg's *Howl and Other Poems* through City Lights, and supported many of the Beat poets in the Bay Area. That Allen's third category contains only four Beat poets, albeit with relatively long selections, means that there are notable absences in this boys' club, such as Diane di Prima, though in Allen's defence the Beat Generation was still very much a growing phenomenon in 1960 when his book went to print.

Like the Beat novelists (Kerouac, along with William S. Burroughs, being the most prominent and enduring of them), the Beat poets drew liberally from wherever they wanted. But often their strongest ancestral ties were to Whitman, and they channelled a Whitmanesque effusiveness into something potent in the cultural climate of 1950s and 1960s America. Kerouac popularized the term 'Beat', but it was left to a *San Francisco Chronicle* writer in 1957 to add the soon-popularized suffix 'nik', an apparent adoption of the Yiddish suffix denoting those who act in a specific manner. However, the term also had other, stronger contemporary resonances. Earlier in the same year, the Russians had put into space the first artificial satellite, Sputnik, proving their dominance in the space race at a time when the US could do no better than explode inferior imitations on the launch pad. The term 'Beatnik' therefore implied, albeit in a rather mixed up way and with tongue pressed into cheek, that they were a potent threat to the American status quo; certainly, Sputnik hurt patriotic, conservative America, and so did the Beatniks. This challenge to established orthodoxies is especially evident in the work of the most prominent Beat poet, Allen Ginsberg, who in the words of Michael Schmidt 'dropped on American poetry like a bomb'.[22] Ginsberg's 'Howl' had, also in 1957, been the subject of a highly publicized obscenity trial and had won the right to be sold (Ferlinghetti was also arrested over his involvement), and *The New American Poetry* gave readers who had not acquired the 1956 City Lights edition the opportunity to read Parts I and II of the long poem in their entirety. 'Howl' remains *the* Beat poem: an inventive, ambitious affront to societal norms, stylistically indebted to Whitman's long lines and subordinate clauses but taking both to something of an extreme and developing also from an Olsonian sense of the breath as a means to measure the line, and with each line delivering one impression hot on the heels of the last. The poem begins by evoking a hostile and uncaring image of modern life, in which the 'best minds of my generation' belong to those 'destroyed' and in the gutter, and continues from there on in to throw one frenzied impression after another. But it was not to the taste even of many who could quite easily look past the authority-offending lines about men being 'fucked in the ass by saintly motorcyclists' and its 'vision of ultimate cunt'.[23] An exasperated John Hollander wrote in *Partisan Review* in 1957, that the poem 'continues, sponging on one's toleration, for pages and pages'.[24] A comparable challenge to societal strictures, and a comparable prolixity, inheres in Gregory Corso's 'Marriage', which makes a stylistic virtue of juggling considerations about whether to 'get married' and therefore 'be good', in a knotted and haphazard line of thought, and ends with him trashing a kind of advertiser's dream of 1950s married bliss: being 'good', he finally determines, *isn't* good, but neither is remaining single.[25]

Whereas poets of the Black Mountain School tended to aim for concision as well as complexity, the Beats made a fetish of diffusion and verbosity. So did some poets of the New York School, such as Kenneth Koch and Frank O'Hara, who, despite their considerable differences as writers, had affinities with the Beats beyond geographical origins. In his 'Preface' paragraph dedicated to introducing the New York School, Allen says nothing about how his fourth group of poets are linked other than by geography: he just points out that some (Ashbery, Koch and O'Hara) 'migrated to New York in the early fifties', and associated with others (Edward Field, Barbara Guest and James Schuyler) who were already there, and leaves it at that.[26] But by the mid-1950s Ashbery was living in Paris, and even this tenuous geographical connection was in practice falling apart. All that can really be said is that most of the New York School poets attended Columbia University; were friends and sometimes collaborators; reviewed art and were connected to the New York School artists; were gay; and lived in New York during the years in which they came to some prominence as writers. Otherwise, they were at least as diverse as any of Allen's other groupings, but shared an observational flourish, a feeling of spontaneity, and often a stream-of-consciousness style.

O'Hara was perhaps the most explicitly 'New York' of the New York School poets, something of a participatory *flâneur* capturing the texture of mid-twentieth-century life in a city that itself feels like a nerve centre of the earth. O'Hara populated his poems with direct, apparently personal perceptions and the goings-on in the city of vendors, artists, and anyone else who entered his sights: the same sorts of people, broadly speaking, who fill the urban landscape of 'Howl'. Like the Beats, O'Hara embraced the first-person pronoun, as in now-familiar poems such as 'The Day Lady Died' and 'Why I Am Not a Painter' – both included in, and in part popularized by, *The New American Poetry*. If the New York poets shared anything in terms of artistic outlook, it might be summed up as a desire to explore and test apparent insignificances, as in the graceful, tumultuous, filmic 'The Day Lady Died'. An elegy for Billie Holliday, this poem is for the first three-quarters a postmodern bricolage of inherently insignificant details, rendered suddenly significant by the human context of a notable death – albeit a death related to the speaker by one of the consumerist fragments that makes up the same postmodern bricolage:

> then I go back where I came from to 6th Avenue
> and the tobacconist in the Ziegfeld Theatre and
> casually ask for a carton of Gauloises and a carton
> of Picayunes, and a NEW YORK POST with her face on it
>
> and I am sweating a lot by now and thinking of
> leaning on the john door in the 5 SPOT
> while she whispered a song along the keyboard
> to Mal Waldron and everyone and I stopped breathing.[27]

This poem is nothing if not a 'high energy-construct', in the words of Olson – though not necessarily in the way Olson imagined.[28] The great gift of Allen's anthology, for all its faults, is that it not only allowed poets as diverse as Olson and O'Hara to appear in one set of covers, it gave the writers a context: each of the four specific groups tumbles into the next, and all become jumbled and redefined in the fifth, a grouping with 'no geographical definition', including LeRoi Jones, Michael McClure and Gary Snyder (who might equally have been in the San Francisco Renaissance section or among the Beats, though he was not a part of the original New York circle).[29] Allen's 'Preface' is again too simplistic: these poets 'evolved their own original styles and new conceptions of poetry', he tells us.[30] This is meant as praise, of course, but is actually an unwarranted and unintended swipe at some of the other poets here, not least Olson, O'Hara and Ginsberg, who manifestly had done just that themselves, to greater or lesser extents.

Some of the failings of Allen's 'Preface' can be put down to his desire to get on with it, to let the work speak for itself. He wanted to present the range of experimentation in American poetry since the Second World War, not to explain it, and it is a tribute both to his prescience and the influence of his book that many of the barely-heard-of poets, poems and statements he included went on to become canonical. As a volume challenging the status quo, the book does have what now seem very clear shortcomings. Only one non-white poet is represented, and there is only one woman for every ten men: one wonders whether, had Diane di Prima (for example) been a man, she might have found her way into the male-only Beats section where she surely belonged. But it is all too easy to approach an anthology more than half a century after the event and pick it apart for what it includes and omits. Allen's book became the touchstone for a new set of approaches in American poetry, audacious in its overwhelming focus on the under-represented. And in its fracturing into groups, its tacit decisions over what matters and what does not, it continues directly and indirectly to shape the way readers conceive of *avant-garde* American poetry from the middle of the twentieth century.

Notes

1. The 1999 reprint is the version of the book referenced in this chapter: Donald Allen (ed.), *The New American Poetry: 1945–1960* (Berkeley, CA: University of California Press, 1999). It is essentially exactly the same book as the 1960 Grove Press edition, with the addition of a short 'Afterword' by the editor.
2. Mark Scroggins, 'From the Late Modernism of the "Objectivists" to the Proto-postmodernism of "Projective Verse"', in Jennifer Ashton (ed.), *American Poetry Since 1945* (Cambridge: Cambridge University Press, 2013), p. 24.
3. Marjorie Perloff, 'Whose New American Poetry? Anthologising in the Nineties', *Diacritics*, 26(3/4) (Autumn/Winter 1996): 104.
4. Donald Hall, Robert Pack and Louis Simpson (eds), *New Poets of England and America* (New York: Meridian Books, 1957).
5. Donald Allen (ed.), *The New American Poetry: 1945–1960*, p. xi.
6. Donald Allen (ed.), *The New American Poetry: 1945–1960*, p. xiv.
7. John Ashbery, 'An Interview with the *Paris Review*', *Paris Review* (1983). Last accessed 4 September 2015. Available at: http://www.theparisreview.org/interviews/3014/the-art-of-poetry-no-33-john-ashbery

8. Allen Ginsberg, *Deliberate Prose: Selected Essays*, ed. Bill Morgan (New York: Harper Collins, 2000), p. 237.
9. Donald Allen (ed.), *The New American Poetry: 1945–1960*, p. xii.
10. Madeline Gleason is the only exception to this date of birth rule: the oldest poet in the book, she is placed only fourth in the 'San Francisco Renaissance' section. Allen's reasoning is not given, and not clear. It can surely have nothing to do with her not being representative enough: the 'San Francisco Renaissance' section is fronted instead by the idiosyncratic balladeer Helen Adam.
11. Donald Allen (ed.), *The New American Poetry: 1945–1960*, p. xiii.
12. Al Alvarez, (ed.), *The New Poetry* (London: Penguin, 1962). This anthology had a broadly similar overarching principle, in some ways, to that of Allen's anthology in the United States, with which it almost shared a name. In order to stand any chance of inclusion in *The New Poetry*, poets needed to be British, to have established their reputation in the preceding decade and no earlier, and to be favoured by Alvarez. Berryman and Lowell, however, fitted only one of these criteria. Alvarez therefore presents them as a sign of what might be possible at home: a yardstick with which to beat his compatriots. Allen, however, pointedly presents no long-established models for his new American poets to follow. Neither American in *The New Poetry* appears in *The New American Poetry*, of course, because they belong to Allen's 'second generation'.
13. What is more, the Black Mountain poets would come directly to influence other significant modernist movements such as the British Poetry Revival, in the work of English and Scottish poets such as J. H. Prynne, Roy Fisher and Gael Turnbull.
14. Donald Allen (ed.), *The New American Poetry: 1945–1960*, p. 387.
15. Donald Allen (ed.), *The New American Poetry: 1945–1960*, p. 2.
16. Donald Allen (ed.), *The New American Poetry: 1945–1960*, pp. 7–8.
17. Williams' ideas were expessed only two years previously, in 1948. See William Carlos Williams, 'The Poem as a Field of Action', in *Selected Essays* (1954) (New York: New Directions, 1969), pp. 280–91.
18. Ezra Pound, 'A Retrospect', *Literary Essays of Ezra Pound*, ed. T. S. Eliot (New York: New Directions, 1935), pp. 3–14, at p. 3.
19. Donald Allen (ed.), *The New American Poetry: 1945–1960*, p. 143.
20. Donald Allen (ed.), *The New American Poetry: 1945–1960*, p. 114.
21. Donald Allen (ed.), *The New American Poetry: 1945–1960*, p. xii.
22. Michael Schmidt (ed.), *The Great Modern Poets* (London: Quercus, 2010), p. 161.
23. Donald Allen (ed.), *The New American Poetry: 1945–1960*, p. 185.
24. Reprinted in Allen Ginsberg, *Howl: Original Draft, Facsimile, Transcript and Variant Versions*, ed. Barry Miles (New York: Harper and Row, 1986), p. 1961.
25. Donald Allen (ed.), *The New American Poetry: 1945–1960*, p. 209.
26. Donald Allen (ed.), *The New American Poetry: 1945–1960*, p. xiii.
27. Donald Allen (ed.), *The New American Poetry: 1945–1960*, p. 265.

28. Donald Allen (ed.), *The New American Poetry: 1945–1960*, p. 387.
29. Donald Allen (ed.), *The New American Poetry: 1945–1960*, p. xiii.
30. Donald Allen (ed.), *The New American Poetry: 1945–1960*, p. xiii.

Further Reading

Allen, Donald (ed.), *The New American Poetry: 1945–1960* (Berkeley, CA: University of California Press, 1999).

Alvarez, Al (ed.), *The New Poetry* (London: Penguin, 1962).

Ashbery, John, 'An Interview with the *Paris Review*', *Paris Review* (1983).

Ginsberg, Allen, *Howl: Original Draft, Facsimile, Transcript and Variant Versions*, ed. Barry Miles (New York: Harper and Row, 1986).

Ginsberg, Allen, *Deliberate Prose: Selected Essays*, ed. Bill Morgan (New York: Harper Collins, 2000).

Hall, Donald, Robert Pack and Louis Simpson (eds), *New Poets of England and America* (New York: Meridian Books, 1957).

Perloff, Marjorie, 'Whose New American Poetry? Anthologising in the Nineties', *Diacritics*, 26(3/4) (Autumn/Winter 1996): 104–23.

Pound, Ezra, *Literary Essays of Ezra Pound*, ed. T. S. Eliot (New York: New Directions, 1935).

Schmidt, Michael (ed.), *The Great Modern Poets* (London: Quercus, 2010).

Scroggins, Mark, 'From the Late Modernism of the "Objectivists" to the Proto-postmodernism of "Projective Verse"', in Jennifer Ashton (ed.), *American Poetry Since 1945* (Cambridge: Cambridge University Press, 2013), pp. 16–30.

Williams, William Carlos, *Selected Essays* (New York: New Directions, 1969).

The Black Mountain Poets

Bertholf, Robert J., and Albert Gelpi (eds), *The Letters of Robert Duncan and Denise Levertov* (Stanford, CA: Stanford University Press, 2004).

Creeley, Robert, *Selected Poems, 1945–2005*, ed. Benjamin Friedlander (Berkeley, CA: University of California Press, 2008).

Duncan, Robert, *A Selected Prose* (New York: New Directions, 1995).

Duncan, Robert, *The H.D. Book: The Collected Writings of Robert Duncan*, ed. Michael Boughn and Victor Coleman (Berkeley, CA: University of California Press, 2012).

Jarnot, Lisa, *Robert Duncan: The Ambassador from Venus* (Berkeley, CA: University of California Press, 2012).

Levertov, Denise, *The Poet in the World* (New York: New Directions, 1973).

Levertov, Denise, *New Selected Poems*, ed. Paul A. Lacey (Tarset: Bloodaxe Books, 2003).

Olson, Charles, *The Collected Poems of Charles Olson* (Berkeley, CA: University of California Press, 1997).

Olson, Charles, *Collected Prose*, ed. Donald Allen and Benjamin Friedlander (Berkeley, CA: University of California Press, 1997).

The San Francisco Renaissance

Adam, Helen, *A Helen Adam Reader: Selected Poems, Collages, and Music*, ed. Kristin Prevallet (Orono, ME: The National Poetry Foundation, 2007).

Ellingham, Lewis, and Kevin Killian, *Poet, Be Like God: Jack Spicer and the San Francisco Renaissance* (Middletown, CT: Wesleyan University Press, 1998).

Everson, William, *The Veritable Years, 1949–1966* (Santa Barbara, CA: Black Sparrow Press, 1978).

Ferlinghetti, Lawrence, *There Are My Rivers: New and Selected Poems, 1955–1993* (New York: New Directions, 1993).

Ferlinghetti, Lawrence, *Poetry as Insurgent Art* (New York: New Directions, 2007).

Ferlinghetti, Lawrence, *I Greet You at the Beginning of a Great Career: The Selected Correspondence of Lawrence Ferlinghetti and Allen Ginsberg 1955–1997* (San Francisco: City Lights, 2015).

Gelpi, Albert, *Dark God of Eros: A William Everson Reader* (Berkeley, CA: Heyday, 2003).

Spicer, Jack, *My Vocabulary Did This to Me: The Collected Poetry of Jack Spicer*, ed. Peter Gizzi and Kevin Killian (Middletown, CT: Wesleyan University Press, 2008).

The Beats

Charters, Ann, *The Portable Beat Reader* (New York: Penguin Classics, 2006).

Corso, Gregory, *Mindfield: New and Selected Poems* (New York: Thunder's Mouth Press, 1998).

Ginsberg, Allen, *Collected Poems 1947–1997* (New York: Harper Collins, 2006).

Ginsberg, Allen, *The Selected Letters of Allen Ginsberg and Gary Snyder* (Berkeley, CA: Counterpoint, 2009).

Kerouac, Jack, and Allen Ginsberg, *The Letters* (New York: Penguin Books, 2011).

Kerouac, Jack, *Collected Poems* (New York: Library of America, Volume 231, 2012).

Knight, Brenda (ed.) *Women of the Beat Generation: The Writers, Artists, and Muses at the Heart of a Revolution* (Newburyport, MA: Conari Press, 1998).

The New York School

Ashton, Dore, *The New York School: A Cultural Reckoning* (New York: Viking Press, 1979).

Ferguson, Russell, *In Memory of My Feelings: Frank O'Hara and American Art* (Los Angeles: The Museum of Contemporary Art / University of California Press, 1999).

Guest, Barbara, *The Collected Poems of Barbara Guest* (Middletown, CT: Wesleyan University Press, 2008).

Koch, Kenneth, *The Collected Poems* (New York: Alfred A. Knopf, 2008).

Nelson, Maggie, *Women, the New York School, and Other True Abstractions* (Iowa City: University of Iowa Press, 2001).

O'Hara, Frank, *Selected Poems*, ed. Mark Ford (New York: Alfred A. Knopf, 2008).

Schuyler, James, *Collected Poems* (New York: Farrar, Straus and Giroux, 1994).

Schuyler, James, *The Letters of James Schuyler to Frank O'Hara* (Brooklyn, NY: Turtle Point Press, 2006).

Younger poets not grouped by affiliation or location

Baraka, Imamu Amiri (LeRoi Jones), *LeRoi Jones / Amiri Baraka Reader*, ed. William J. Harris (New York: Thunder's Mouth Press, 1991).

Baraka, Imamu Amiri, *Somebody Blew Up America and Other Poems* (Philipsburg, St Martin: House of Nehesi, 2003).

McClure, Michael, *Of Indigo and Saffron: New and Selected Poems* (Berkeley, CA: University of California Press, 2012).

Snyder, Gary, *Look Out: A Selection of Writings* (New York: New Directions, 2002).

Snyder, Gary, and Jim Dodge, *The Gary Snyder Reader: Prose, Poetry and Translations, 1952–1998* (Berkeley, CA: Counterpoint, 1999).

Whalen, Philip, *The Collected Poems of Philip Whalen* (Middletown, CT: Wesleyan University Press, 2007).

12

Not Quite The End Of The World: American Poetry since 2000

Stephen Burt

In James Merrill's final book of poetry, *A Scattering of Salts* (1995), the poet and his lover visit a residential twelve-step facility called Oracle Ranch, as if the place could predict some larger future. Their time there prompts a series of sonnet-like poems that intersperse the all too simple, therapeutic language of the programme with Merrill's own typically elaborate wordplay, rhyme, allusion and irony. At the end of 'Family Week at Oracle Ranch', the guests and patients receive alarming advice: '(a) you are a brave and special person (b) / There are far too many people in the world / For this to still matter for very long.[1] What could matter instead?

As in much of Merrill's late work, the quoted solecisms ('to still matter', 'for ... for') and mismatch between line shape and sentence shape (the line break between '(b)' and what '(b)' indicates) portray a technically gifted sophisticate both attentive to, and far out of step with, the language of his own time. Merrill played with that portrayal throughout this last and best book, while making the book itself resolutely contemporary, with personal computers, up-to-date materials science ('a new synthetic substance / Crystallized in Sacramento for the first time'), HIV/AIDS (Merrill himself was HIV positive), anthropogenic species extinction, and global climate change.[2] Perhaps its most ambitious poem, 'Self-Portrait with Tyvek Windbreaker', envisions the poet, his poetry, European and trans-Atlantic high culture, and indeed human civilization, as endangered anachronisms, 'Songs of Yesterday'.[3] At once meditation on generational change (the ageing poet fears he has nothing in common with a teenager, even though they are wearing 'the same' windbreaker), an ambivalent poem about democracy (Merrill quotes Pascal: 'while all humans aren't / Countable as equals, we must behave / As if they were or the spirit dies'), and a poem that contemplates the end of the inhabitable world, despite our resolve 'to keep the blue wave dancing in its prison', 'Self-Portrait' claims to be the last poem of its kind. What kind of poetry would replace it?

To survey the American poetry of the two decades after Merrill's death is to survey a bafflingly wide array of styles, schools, backgrounds, approaches to poetry, and definitions of 'poetry'. New poets, celebrated poets, poets imitated across regions, institutions, and generations can hardly agree on a set of forebears more recent than Walt Whitman and Emily Dickinson (and some would not even agree on those). Even the division, familiar since the 1960s (and anatomized, for example, by Christopher Beach), between 'experimental' or 'New American' poets, indebted to Pound or to Stein, and 'traditional' or 'mainstream' writers, who looked to Frost, Stevens or Eliot, failed to hold. By 2000, poets such as Jorie Graham and C. D. Wright had emerged as supposed 'hybrids' between lines of poetry that made prose sense, focused on individual states of feeling, or drew on the pre-modern past, and those that did not.

Still other lines of challenging poetry seemed to grow farther and farther from the formal repertoire of the European past. US Latino, Hawai'ian, Asian American, and Native American poets articulated linguistic strategies that drew on their polyglot backgrounds. Poets – black, Latino, white Anglo, Native, Arab- and Asian American, among other backgrounds – who first wrote for oral performance on stage developed an increasingly prominent body of work; some of these poets (such as Patricia Smith) grew closer to the page-based 'mainstream' as the new century wore on. *Avant-garde* theatre work (Ariana Reines), strategies drawn from movements in visual art, especially FLUXUS and Conceptualism (CAConrad, Kenneth Goldsmith), and tactics from computing and cognitive science (Aaron Kunin, Nick Montfort) led to what look like new kinds of poetry, or writings that stretch the definition of 'poetry' beyond some readers' recognition. Juan Felipe Herrera, named US Poet Laureate in 2015, combines English, Spanish, and Chicano ('Spanglish'); storytelling and epistemological exploration; fragmentation and theatrical effect; and miniatures and expanded, book-length projects, from prose-and-verse travelogues to litanies dubbed 'undocuments' (such as '187 Reasons Mexicanos Can't Cross the Border') to a series of quasi-sonnets based on *lotería* (sometimes called Mexican Tarot) cards. Without him many strands of American poetry – the 'hybrids' of the 1990s and afterwards, the heritage of 'spoken-word' or performance-based poetry, the responsible journalistic impulse and the wild odic one – might seem impossible to reconcile.

They seem quite hard to reconcile still: nobody could ride all of those waves at once. Certainly we cannot say there is one current, one 'mainstream' in American poetry now (if we ever could): nor can we say there is just one counter-tradition, one meaningful *avant-garde*. And yet we can still see the poetry as a whole, if we take the right angle and watch carefully: the books that stand out from the most recent years continue to address – even as they develop a new repertoire for – the concerns in *A Scattering of Salts*. They ask about the fate of the individual, and the place of poems that describe the poet's individual life, in a world that seems faster paced, more crowded, less hospitable to individual agency, than before. They ask about the future of poetic forms, new or old, virtuosic or seemingly natural. They ask about the place of human language – especially impractical language, figurative language, the language of poems. They notice that human beings (especially American human beings) are wreaking catastrophic damage on the environment and the non-human world. And they ask whether poetry can imagine a future, for itself and for the people who read it. To bring them together is to see how many poets anticipate something like a quiet apocalypse: the end of their kind of poetry, or the end of the form of life that they know, or the end of the world.

★

So closely tied to ideas of the individual as the unit of analysis, to the idea that a poem should project a 'voice', and that it ought to imply a narrative, the 'confessional' and the autobiographical seemed to many twenty-first-century observers like obsolescent modes. Yet their leading practitioners made them new, and none more so than the Michigan-based poet Laura Kasischke, whose poems start from lives like her own, and who tends to focus on middle-class women's life course: on high and low points in the lives of teenage girls, of mothers of small children, of middle-aged couples, of adults whose parents are elderly or ill. Kasischke's fourth book of poems, *Dance and Disappear* (2002), begins with 'Kitchen Song', a kind of montage, a series of sounds and images around the destruction of a paradigmatic nuclear family in a car accident:

> The pantry
>
> full of lilies, the lobsters scratching to get out of the pot, and God
>
> being pulled across the heavens
> in a burning car.

They were just driving along. Dad
turned the radio off, and Mom
turned it back on.[4]

Kasischke's formal signature involves the play of irregular, prominent rhyme, at line-ends and within lines, across a jaggedly enjambed free verse whose lines vary widely in length. Her acoustics suggest the emergence of patterns from chaos: the impulsive teenaged girl; the self-sacrificing, passive-aggressive mother. Like the many realist novelists, she aims to make incidents from a particular life not stereotypical, yet representative: strange enough to stand out, and yet similar to what many readers experience or expect. (Not coincidentally, Kasischke is also a commercially successful novelist: three of her books have been made into films.) The sounds in Kasischke's poems could belong to nobody else, but the incidents certainly could, and that is part of her point. Sometimes the incidents show what did not take place, what happened to other brave or special or damaged people, but did not happen to her, as in the poem – reprinted and shared frequently online as of 2014 – entitled 'Bike Ride with Older Boys'. That poem begins,

The one I didn't go on.

I was thirteen,
and they were older.
I'd met them at the public pool.[5]

The young Laura never goes out to meet the boys: she has missed out, perhaps on 'the best/ afternoon of my life. Two / cute and older boys / pedaling beside me – respectful, awed.' Or perhaps she has avoided sexual assault, 'bits of glass and gravel / ground into my knees. / I will never love myself again.' Both of these avoided possibilities, because she has avoided them, have made her the older person she has become, 'thirty-seven, wiping / crumbs off the kitchen table with a sponge'. Who has not done likewise? What fortunate citizen, what middle-class parent or professional, cannot understand the process of ageing, of becoming an adult, in terms of what did not happen, what lives were not lived?

The mother in Kasischke's poem 'Day' appears to have missed her life too, to have experienced an end of life without any middle. She contrasts the struggles of her 'civilian life' to the apocalyptic events in fairy tales, in horror stories:

> Thursday, a star
> falls out of the sky as I
> wheel the child's bike
> to the garage – the garage, which is a darkness
> like the father
>
> of my son, glittering
> with wrenches, the smell of rags and oil. He keeps
>
> a hat he wore in the jungle
> hanging from a nail on the door.[6]

The apocalypse takes place elsewhere; she stays home, as if to fill out Randall Jarrell's resigned aphorism, 'The ways we miss our lives are life.'[7] The star that falls unnoticed, the struggle of domesticity (hard or impossible to see from outside), are at once like the 'boy falling out of the sky' in Auden's 'Musée des Beaux Arts' and the feminine counterpart to such a macho doom.

Motherhood was until recently (for many poets it is still) a new subject, a dangerous subject, one without modernist precedents, full of ethical and emotional risks, 'a playground full of unexploded mines'.[8] It became a prominent subject during the 1990s and 2000s, examined in the important anthologies *The Grand Permission* (2003), edited by Patricia Dienstfrey, and *Not for Mothers Only* (2007), edited by Rebecca Wolff. The poetry of motherhood – of poets who (like it or not) define themselves by how they care for the children they bore – continues up to the present in, for example, the unruly, raw verse and essays of Rachel Zucker.

Yet what Kasischke's characters cannot escape is not just a specific maternal role, what Adrienne Rich in *Of Woman Born* (1976) called 'motherhood as institution'; it is also the idea of a role in general, the idea that the mother can be explained by a sociological stereotype, like a minor character in a novel. If she does not devote herself to 'lost keys', to 'the breathing sweetness / of macaroni and cheese', to 'the home she's made for herself // out of Kleenex / and twigs' (like the sparrow in her eaves), how should she live? Who can she be?[9]

Poetry for Kasischke remains a way to think about an individual consciousness, an individual life; her methods of focus, of showing and telling, overlap with the methods of novels, of memoirs, of other kinds of prose life-writing. And yet – in an era when the personal has been political for some time; when the idea that 'personal' poetry should contain a sexual charge, or a sexual revelation, has become a cliché – Kasischke's poetry not only updates, but challenges, the confessional, and the psychoanalytic, and the memoristic, conceptions of poetry; it is a challenge (like Merrill's 'Family Week') not only to Freud, or to Lowell, but to Wordsworth, and to the whole idea that we are unique and worth examining because of what we felt and what we did. A writer for *Cosmopolitan* magazine enthuses, plausibly, about Kasischke's earlier volume *Housekeeping in a Dream*, 'Kasischke knows girls ... these are the poems your best friend from high school would write if she could translate her inner world into language': it seems like a fine way to recommend a good book, and yet such praise implies – as the poems imply – that the inner worlds of girls, and of best friends from high school, and of their grown-up alter egos, are very much alike.[10] Kasischke's character 'Miss Weariness' (one in a series of allegorical 'Misses') imagines herself trapped, exhausted, just like all the other people in her social position, in her psychologically – and, perhaps, economically and environmentally – limited world. She feels like 'all / those goldfish in their plastic / baggies at the fair', who feel 'as if the world were divided / into small, warped dreams, nowhere // to get to, and nothing to do but swim'.[11]

Death is one way we can disappear (along with our poems), giving the lie to the promise in our hopeful song. We can also disappear into that very future, if it is a future where no one will find us, no one will remember us, a future vexed by a surfeit of information, in which individual lives and poems are 'statues dumped / into the sea, the sea is full of these': that is the apocalyptic metaphor in Kasischke's poem 'The Internet', in which not drugs, not adulthood, not disease, but the Information Age spells out the end. 'This strange haze / made of information', worked uneasily into Kasischke's uneven lines, 'expands to contain // everything', and therefore denies the poet's assertion that 'there are things I've said and done that still belong to me', things that could only prompt her poems, pertain to her.[12] If Kasischke's forebears are 'confessional', or autobiographical, her emotional tenor is (like theirs) sometimes extreme, anxious, passionate, full of fear; it is, on the other hand, almost always *responsible*, alert to what she now owes other people (as a mother and as a writer), determined that she will not be the one who breaks down. Instead, they imagine the breakdown of other people, of alternative versions of herself, or of everyone all at once, in some near future. Built on a template that valorizes individual expression, Kasischke's poems contemplate a future from which she herself has been erased.

As they contemplate the limits of individuality, the ways in which the troubles that define us might make us alike, Kasischke's poems also contemplate an apocalypse, the end of the kind of life we know. 'Credit Card in My Hand' identifies its poet with 'the shepherd // who claimed his sheep / climbed to the top of a hill one day // and never came back down'.[13] 'Miss Post-Apocalypse' imagines a poet under a toxic cloud, interrogated by her empty shoes, which ask 'Girl, / where // are all your little trashy daydreams now?'[14] The end of life, and the dilemmas of end-of-life care, motivate much of the poetry in Kasischke's *Space, in Chains* (2013): in her recent poem 'Ativan', that painkilling drug – and poetry itself – are compared to a

Little, hopeful, insistent
song
about the future
sung
to a hanged man's boots.[15]

★

Merrill asked about the continuing viability of a poetry based on the individual, on individual lives; he also asked (and he was far from alone) about the viability of complicated or inherited forms. Can poets come up with patterns that might replace these forms? Can poets make them seem modern, or appropriate to our crowded, fast-paced era, or just less Anglo-European-white? Terrance Hayes can do all these things: his career since his second book, *Hip Logic* (2002), has attempted to integrate (the verb is no accident) specifically African American lines, traditions, and aesthetic effects with other, supposedly European, or newly invented, almost mathematical forms.

These integrations do not, however, suggest any kind of endpoint, any single voice consistent in affect and attitude (as in, for example, Seamus Heaney or Yusef Komunyakaa). Instead, Hayes' imbrications of recollection with novelty, of seemingly natural voice with odd barriers to it, of multiple kinds of form with multiple racially marked histories, suggest that everything in his poems, no matter how strong the feelings it provokes, may be regarded as artificial, contingent, bizarre, perhaps subject to strenuous change. Hayes, who now teaches in Pittsburgh, grew up in South Carolina, and moved north only after college; African American, and especially Southern black, identity – embraced but detourned, celebrated, and taken apart – becomes a raw material for Hayes' homages, *détournements* and reconstructions almost as Northern Irish and Catholic identity became a raw material for Paul Muldoon.

All Hayes' books after his first are, in effect, cyclopedias of forms; they are also, more or less enthusiastic, more or less frustrated attempts to figure out what, if any, form will put the poet into the right, enabling, relationship to the historical and personal past, what way of writing will let him both claim, and escape, it. *Hip Logic* got attention in part for its overtly ludic or mathematical forms: in a sequence of eleven-line poems entitled collectively 'A Gram of &s', each line-end could use only anagrams formed of the one-word title ('Bowling', for instance, used the end words *wing*, *lion*, *gown*, *bingo*, *glow*, *glib*, *long*, *blow*, *boil*, and *bowl*).[16] *Hip Logic* also included a sonnet called 'Sonnet' in which fourteen identical lines, 'We cut the watermelon into smiles', built up an objection to racist stereotypes, and then an objection to the objection, as if protesting against the monotony of a literary world where black poets were asked, always, to protest.[17] *Lighthead* (2010) introduced a form called the Golden Shovel, in which each line had to end with one of the words from Gwendolyn Brooks's much-anthologized poem 'We Real Cool'; the Golden Shovel has already become a form that other poets appropriate, while Hayes has moved on.[18] Hayes' third book, *Wind in a Box* (2006), begins with 'Woofer (When I Consider the African-American)', an allusion to John Milton's sonnet 'When I consider how my light is spent':

> When I consider the much discussed dilemma
> of the African-American, I think not of the diasporic
> middle passing, unchained, juke, jock, and jiving
> sons and daughters of what sleek dashikied poets
> and tether fisted Nationalists commonly call Mother
> Africa, but of an ex-girlfriend who was the child
> of a black-skinned Ghanaian beauty and Jewish-
> American, globetrotting ethnomusicologist.[19]

The sentence becomes a mouthful; it incorporates densely alliterative wordplay, of a kind that might 'sound' African American, but it does not confine itself to that register, nor to any other. Rather than accept an inherited way to think about black identity, or about poetry, or about life writing, rather than believe that 'we were assigned some lousy fate / when God prescribed job titles at the beginning of Time' (another allusion to the same sonnet of Milton's), Hayes asks 'if out-running your captors is not the real meaning of Race', and imagines African Americans as 'a string of people connected to one another', 'linked by a blood filled baton in one great historical relay'. Kinds of poems and kinds of forms, like kinds of persons and ways of speaking about them, come down to Hayes through history, as in a relay, and he will neither ignore them nor take them up uncritically.

Hayes treats the history of the bodies in his poems almost as he treats poetic form. Both are in flight from the constraints of their histories; both are trying to become something else. One sequence in *Wind* addresses Michael Jackson; part of that sequence bears the subtitle 'A Few Rumors Concerning Mr. Potato Head', and it uses a hortatory, anaphoric prose:

> Bet in his diary there are blueprints of his faces. *Yep, and a little arrow pointing to where his eyeball rolled from the page.* Yep, and bounced once on the floor. *Bet a diamond glistens in the ear floating in the mason jar on his desk.* Bet his collar-bone is made of gold.[20]

The pop star Michael Jackson, with his virtuoso dance routines and his cosmetic surgeries, took himself apart and put himself back together on his own terms; you could say the same thing of Mr. Potato Head, who has made his real self (whatever that means), the self behind the disassembled parts, unreachable: 'bet no one finds the diary. *Bet no one finds the face.*' Hayes' 'Harryette Mullen Lecture on the American Dream' imitates and defends the African American poet Harryette Mullen's puns and her Oulipian methods (for example, the substitution of nouns by rough homonyms): 'Mud is thicker than what is thicker than water. Pull your head up by your chin straps ... Father knows beds, but I am not my breather's keeper.'[21]

Forms and devices – rhetorical, poetic, acoustic, generic – are for Hayes not obsolescent so much as inescapable, just like classification and kinds of persons: you can try to outrun the classifications other people assign you, to contest and change and even replace them, but you cannot live among other people without being classified in some way or other, without having to find a form. In the same way, you can give your poem a familiar shape or strange shape, but you cannot give it no shape at all. You can, however, give it a disorientingly playful set of alterable shapes, a conjunction of sound-effects and allusions that make the speaker hard to place: you can reject 'far right- / wing indicators blinking / white&black, white&black, white&black' by trying to 'be best friends / or fried fiends' with 'floundering interiors, be all these things / at once'.[22]

Those lines come from a poem called 'The Blue Baraka', whose sounds are part homage, part caricature, of the black nationalist and revolutionary leftist poet Amiri Baraka. Hayes' 'Blue Baraka' is the first in a series of incompatible role models, disparate acoustic models, persons thanked and attacked, in a series of poems with 'Blue' titles: 'The Blue Bowie', named for David Bowie; 'The Blue Etheridge', for Etheridge Knight; and 'The Blue Seuss'. That last poem alludes to Seuss's *Fox in Socks* as it envisions, first, the Middle Passage – 'Blacks stacked in boxes stacked on boxes' – and then residential segregation: 'Blacks beside / Blacks in rows of houses are / Blacks in boxes too'.[23]

William Butler Yeats said that a finished poem snapped shut with a click like a closing box; are poetic forms and subgenres just more boxes? Are inherited classifications traps? Hayes' whole way of writing answers that question over and over, and his answers are at once yes and no. He remakes the boxes, as he remakes what could have been a predictable life story, as he remakes (for example), in a poem called 'The Blue Terrance', both *terza rima* and blues. The poem begins:

> If you subtract the minor losses,
> you can return to your childhood too:
> the blackboard chalked with crosses,
>
> the math teacher's toe ring. You
> can be the black boy not even the buck-
> toothed girls took a liking to:
>
> this match box, these bones in their funk
> machine, this thumb worn smooth
> as the belly of a shovel. Thump. Thump.[24]

Note the concealed pun on *subtract – minor/minus – losses*; the black-and-white of the third line, with its imaginary cemetery; the consonant patterns that echo the *terza rima* midline *in childhood – chalked, black – buck – box, math – toothed – match*. (*Buck – funk – thump* are vowel rhymes; and note the avoided rhyme-word *fuck*.) And if this poem adopts – even while it transforms – that European formal device, *terza rima*, other poems in *Wind in a Box* also adopt and transform old subgenres, among them the verse testament, as in Donne and Villon, in which the poet explains, with some irony, who will inherit what after his death: 'To the boy with no news of my bound and bountiful kin, / I offer twelve loaves of bread ... To the mirror, water; to the water, a book with no pages, / the author's young face printed on the spine.'[25] Many of the forms and subgenres Hayes takes up (including the *terza rima* above, the verse testament, and the Seuss in boxes) seem to take place, as it were, posthumously: *Wind in a Box* also means speech from a coffin, speech to and about a grave.

And that is what seems apocalyptic about Hayes' otherwise fruitful, promising (and, by now, much-imitated) work: it often seems about to be consumed by the stereotypes and the bad history that its ingenuity keeps on trying to outrun. The poems are not just virtuosic, but enthusiastic: they have fun with their forms – and yet that fun (as in the impersonations of Michael Jackson) can seem almost desperate – they don't stop till they can get enough, and they can never get enough. We can find the same fast-paced synthesis, and sometimes a similar effect, in other formally versatile African American poets who began in the 1990s: some of those writers (Hayes, Tracy K. Smith, Kevin Young) emerged from specifically African American poetic institutions, such as Boston's Dark Room Collective and the Cave Canem workshop, founded in 1996, initially a writers' retreat in upstate New York, now a larger set of retreats and fellowships. Kasischke's poetry represents the near future of 'confessional' poetry, of poetic autobiography. Hayes' poetry – while it also holds aspects of autobiography – provides occasion to ask not just (as all his critics note) about the future of African American poetry, but about the future of poetic subgenre (testament, Oulipian word-scramble, persona poem, anthem), and the future of form.

⋆

Hayes (like Kasischke) remains invested in the history of what we now call lyric, in models of individuality that apply to persons and to poems. His short poems have lines or stanzas, clear beginnings, strong closure at the ends, and most of them (even the parts of his 'Blue' or his anagram series) could be reprinted alone. What would a poetry look like, how would it sound, that tried to get past the category of the individual voice, the individual poem? How could it use, in extended ways, ways that go beyond allusion, the resources of scientific and technical prose, or of cartography, or of other ways in which human beings chart the non-human world? Could such new poetry respond to changes not just in how we see individuals and kinds of individuals (girls, boys, mothers, fathers, rural people, bowlers, African Americans) but in how we see fish, plants, birds, soil? Other poets now try to answer such questions by incorporating non-fiction reportage, as in Mark Nowak's books of documentary poetry about unions and miners; by presenting as poetry work that looks and feels like something else – like visual art, or like a diary, or like a stage script, or like a personal essay, or like a film, or like all of these together, as in Claudia Rankine's book-length verse-and-prose projects *Don't Let Me Be Lonely Tonight* (2004) and *Citizen* (2015); by working in very short forms that therefore highlight their dependence on interpretive frames, as in Craig Dworkin's *Motes* (2011) or Joseph Massey's *To Keep Time* (2014); and by working in long forms that defy the closure, the reliance on 'voice' and on compressed patterns, that have characterized lyric modes.

Not the most extreme, but one of the most aesthetically successful, among such efforts is the recent work of Juliana Spahr, especially the seven verse and prose essays, documents, lines, lists and pictures collected in *Well Then There Now* (2011). Four of them reflect Spahr's residence in Hawai'i, where she taught in the early 2000s; others consider global species extinction, intercontinental travel, (supposedly) natural beauty, and class privilege. 'Dole Street' began as a zine or chapbook, with photographs, about the street on which she lived in Honolulu. 'The Incinerator', the final poem-essay, starts from the polluted Appalachian vistas of Chilicothe, Ohio, where Spahr spent her childhood. Some of the poems use long, Whitmanian lines, others blocks of prose, and others the short, sometimes asyntactic lines familiar from Spahr's earlier work. And every one of the sequences reminds us that we are connected to one another, and to the places we live, in ways that reflect existing power relations, and that produce power relations in turn. 'Power clusters in close patterns on top of geography',[26] highlighting 'connections between humans and humans or between humans and the land', as Spahr shows: those patterns, those connections, get harder to see if we look only for distinctions among individuals, or among singled-out, well-made poems.[27]

'Things should be said more largely than the personal way', 'larger than the personal way of telling', Spahr declares; 'We are situated with some and not with one against confession.'[28] In 'Sonnets' (from which this declaration comes) such claims, arranged in brisk fourteen-line groups, are printed *en face* with biomedical information about human blood ('bilirubin total at 0.5 milligrams per decaliter / high density lipoprotein at 52 milligrams per decaliter').[29] The juxtapositions imply that human beings and language circulate in society and on Earth as blood circulates in the human body, and people (even authors) can no more act alone than blood cells can work effectively on their own. 'Who authorizes so one is not what one individual one says one is'.[30] Spahr, no less than Hayes or Kasischke, invokes a particular, partly American heritage, in her case including expansive, inclusive, yet challenging poets such as Walt Whitman, Bernadette Mayer and Gertrude Stein. It is hard not to hear Stein in the limited, repeated vocabulary of Spahr's longest sentences, one of which concludes:

> because we could not begin to understand that this place was not ours until we grew and flowed into something other than what we were we continued to make things worse for this place of growing and flowing into even while some of us came to love it and let it grow in our own hearts, flow in our own blood.[31]

Another long prose work, Spahr's 'Unnamed Dragonfly Species', interlaces a calm, unnerving memoir, rinsed of details and told in the third person plural, with a catalogue of names (printed in bold face) of species that may go extinct: 'They were anxious and they were paralyzed by the largeness and the connectedness of systems, a largeness of relation that they liked to think about and often celebrated but now seemed unbearably tragic. **Upland Sandpiper** The connected relationship between water and land seemed deeply damaged, perhaps beyond repair in numerous places. **Vesper Sparrow**'.[32]

This strand of Spahr's volume belongs to another burgeoning, and frightening, new subgenre within American poetry, the long elegy on climate change. Many parts of D. A. Powell's *Chronic* (2008), Jorie Graham's *Place* (2012), Peter O'Leary's *Phosphorescence of Thought* (2013) and Betsy Andrews' *The Bottom* (2015) occupy that fragile space (as does so much of *A Scattering of Salts*). Almost all such poems look outward at least from a site to a watershed, sometimes to a continent or to the globe: all use long lines, long sentences, or other large sizes to indicate the seriousness of their project (both Andrews and O'Leary write book-length poems). All are rooted in a particular place (Powell in California's Central Valley, Andrews in Florida's Gulf Coast), and many respond (as Graham and Spahr both do) to the argument that we need new ways of thinking and writing about a new Earth (what the organizer Bill McKibben calls 'Eaarth'), a globe changed beyond our ken by what we have done.

Spahr's eco-elegies try to achieve such thinking. 'Attempting to grow some other eyes', in very long and sometimes quite flat lines, in iterative phrases that feel, now like outcries, and now like accounting, Spahr puts forward a series of works that reject – or at least try to reject – the idea that poets write separable poems that reflect the emotions of individuals.[33] Spahr tries to make works attuned to big systems instead, making poems larger and stranger, and in some ways less personal, less introspective, than the lines represented by Lowell and Plath, Powell, or Hayes, demand.

In that way Spahr now seems representative, not only of her era, but of one way to tell the story of the poetry that came just before it. The earlier American poets who have been 'recovered', re-appreciated, raised to new prominence in the past twenty years, have in common their sustained attempts to work outside the lyric mode, the individualism and the likeness to memoir implied by confessional, autobiographical, songlike, and post-Romantic poems. If Stein is one such poet, Jack Spicer is another, as the collection of essays *After Spicer* (2011), edited by John Emil Vincent, reveals. Spicer died in 1965, but his complete poems, edited by the prominent poet Peter Gizzi, appeared only in 2008. Violently of two minds about whether a large audience was possible or desirable ('No one listens to poetry ... No / One listens to poetry' he repeated).[34] Spicer also insisted on the indissolubility, the greater ambition, and the independence from mere personality, in his mature work: 'There really is no single poem,' he wrote.[35] Spahr is not uniquely influenced by Spicer (she remains far closer to Stein) but just for that reason her work shows the broad utility of a revisionist, West Coast-based account of American poetic history that sees Spicer and Stein among its great sources, and Lowell, Jarrell, Plath, and Bishop as a dead end. Among the many poets who try for larger, less introspectively personal modes, Spahr is not the most extreme by any means, but rather the most careful, and one of the most receptive in her use of expository and polemical prose.

★

What would it mean to try for the extreme? What would it mean for a poet to try to attack the inherited domain of 'poetry' in America – not just to attack the recognizable subgenres (confessional, blues, prospect poem, love sonnet, epigram, sexual apology, ecological ode), but to attack, while remaining inside, 'poetry' as we understand it, poetry as a means of expression in words? Would it be worth it? How would it sound? Such goals are not new – they go back at least to Tristan Tzara and Dada, to Ezra Pound and the magazine *Blast* (1914), if not to Arthur Rimbaud, or to Jonathan Swift. But they have gained attention recently, in part because partisans of the language writers from the 1970s and 1980s have sought further extensions of their modernist, boundary-breaking project, sought more poems that can make us ask what 'poetry' is.

Some such poems came in the 2000s from writers (such as K. Silem Mohammad and Katie Degentesh) associated with a movement called Flarf, who wrote (or 'sculpted') deliberately offensive, banal, or bizarre poetry based on outcomes from Internet searches.

Other such poems, or verbal objects, came from creators of what was called Conceptual poetry, by analogy with Conceptual art: Kenneth Goldsmith's 'uncreative writing' presented found texts (as when he re-typed a day's issue of the *New York Times*), unreadable texts meant to document an activity (as in *Fidget*, where Goldsmith wrote down every action his body undertook for a day). While these projects have become unavoidable in academic discussions (sometimes in debates on 'Conceptualism vs. Flarf'), other poets have mounted other attacks on lyrical individualism, on the insistence that a poet is a very brave and special person, on the idea that a poem simulates and elevates an individual voice.

If that mode survives anyway, we may conclude that what does not kill lyric makes it stronger; we may conclude that the category of poetry (like other large categories, other art forms) expands by coming to include objects and projects that first seemed designed to attack it. And few attacks seem fiercer or more memorable, at the level of the individual phrase, than the prose and verse in *The Book of Interfering Bodies*, by Daniel Borzutsky (2014). Borzutsky folds the left-wing outlook he seems to share with Spahr, the undertone of rage he shares with Degentesh, the attention to history that he shares with Hayes, and the ambition to describe a whole culture that he shares (*inter alia*) with Whitman, into works that cannot stop telling us how frustrated, impotent, guilty and violent this poet feels. 'From now on all culture will be body parts floating in milk, shouts the miniscule hermaphrodite poet terrorist through his bullhorn. ... An illegal immigrant girl from a nameless country in a featureless part of the world smashes the heads of the residents of New York City with bottles of Coca-Cola.'[36]

No parts of the world are really featureless, of course, and the girl is not real (not even intradiegetically real); she is a projection, as so much of Borzutsky's work amounts to projection, of the bad conscience that readers and writers who have time for poetry now entertain. Just by living in the world and reading, by drinking coffee or tap water or buying a book, we take part in a system of self-gratification, of non-renewable consumption, of exploitation. It is a system that Borzutsky's corrosive tone and his loud stanza try and almost fail to denounce. In this crowded system, symbolized by New York City (but hardly limited to it), 'we fear the towers of trash on our streets', and 'we connect to the world by shining our headlights at the men who sit in their cars and masturbate to the image of darkness' (a line that may allude to Lowell's 'Skunk Hour').[37]

Borzutsky has also translated the work of the Chilean poet Raúl Zurita, and his own work insists that we look not only outside the frame called 'poetry', but outside the frame of the United States. Some of the sites in Borzutsky's *Book* suggest the lawlessness of open civil war, or of failed states: 'poets in the trash, imploding, and glass blowing out of storefront windows, and in the rubble the origins of a stanza: the putrefaction of a silent word'.[38] The title of that poem, 'Love in the Time of Poetry', alludes to Gabriel Garcia Marquez's *Love in the Time of Cholera*: in Borzutsy's 'poetry of infestation ... the verses swarmed and reproduced around any old mouth that belched or wept or driveled'.[39] Poetry here feels like a disease, or a symptom, both of a failed modernity (a social condition) and of a failed modernism (literary response to that condition). It makes us sick as it complains that there is nothing we can do. Borzutsky's prose blocks attack and unsettle, provoke bad associations and 'bad taste', even as they complain (much as Merrill complained!) that poetry seems helpless, both elite and obsolete. And their extremes respond to twin pressures that do seem peculiarly modern: first, the dense and fast-moving media-scape, in which more and more actors (most of them out for a profit) attempt to catch our attention, to monetize eyeballs; second, the extreme conditions of environmental menace everywhere, and of open violence always somewhere.

If Borzutsky's *Book* hopes to be something other than 'poetry', to do something previous poets have not done, to get outside the system by which art is only about its readers' experience, or only about other art, then the book confesses angrily over and over that it has already failed – it is a 'dead book', in which radical and liberal and professedly apolitical defences of poetry are wishful thinking, nothing more: 'It's comforting to think you might have spoken in code but you did not know how to speak in code and neither do I.'[40] With its code broken, its aspirations smashed, Borzutsky's work presents itself as symptomatic, as an almost involuntary reaction to the extreme, systemic distress of a contemporaneity that it cannot escape.

In this strategy it resembles other recent poets devoted to violent extremes, to acts of 'bad taste', to provocations, abjections, and marks of violence, especially some of the poets associated with Fence Books (Catherine Wagner and Nick Demske); with the feminist movement called the Gurlesque (Wagner, Danielle Pafunda, and Lara Glenum); and with Joyelle McSweeney and Johannes Göransson, who have argued strenuously for a modern aesthetic of violent extremes and of conscious internationalism through their web journal Montevidayo and their publishing house Action Books. These clusters of poets in turn speak to one another: Wolff, who anthologized Pafunda and Wagner in *Not For Mothers Only*, also runs Fence. One of Göransson's own prose poems, 'Dear Ra' (2008), explains 'That's the kind of poem this is. The kind raised on excess television violence. All that's left are ads for brotherhood and blowjobs ... This poem is dedicated to the man who put a gun in my gullet ... This poem is a pay phone. Someone has slashed its chords [*sic*] and ripped out its face.'[41]

Earlier poets also sought ever more violent excess; earlier poets, too, have resented the fact that poems are made of words, that they do not do much physical, literal work, and that at most times, in most rich countries, they are not especially effective ways to make large-scale political change. Spicer aspired in *After Lorca* 'to make poems out of real objects', to create 'a poetry that would be more than the expression of my hatred and desires'.[42] Baraka's single best-known poem, 'Black Art', announced in 1969, 'Poems are bullshit unless they are/ teeth or trees or lemons'; he went on to ask for 'dagger-poems in the slimy bellies / of the owner-jews'.[43] Even readers who would not want to emulate poems of that kind (whatever we call that kind) can find them hard to forget: they get noticed, and to get noticed as a poet nowadays seems easier in one way (thanks to the Internet) but harder in others (thanks to the Internet, to the sheer size of the country, to the declining importance of older verbal arts, to the blaring news) than ever before.

Jahan Ramazani has shown how much contemporary poetry, perhaps all poetry, tends to situate itself between the goals of prayer and the goals of news, working with and against 'the secular, mimetic and empirical imperatives of journalism'.[44] Poetry wants to distinguish itself from journalists' imperative to record mere fact, and yet it also wants (as journalism wants) to respond to the world *right now*, from the news-flash death of Michael Jackson, to the gradual collapse of privacy online, to the Great Recession of 2007 and after, which (as Christopher Nealon has convincingly argued in *The Matter of Capital*) produced left *avant-garde* styles of its own. To write a poetry that ignores the headlines, poem after poem, seems harder in twenty-first-century America (where the headlines follow us, on Facebook and in the weather reports) than it was before. To write with an aspiration to change the headlines would be to court frustration, or delusion. But to write a poetry that views the headlines without aspiring to change them is to write – as Spahr and Borzutsky and Kasischke and Hayes understand, as Merrill understood – a poetry either of elegy, or of thrashingly impotent anger, or of despair, in which we make litanies of the vanishing species, or imagine the whole of humanity as – in Merrill's figure – a very dangerous baby. In Merrill's poem 'A Downward Look', we are to the Earth as a young child is to a bathtub, 'When, far beneath, a wrinkled, baby hand / Happens upon the plug.'[45] Andrews echoes the metaphor, and the anxious, almost giddy lament for the Earth and its oceans, just at the end of *The Bottom*: 'When we've managed to pirate every molecule of the seas, / and replaced them with replicas rendered in plastic … will they witness our bathtub-ring finish, from space?'[46]

To scatter the Earth with salts is to make sure that nothing grows, to verify that we have no future. Such apocalyptic thinking dominates – with more aggression and less regret – Borzutsky's devastated, thought-provoking, on occasion disgusting exclamations, and poems. The same apocalyptic ideation – focused now on America, now on the end of an individual life – runs through Kasischke's work too, and even through Hayes, with his images of lynchings, his fugitives, his bloody relay. Apocalyptic thinking, the idea that this poem might be the last of its kind, describing the last human beings of their kind, even controls the aesthetic, and the effect, of poems whose subgenres might seem to place them far from it: Monica Youn's sequence *Ignatz*, for example, seems to be an ekphrastic response to George Herriman's modernist comic *Krazy Kat*, whose characters are constantly hit by bricks but never die, and a series of poems about erotic pursuits, in the tradition of *Astrophel and Stella*. And yet Youn, too, keeps imagining the end of everything, the hopelessness of every pursuit, and the collapse of lyric into a dense supermassive arrangement of just a few words 'scratched' on a page as in her poem 'The Death of Ignatz'.[47] The echo of Kasischke's 'Kitchen Song' in the phrase '*simple song*' may be coincidence, but the shared sense of an ending is not; nor is the sense that what ends is a medium of communication (radio, jukeboxes, records, poetry) not only a life.

Ideas of apocalypse, ideas that we are at the end of something big, coexist with ideas of futility, with protests against the impotence of the poetic mode that the poet nonetheless chose, exist 'all over the landscape' (to quote John Ashbery) of recent American poetry. Consider, for one more recently prominent example, the mutants and fairy-tale monsters that populate Patricia

Lockwood's *Motherland Fatherland Homelandsexuals* (2014), along with the bleak humour of her popular Tweets, which may or may not be rightly considered as poems: 'Sext: The apocalypse has happened and most people are dead. I crawl into a Bath & Body Works and finally have all the lotion I want.'[48] Or take Elizabeth Colen's *Waiting Up for the End of the World*, a whole book of verse organized in response to conspiracy theories and disasters (Pan Am 103, 'chemtrails') where 'history rises / or circles back to meet us', 'what were words become images' (as if her poem were the last poem anyone wrote),[49] and 'houses burn like winter / until winter blows them out'.[50]

Ours are not the first poets animated by the idea of apocalypse, by the notion that their ways of life or ways of writing are near the end. Prior poets feared the Second Coming and the End of Days, the French Revolution, the Napoleonic Wars, World War I and its aftermath, the A-Bomb and the H-Bomb. But the current apocalypse has distinct causalities, which lead to distinct modes of writing: the apparent exhaustion of poetry itself as a way to highlight the individual (eclipsed by the crowded Internet, by the monetization of everything, by our fast pace); the apparent demise of so many old forms; the apparent saturation of culture by commerce and capitalism, with (as Nealon complains) no apparent outside; and, above all, manmade damage to Earth and its climate, a story that has gone on for so long that it's hard to craft new poetic response. The poetry in response to these particular versions of apocalypse wonders how and when to depict an individual life; asks how to imagine history, including the history of poetic forms; pays attention to place, to environment, to the non-human world; and pushes back against the supposed impotence of poetry as we know it, testing the boundaries of taste, of 'poetry' with compensatory extremes.

'It is immodest of a man to think of himself as going down before the worst forces ever mobilized by God,' quipped Robert Frost, rejecting what he saw as the unearned apocalypse of *The Waste Land*.[51] And yet these perhaps immodest contemporary poets can think of themselves that way, and their poems can depend on it, in their reactions to entities (from global climate change to 'sexts' to unlimited credit card debt) that do seem very much of our day. 'What is the future / beyond a premonition?' asks Hayes's verse testament, and it continues: 'Here in the last moments of my illiterate future / may the people know I did not matter.'[52] Nealon quotes Rankine's *Don't Let Me Be Lonely Tonight*: which complains of 'a deepening personality flaw: IMH, the Inability to Maintain Hope'.[53] Seen in one light, all these poets' projects – an updated, apocalyptic confessionalism, a remixed and passionate formalism, a poetic documentary, a violent anti-poetry – look quite new: none of these books could have been written fifty, or even thirty, years ago. In another light they seem familiar, continuing paths laid down by Plath and Jarrell, by Whitman and Stein, by Hughes and Frost, by Artaud and Césaire. All of them find new tones and new sounds for a late Anthropocene, or late capitalism, or a late information age; all find figurative language, completing (to quote William Carlos Williams) 'emotional machines made of words', that will make sense in what they, too, see as a crowded, imperiled, complicated, unjust, information-rich, irresponsible, fossil-fuel-burning, torture-ridden, hierarchical, exhilarating, complicated nation, whose national literature occupies an even more imperiled, and more complicated world.

Notes

1. James Merrill, 'Family Week at Oracle Ranch', in J. D. McClatchy and Stephen Yenser (eds), *Collected Poems* (New York: Knopf, 2002), p. 659.
2. James Merrill, 'Press Release', in J. D. McClatchy and Stephen Yenser (eds), *Collected Poems*, p. 638.
3. James Merrill, 'Self-Portrait with Tyvek Windbreaker', in J. D. McClatchy and Stephen Yenser (eds), *Collected Poems*, p. 669.
4. Laura Kasischke, 'Kitchen Song', *Dance and Disappear* (Amherst, MA: University of Massachusetts Press, 2002), p. 3.
5. Laura Kasischke, 'Bike Ride with Older Boys', *Dance and Disappear*, p. 48.
6. Laura Kasischke, 'Day', *Dance and Disappear*, p. 5.
7. Randall Jarrell, *Complete Poems* (New York: Farrar Straus and Giroux, 1969), p. 9.
8. Laura Kasischke, 'Sennacherib of Assyria', *Dance and Disappear*, p. 60.
9. Laura Kasischke, 'Day', *Dance and Disappear*, p. 4.
10. Julie Buntin, '12 Poetry Collections Every Woman Should Read', *Cosmopolitan* (16 April 2014). Last accessed 3 September 2015. Available at: http://www.cosmopolitan.com/advice/tips/poetry-collections-women
11. Laura Kasischke, 'Miss Weariness', *Lilies Without* (Keene, NY: Ausable, 2007), p. 69.
12. Laura Kasischke, 'The Internet', *Gardening in the Dark* (Keene, NY: Ausable, 2004), p. 77.
13. Laura Kasischke, 'Credit Card in My Hand', *Dance and Disappear*, p. 58.
14. Laura Kasischke, 'Miss Post-Apocalypse', *Lilies Without*, p. 80.
15. Laura Kasischke, 'Ativan', *Poetry Foundation*. Last accessed 3 September 2015. Available at: http://www.poetryfoundation.org/poetrymagazine/poem/244578

16. Terrance Hayes, 'A Gram of &s' (Bowling), *Hip Logic* (New York: Penguin, 2002), p. 32.
17. Terrance Hayes, 'Sonnet', *Hip Logic*, p. 13.
18. Terrance Hayes, 'The Golden Shovel', *Poetry Foundation*. Last accessed 3 September 2015. Available at: http://www.poetryfoundation.org/poem/244278
19. Terrance Hayes, 'Woofer (When I Consider the African-American)', *Wind in a Box* (New York: Penguin, 2007), p. 3.
20. Terrance Hayes, 'A Few Rumors Concerning Mr. Potato Head', *Wind in a Box*, p. 14.
21. Terrance Hayes, 'Harryette Mullen Lecture on the American Dream', *Wind in a Box*, p. 27.
22. Terrance Hayes, 'The Blue Baraka', *Wind in a Box*, p. 19.
23. Terrance Hayes, 'The Blue Seuss', *Wind in a Box*, pp. 43–4.
24. Terrance Hayes, 'The Blue Terrance', *Wind in a Box*, p. 69.
25. Terrance Hayes, 'Wind in a Box', *Wind in a Box*, p. 80.
26. Juliana Spahr, 'Dole Street', *Well Then There Now* (Santa Barbara, CA: Black Sparrow, 2011), p. 41.
27. Juliana Spahr, 'Dole Street', *Well Then There Now*, p. 39.
28. Juliana Spahr, 'Sonnets', *Well Then There Now*, p. 23.
29. Juliana Spahr, 'Sonnets', *Well Then There Now*, p. 22.
30. Juliana Spahr, 'Sonnets', *Well Then There Now*, p. 27.
31. Juliana Spahr, 'Sonnets', *Well Then There Now*, p. 29.
32. Juliana Spahr, 'Unnamed Dragonfly Species', *Well Then There Now*, pp. 92–93.
33. Juliana Spahr, 'The Incinerator', *Well Then There Now*, p. 135.
34. Quoted in John Emil Vincent (ed.), *After Spicer: Critical Essays* (Middletown, CT: Wesleyan University Press, 2011), p. 1
35. Quoted in John Emil Vincent (ed.), *After Spicer: Critical Essays*, p. 5.
36. Daniel Borzutsky, *The Book of Interfering Bodies* (New York: Nightboat, 2011), p. 11.
37. Daniel Borzutsky, *The Book of Interfering Bodies*, p. 69.
38. Daniel Borzutsky, *The Book of Interfering Bodies*, p. 33.
39. Daniel Borzutsky, *The Book of Interfering Bodies*, p. 33.
40. Daniel Borzutsky, *The Book of Interfering Bodies*, p. 96.
41. Johannes Göransson, 'Dear Ra', *Poetry Foundation*. Last accessed 3 September 2015. Available at: http://www.poetryfoundation.org/poem/246198
42. Jack Spicer, *After Lorca* (San Francisco, CA: White Rabbit Press, 1957). Last accessed 3 September 2015. Available at: http://cuneiformpress.com/wp-content/uploads/2014/10/After-Lorca-Spicer.pdf
43. Amiri Baraka, 'Black Art', in William J. Harris (ed.), *The LeRoi Jones / Amiri Baraka Reader* (New York: Thunder's Mouth Press, 1991), p. 219.
44. Jahan Ramazani, *Poetry and Its Others: News, Song, Prayer and the Dialogue of Genres* (Chicago, IL: University of Chicago Press, 2013), p. 124.
45. James Merrill, *Collected Poems*, p. 589.

46. Betsy Andrews, *The Bottom* (South Bend, IN: 42 Miles Press, 2015), p. 52.
47. Monica Youn, 'The Death of Ignatz', *Ignatz* (New York: Four Way, 2010), p. 51.
48. Patricia Lockwood (@TriciaLockwood), Twitter, 4 July 2011. Last accessed 3 September 2015. Available at: https://twitter.com/TriciaLockwood/status/87929158902099968
49. Elizabeth Cohen, 'Skybusters Triggering Tiny Signals', *Waiting Up for the End of the World* (Seattle, WA: Jaded Ibis, 2012), p. 101.
50. Elizabeth Cohen, 'Day After, Over London', *Waiting Up for the End of the World*, p. 89.
51. Robert Frost, *Selected Prose*, ed. Hyde Cox and Edward Connery Lathem (New York: Holt, Rinehart and Winston, 1966), p. 106.
52. Terrance Hayes, 'Wind in a Box', *Wind in a Box*, p. 80.
53. Quoted in Christopher Nealon, *The Matter of Capital: Poetry and Crisis in the American Century* (Cambridge, MA: Harvard University Press, 2011), p. 149.

Further Reading

Andrews, Betsy, *The Bottom* (South Bend, IN: 42 Miles Press, 2015).

Baraka, Amiri, *The LeRoi Jones / Amiri Baraka Reader*, ed. William J. Harris (New York: Thunder's Mouth Press, 1991).

Beach, Christopher, *Poetic Culture: Contemporary American Poetry between Community and Institution* (Evanston, IL: Northwestern University Press, 1999).

Borzutsky, Daniel, *The Book of Interfering Bodies* (New York: Nightboat, 2011).

Colen, Elizabeth, *Waiting Up for the End of the World* (Seattle, WA: Jaded Ibis, 2012).

Graham, Jorie, *Place: New Poems* (Hopewell, NJ: Ecco, 2012).

Hayes, Terrance, *Hip Logic* (New York: Penguin, 2002).

Hayes, Terrance, *Wind in a Box* (New York: Penguin, 2007).

Hayes, Terrance, *Lighthead* (New York: Penguin, 2010).

Herrera, Juan Felipe, *187 Reasons Mexicanos Can't Cross the Border* (San Francisco, CA: City Lights, 2007).

Kasischke, Laura, *Dance and Disappear* (Amherst, MA: University of Massachusetts Press, 2002).

Kasischke, Laura, *Gardening in the Dark* (Keene, NY: Ausable, 2004).

Kasischke, Laura, *Lilies Without* (Keene, NY: Ausable, 2007).

Longenbach, James, *The Virtues of Poetry* (Minneapolis: Graywolf, 2013).

Merrill, James, J. D. McClatchy and Stephen Yenser (eds), *Collected Poems* (New York: Knopf, 2002).

Nealon, Christopher, *The Matter of Capital: Poetry and Crisis in the American Century* (Cambridge, MA: Harvard University Press, 2011).

Perloff, Marjorie, *Uncreative Writing* (Chicago, IL: University of Chicago Press, 2011).

Ramazani, Jahan, *Poetry and Its Others: News, Song, Prayer and the Dialogue of Genres* (Chicago, IL: University of Chicago Press, 2013).

Spahr, Juliana, *Well Then There Now* (Santa Barbara, CA: Black Sparrow, 2011).

Vincent, John Emil (ed.), *After Spicer: Critical Essays* (Middletown, CT: Wesleyan University Press, 2011).

Youn, Monica, *Ignatz* (New York: Four Way, 2010).

Index